the distinctive voice

the distinctive voice

TWENTIETH-CENTURY AMERICAN POETRY

WILLIAM J. MARTZ · RIPON COLLEGE

SCOTT, FORESMAN AND COMPANY

Conrad Aiken   "All Lovely Things," "Improvisations: Lights and Snow," "Changing Mind." From
Collected Poems, copyright 1953, by Conrad Aiken. Reprinted by permission of Oxford
University Press, Inc. "Limericks 1, 7, 11, 12, and 27." From *A Seizure of Limericks,* copyright
© 1963, 1964, by Conrad Aiken. Reprinted by permission of Holt, Rinehart and Winston,
Inc.

Elizabeth Bishop   "Wading at Wellfleet," "A Miracle for Breakfast," "Insomnia," "At the Fish-
houses." From *Poems: North and South—A Cold Spring* by Elizabeth Bishop. Copyright 1955.
Reprinted by permission of Houghton Mifflin Company. "Visits to St. Elizabeths"; "The
Armadillo," which appeared originally in *The New Yorker.* From *Questions of Travel* by Eliza-
beth Bishop. Copyright © 1957 by Elizabeth Bishop. Reprinted by permission of Farrar,
Straus & Giroux, Inc.

Philip Booth   "Convoy," "Maine," copyright © 1960 by Philip Booth; "First Draft," copyright ©
1961 by Philip Booth. From *The Islanders* by Philip Booth. "First Lesson." From *Letter from
a Distant Land,* copyright 1957, by Philip Booth. All reprinted by permission of The Viking
Press, Inc.

John Ciardi   "Bedlam Revisited," "A Plea," one line from "Showing a Foreigner Through His
Studio, Leonardo Answers a Question," five lines from "Damn Her," two lines from "A
Voice Said," one line from "Joshua on Eighth Ave." From *In the Stoneworks.* Copyright
Rutgers, The State University, 1961. "In Place of a Curse," "The Baboon and the State,"
"To W. T. Scott," three lines from "A Thousandth Poem for Dylan Thomas." From *39
Poems.* Copyright Rutgers, The State University, 1959. "Gulls Land and Cease to Be,"
"Men Marry What They Need. I Marry You," "Two Hours," "Tenzone." From *Person to
Person.* Copyright Rutgers, The State University, 1964. "On Being Sure and Of What,"
"A Missouri Fable," "In Pity as We Kiss and Lie." From *In Fact.* Copyright Rutgers, The
State University, 1962. All reprinted by permission of the author. "Manner of Speaking."
From *Saturday Review,* 1965, October 9: 41. Reprinted by permission of the author and
Saturday Review.

Hart Crane   "The Harbor Dawn," "Virginia," "Chaplinesque," "Passage," "Voyages: VI," "Imperator Victus." From *The Collected Poems of Hart Crane.* Copyright © renewed 1961, by
Liveright Publishing Corp. Reprinted by permission of Liveright, Publishers, N. Y.

E. E. Cummings   "I Thank You God For Most This Amazing," copyright 1950 by E. E. Cummings;
"At the Head of This Street a Gasping Organ is Waving Moth-," "The Cambridge Ladies
Who Live in Furnished Souls," copyright 1923, 1951 by E. E. Cummings; "If You Can't
Eat You Got To," copyright 1940 by E. E. Cummings. From *Poems 1923-1954.* "Thanksgiving (1956)," copyright © 1957 by E. E. Cummings; "Rosetree, Rosetree," copyright
1952, by E. E. Cummings; one half line from "Because You Take Life In Your Stride,"
copyright 1952. From *95 Poems.* All reprinted by permission of Harcourt, Brace & World, Inc.

James Dickey   "The Life Guard," "In the Mountain Tent," copyright © 1961 by James Dickey;
"A Birth," copyright © 1960 by James Dickey, and appeared originally in *The New Yorker.*
From *Drowning with Others* by James Dickey. "Cherrylog Road." From *Helmets,* copyright
© 1963, by James Dickey, and appeared originally in *The New Yorker.* All reprinted by
permission of Wesleyan University Press. "Reincarnation 2." From *Two Poems of the Air*
by James Dickey. Copyright 1964. Reprinted by permission of the author. "Shark's Parlor."
From *Buckdancer's Choice,* copyright © 1965, by James Dickey. Reprinted by permission
of Wesleyan University Press. Appeared originally in *The New Yorker.* Extracts from various
poems by James Dickey are reprinted from his books *Drowning with Others* and *Helmets*
by permission of Wesleyan University Press, and are copyright © by James Dickey as
follows: "Inside the River" (1960); "The Change," "The Summons" (1961); "On the Coosawattee," "Springer Mountain," "Armor" (1962); "A Folk Singer of the Thirties," "The
Being," "Drinking from a Helmet" (1963); and "Approaching Prayer" (1964).

Alan Dugan   "Tribute to Kafka for Someone Taken." From *Poems.* Copyright 1961. "Fabrication
of Ancestors," "Variation on a Theme by Stevens." From *Poems 2* by Alan Dugan. Copyright 1963. First published in *Poetry.* All reprinted by permission of Alan Dugan. "On a
Seven-Day Diary." From *Poems 2* by Alan Dugan. Copyright 1963. Reprinted by permission
of Yale University Press.

Preface

■ The first assumption upon which this anthology is based is that literature is conveniently studied in historically definable periods. The contrast between *romantic,* nineteenth century, and *modern,* twentieth century, is now a stock one and does anything but deny that the second period has strong antecedents in the first. Modern American poetry is said to begin with Whitman, a good and a fair generalization, but to speak of modern American poetry is to speak not only of achievements which go back to Whitman but of achievements which stand fulfilled in the first half (in round figures, of course) of the twentieth century. Thus Robert Frost, Wallace Stevens, William Carlos Williams, Ezra Pound, T. S. Eliot, and Hart Crane are now names, though not the only names, which serve to define a period of our literature. But an editor's problem inevitably is to select. My choice for the present collection is to emphasize four poets who seem clearly to be major poets—Frost, Stevens, Williams, and Eliot—recognizing at the same time that they are not the only four who are or may come to be regarded as major poets of the period. Then to round out the representation of the period I have selected seven of their contemporaries—Pound, Cummings, Moore, Jeffers, Ransom, Aiken, and Crane. The eleven taken together ought to provide an abundant suggestion of the achievement of American poetry in the first half of the twentieth century without producing a book that is unreasonably bulky.

Beside this period I have chosen to juxtapose what might be called an achievement in the making or an achievement more immediately in the process of evaluation—that is, a period evolving. An achievement in the making involves by definition living poets; an achievement more immediately in the process of evaluation involves both living poets and such a poet as Theodore Roethke, who died suddenly in 1963 at the height of his powers. The poets whose achievements are in the making or who have not yet been evaluated with some of the perspective that only time can give were born mainly in the first quarter of the twentieth century or fairly early in the second quarter. There are many of them. The present collection offers nineteen— by no means on the assumption that the choice is an infallible choice of the nineteen best. On the other hand, some consensus is possible, and it is hoped that a glance at the Table of Contents will confirm this fact, as well as the fact of abundant variety. Here are poets of reputation, but they do not comprise a list of all living American poets of reputation. An editor can only hope that his readers will accept his selection as an adequate point of departure for personal adventuring in a period, or in periods, offering many poets to adventure among and to see in juxtaposition with one another.

■ The second assumption upon which this anthology is based is that the student of twentieth-century or modern American poetry must come to that poetry in terms of reading *experience*. Thus the critical introduction concentrates on the voice of the poet. Commentary is made on seventeen voices which seem to orchestrate well for comparison and contrast. For the four poets identified as major—Frost, Stevens, Williams, and Eliot—there is focus on one poem. Following a fairly brief commentary on their selected contemporaries, six of the nineteen poets of today are selected for commentary, with the focus broadening from one poem to several. Whole poems are freely quoted and commented on. There is no pretension that the six chosen are the best six of the nineteen or that an anthology of this kind is the place to do such choosing, except, of course, insofar as full representation tends to imply the quality of such poets as Roethke and Lowell. The six are selected as an interesting orchestration of poetic voices and as an introduction to part of what it means to be a contemporary American poet. Each of the six is a poet of competence with strengths and some weaknesses, both deserving commentary. Thus to the assumption that poetry is best experienced in terms of an awareness of the differences between and among poets is added the assumption that poetry is best experienced in terms of an awareness of the individual poet's weaknesses and strengths. The aim of the introduction is, then, to provide the student with a useful experience in the *actual reading* of poetry so that he may acquire some of the awarenesses necessary for a truly meaningful response.

■ The third assumption upon which this anthology is based is that the study of poetry is highly complex and that no introduction to an anthology can be an exhaustive critical study nor a really engaging and comprehensive historical study, much less a combination of the two. Thus the choice was made to separate the two basic approaches, critical and historical, and to place "A Note on the History of American Poetry Since Whitman" in an appendix. Thus also the choice, applying to both approaches, to include a fairly extensive bibliography, as well as "Poets Reading Their Own Poems: A List of Recordings." The large assumption is, of course, that for some readers and listeners poetry can become a lifetime event.

Based on these three assumptions, this collection of twentieth-century American poetry ought to lend itself for use in courses in twentieth-century literature, American literature, and modern poetry. I hope that teachers who use *The Distinctive Voice* will feel invited to send their suggestions for essential additions to the Nineteen Poets of Today; a future edition might then be able to offer a consensus from opinions not otherwise available.

Finally, I wish to thank the poets who generously gave me their personal statements on the voice of the poet, or what they aim to be as a poetic voice. These statements, placed in the headnote for each author, add, in my view, a good dimension to the experience of all modern American poetry and may in time have historical value.

William J. Martz

Contents

APPENDICES

INDEX OF TITLES AND FIRST LINES

for Bill Ingersoll

INTRODUCTION

The Problem: Individual and Value

The basic problem of the twentieth century—political, social, religious, philosophical, or personal—is the location of the individual in his world, or the problem of what values an individual can or must maintain in a century of severe pressures and bewildering diversity. For the twentieth century is not a century that is philosophically integrated in the sense that many individuals find themselves making a single affirmation. What integration it has seems rather to stem from the fact of the *problem* of the individual, not its solution. The problem is commonly described in phrases that have become the stamp of the age. We are said to live in an age of anxiety, an age of ethics made relative, and of the Freudian truth that all social relations are coercive. We are described as feeling exiled and alienated; as anguished and guilty creatures lost in a desert of meaninglessness; as individuals paradoxically lonely in a crowd, conscious of being disinherited, lacking an authentic world; or, in the archetypal metaphor that perhaps sums it all up, as homeless.

Whatever the terms, the problem is, of course, the whole question of human identity and therefore as old as man. Sophocles asked it in *Oedipus Rex,* "Who am I?" in the deepest sense of self-knowledge. And in *Death of a Salesman* Arthur Miller echoes the demand for identity in Willy Loman's eloquent assertion that a man is not a piece of fruit. But the problem is also newly articulated by the fact of nuclear weaponry. It is a fact that our personal identity can be erased in a matter of hours, that the casualties in a nuclear exchange would easily exceed all losses of life in World Wars I and II combined. Like Oedipus, we are too successful at scientific measuring, threatening to measure ourselves either, ironically, out of existence or, more hopefully, into a new awareness of how we can locate as individuals in a complex and diversified but scientifically unified world—if we may take the growing control over environment characteristic since the age of Galileo as a form of unity. Science, we know, does not offer us value, the sine qua non of the meaningful life. Twentieth-century man is thus asking where his spiritual center is, or if there can be one at all. Or as E. M. Forster put it as early as 1910 in a beautiful metaphor in *Howards End,* can we build a rainbow bridge that will connect the prose in us with the passion? Such in general terms is the context in which the modern poet writes and the problem to which in one way or another he comes to address himself.

Four Major Poets

From American poetry of the first half of the twentieth century, we may select four poets whose achievements stand among the best. In order of their birth: Robert Frost (1874-1963), Wallace Stevens (1879-1955), William Carlos Williams (1883-1963), and T. S. Eliot (1888-1965).[1] Although a full description of their complex individual achievements is beyond the scope of a brief introduction, it is possible to select a short poem by each poet which is reasonably representative first of his particular approach to the problem of the location of the individual in his world, or to the problem of value, and second of how each speaks as a distinctive voice. We may begin with the radical individuality of William Carlos Williams. Here is *A Sort of a Song:*

> Let the snake wait under
> his weed
> and the writing
> be of words, slow and quick, sharp
> 5   to strike, quiet to wait,
> sleepless.
>
> —through metaphor to reconcile
> the people and the stones.
> Compose. (No ideas
> 10   but in things) Invent!
> Saxifrage is my flower that splits
> the rocks.

This is not a poem about a snake, a nature poem, but rather an analogy. The speaker is comparing the act of writing, the job of the poet, to a snake. The first stanza reads like a list of qualities he thinks words, as they are combined in "the writing" (of a poem), ought to have: *slow, quick, sharp, quiet,* and *sleepless.* But by introducing the snake in the first line, he forces us to feel the qualities of words as we would the potential of the snake. His value is, then, by implication, a tremendous sense of personal action. It is as if the speaker is sleepless himself as he struggles with inchoate words and would, by the shaping power of the imagination, give them life, as he does in the poem by

1 The question of whether T. S. Eliot is an American or a British poet seems academic. He was born in St. Louis, educated at Harvard, and became a British subject in 1927.

transforming a list into a demonstration of the qualities being listed, especially in the phrase "sharp to strike."[2] He is sleepless in the sense of feeling nervous unrest, in the sense of being resolute, and in the sense of being poised ("quiet to wait"). The stanza as a whole is built on a contrast between *waiting* and *striking,* which is to say that the speaker by implication is giving value to balance, or to a control of his great sense of urgency.

In the second stanza we learn more specifically what the urgency is all about; we become, that is, more specifically aware of the intent of the analogy at the abrupt mention of *metaphor* and then of its purpose, "to reconcile the people and the stones." It is, of course, nowhere previously suggested in the poem just who "the people" are or what "the stones" are other than stones. No such specific identification is intended. The speaker is thinking of all of humanity and of environment as it is hard and puzzling. His purpose is reconciliation, which thus reiterates balance as a value. He is thinking of the poet as an intermediary, as performing the secular equivalent of the religious function of reconciling man to God. He in effect makes the creation of metaphor a religious act, especially when he insists on the *unity* of idea and thing. Similarly, his call to *Invent* must be viewed in the context of reconciliation as his purpose; a religious equivalent might be "transcend" or "let the will seek God." His final statement is necessarily an attempt to realize his purpose; his possession of saxifrage is a triumphant insistence on his own power as a poet. But crucial to his emphasis is the fact that it is the wild flower, not himself, that does the splitting. His function is that of observer who perceives the relation of ideas to things; his function is to create metaphor and, like the snake, be sharp to strike—at our sensibility, at our overwhelming need for meaning, for location and value in our world. In broad terms Williams is a secular romantic poet, recalling Shelley and Whitman. *A Sort of a Song* is in the general classification of a song about himself as a poet, but a poet who is daring and individual, who is as irreducibly specific as saxifrage.

Williams thus locates the individual in his world as the individual seeking to be reconciled. His voice is necessarily that of a strong and determined man. It is a voice of will, a voice that insists on the power of the individual to come to terms with his own life. It is also self-

---

2 The technique, or ideal, is not a new one. Alexander Pope sums it up and gives what has become a classic illustration in Part II of his *Essay on Criticism*:

> True ease in writing comes from Art, not Chance,
> As those move easiest who have learn'd to dance.
> 'T is not enough no harshness gives offence;
> The sound must seem an echo to the sense.
> Soft is the strain when zephyr gently blows,
> And the smooth stream in smoother numbers flows;
> But when loud surges lash the sounding shore,
> The hoarse rough verse should like the torrent roar.
> When Ajax strives some rock's vast weight to throw,
> The line, too, labours and the words move slow:
> Not so when swift Camilla scours the plain,
> Flies o'er th' unbending corn, and skims along the main.   (lines 162-173)

ironic. Thus the wry title, not a song, which might be taken as traditional (no strict iambic tetrameter for him), but a *sort* of song; he is amused at himself, at his own desire to be different. He is also aware that he might appear absurd, absurdly serious, if he did not incorporate some wry humor or some self-irony into his poem. His last statement thus has to be read in the context of an almost silly title, as if he were seeing the great, his serious ambition, in terms of the small, a little wild flower. Likewise, he seems aware of the absurdity of the fact that it is a flower *splitting* a rock, a power which, of course, flowers do not ordinarily have. He must, moreover, be wittily aware of the saxifrage-rock relationship as a sexual symbol. It is wholly consistent with the rest of the poem that he would both affirm his sexual power and be amused by it too; this being the case, the snake in the first line is a standard sexual symbol, and he is seeing the act of writing as humorously analogous to an erection. The wit is compounded when he thinks of saxifrage, thus creating, by witty ironic contrast of snake and flower, his personal metaphor. His tone of voice is, then, a balance between the over-serious and the under-serious. As such it is a mature voice, even though at first it might seem egocentric or heedlessly overconfident. In other words, his extreme tone is dramatically functional.

T. S. Eliot makes an appropriate contrast with William Carlos Williams. Whereas Williams is a radical individual separated from the mainstream of religious tradition, Eliot is a distinctly religious poet, in his personal life a devout Anglican. His values, essentially, are those usually associated with the mainstream of Christian thought: man as a sinner seeks salvation which with the aid of grace he may find. But his problem is *to dramatize* the reality of the contemporary condition in relation to Christian belief. He puts the matter succinctly in *After Strange Gods* (1934) when he suggests that people writing devotional verse usually write as they want to feel rather than as they do feel.[3] In his early works, such as *The Waste Land* (1922) and *The Hollow Men* (1925), what he dramatizes is the condition of things when man cannot believe or when belief is absent from experience. He thus comes to affirmation through what might be called negative example. At the center of his later work are the *Four Quartets* (1943), poems which are religious meditations of a high order of abstraction. Somewhere in between is the great religious meditation *Ash Wednesday* (1930). It is too long to quote in full, but here is a passage from the second of its six parts that can be read almost as a complete poem in itself, a characteristic of many parts of Eliot's works. Our concern, of course, is to examine Eliot's manner of dramatizing the twentieth-century religious experience in order to suggest the nature of his voice as a poet:

> Lady of silences
> Calm and distressed

---

3 P. 29. See also F. O. Matthiessen, *The Achievement of T. S. Eliot, An Essay on the Nature of Poetry* (New York, Oxford University Press, Inc., 1959), pp. 120-121.

```
        Torn and most whole
        Rose of memory
   5    Rose of forgetfulness
        Exhausted and life-giving
        Worried reposeful
        The single Rose
        Is now the Garden
  10    Where all loves end
        Terminate torment
        Of love unsatisfied
        The greater torment
        Of love satisfied
  15    End of the endless
        Journey to no end
        Conclusion of all that
        Is inconclusible
        Speech without word and
  20    Word of no speech
        Grace to the Mother
        For the Garden
        Where all love ends.
```

Since we have observed the self-ironic tone of William Carlos Williams, it ought to be mentioned that this passage is in a self-ironic context. The speaker of the poem is a penitent meditating his way toward a religious affirmation, but he is aware of the excess to which introspection may be carried: "And I pray that I may forget / These matters that with myself I too much discuss / Too much explain." Moreover, the "Lady of Silences" passage is presented as the chirping of bones, a song in defiance of death; it is a witty view of happy dead bones, without fear of either life or death.

Although we expect any song to be strongly rhythmical, this song is overpoweringly so. The reason is not hard to find. With each line containing two strong stresses in balance with one another, there is strong rhythmic repetition yet enough variety to avoid monotony—for example, in the first two lines, the second stress in line 1 falls on the third from last syllable, and in line 2 on the last syllable. In addition to the auditory appeal of rhythm, Eliot is exploiting in an emphatic way the appeal of sound relationships; of these, perhaps the most obvious is the alliteration of "Terminate torment" (line 11). Slightly less obvious is *Grace* and *Garden* (lines 21-22). Similarly, assonance is everywhere, as in the unaccented last syllable of the first line and the accented last syllable of the line following, or the *o* sound in the third and fourth lines. Of course, such things can be pointed out in a quite mechanical way; one must make a leap to an estimate of effect. If we ask how the rhythm suggests the consciousness of a speaker, we are prompted to say that the consciousness is in a state of balance, a consciousness suspended—at least until the last line brings that balance, momentarily, to an end.

Moving to the rationally explicable meaning of the lines, we find that the speaker's thought is a succession of paradoxes (e.g., *Torn* and *whole, End* and *endless, Speech* and no *word*), culminating in "the Garden/Where all love ends," except that paradoxically the end of love is a beginning. The last line, in other words, expresses a climactic paradox. But to see *in what sense* the end of love is a beginning, we must examine the main symbols in the song and the manner in which they are presented.

The main symbols are clearly the *Lady* (later *Mother*), the *Rose*, and the *Garden*. One is prompted immediately to assume that they *are* symbols, because there is no highly concrete situation being developed into a symbolic one. Here we come to one of the basic facts of Eliot's technique as a poet. He is capable of precision in vagueness.[4] And since precision in vagueness is perfectly appropriate to the speaker's concern for the paradoxical nature of reality, Eliot is matching form and content. The effect of precision in vagueness is something that has to be felt; by definition it cannot be fully explicated since what is vague stays vague.

But perhaps some light can be thrown on the matter by observing another aspect of Eliot's technique, namely, the *free association* of ideas and images which define the structure of this song. His dramatic device is that of the mind working as, particularly from modern psychology, we know it works. Thus the third line "Torn and most whole" refers to both the *Lady* preceding and to the *Rose* following. Line 6, "Exhausted and life-giving," refers immediately to *forgetfulness* and more largely to the whole passage preceding, as well as being a sudden thought of the speaking bones. Likewise, "reposeful" (line 7) refers to "The single Rose" following as well as to the Rose—or is it two Roses?—preceding. Then, is or are the "Rose of memory" and the "Rose of forgetfulness" the same as "The single Rose" which is now, in the speaker's mind, "the Garden"? It is impossible to give a final definite answer to such questions. Such indefiniteness becomes an abstract metaphor of spiritual quest.

Such a quest, or *Journey* (line 16), ends in a *Garden*. Is it Gethsemane, an earthly paradise glimpsed by the believer, or a metaphor for man's union with God—that is, for immortality? All three, at least; in each case the end of love is a beginning. The *Rose*, traditional symbol of love, unites and concentrates the speaker's mind with its object, the *Garden*, or it could as easily be said that the *Garden* is moved inside the speaker's mind. The *Lady* and *Mother* seem to suggest, in psychological terms, the parent from whom the child (the penitent is easily imagined as childlike in his helplessness) seeks love and approval and, in religious terms, a saintly lady or Jesus' mother. But of course we must remember the ironic fact that the speaker is the bones. We are in effect asked to imagine how it feels to be dead and yet have an awareness of the final meaning of life and, perhaps, hunger to affirm that meaning.

How, then, may we describe Eliot's voice as a poet? Eliot, like Williams, locates the individual in his world as one seeking to be recon-

---

4 See Matthiessen, p. 116.

ciled but, unlike Williams, reconciled within a traditional religious framework which is, to be sure, newly experienced. Eliot's voice is clearly less his own personal voice than that of Williams. Eliot felt, in fact, that the emotion of art is impersonal.[5] Yet his own voice is surely implied, even if implied only by his chosen *persona*. It is a voice of prayer and devotion, of intense mental exercise and discipline. It is a somewhat formal, even academic, voice, as opposed to the more colloquial Williams. And, like Williams, Eliot has a self-ironic voice. It is the voice of a man who locates the individual in his world by emphasizing dislocation. It is a voice of honest recognition, as is particularly well seen in other parts of *Ash Wednesday* which emphasize the speaker's weakness as a creature of the senses as well as of religious will, "the fig's fruit" being a principal symbol of the former. It is a voice which can, without a hint of the stale or the sentimental, exclaim, "And let my cry come unto Thee."

To move from T. S. Eliot to Wallace Stevens is to move from a poet who accepts revealed religion to a poet who emphatically rejects it. Stevens, whose first book of poems, *Harmonium* (1923), includes a poem called *Nuances of a Theme by Williams,* is a cousin to Williams in radical individuality, in a desire to have the self reconciled with all other reality, what might conveniently be called the non-self. How then does Stevens differ from Williams? A reading of *Anecdote of the Jar,* one of several "anecdotes" from *Harmonium,* will suggest differences and similarities:

> I placed a jar in Tennessee,
> And round it was, upon a hill.
> It made the slovenly wilderness
> Surround that hill.
>
> 5   The wilderness rose up to it,
> And sprawled around, no longer wild.
> The jar was round upon the ground
> And tall and of a port in air.
>
> It took dominion everywhere.
> 10   The jar was gray and bare.
> It did not give of bird or bush,
> Like nothing else in Tennessee.

We notice first that whereas *A Sort of a Song* proceeds from the voice relatively impersonal to the voice most emphatically personal—"Saxifrage is my flower," with a strong emphasis on *my*—*Anecdote of the*

---

5 Perhaps the most illuminating clarification of his theory of impersonality is his idea that the bad poet is unconscious when he ought to be conscious and conscious when he ought to be unconscious, with both errors tending to make him personal. "Tradition and the Individual Talent," in *The Sacred Wood* (London, Barnes & Noble, Inc., 1920). See also his "The Three Voices of Poetry," in *On Poetry and Poets* (New York, Farrar, Straus & Giroux, Inc., 1957).

Jar begins with the personal *I* but then becomes impersonal. The difference, as one may test or discover from a larger reading of the two poets, is typical. For Williams, a poem, whatever else it is, is a direct expression of personal emotion. Stevens, by contrast, is detached, smooth, urbane—though this is not meant to suggest that Williams is rustic, since in his own way he is extremely sophisticated. Stevens, like any poet, is after emotion, but he tends to choose an impersonal *point of view.*

The *Anecdote* is not a poem about a jar but, like *A Sort of a Song,* an analogy. In the first stanza the speaker focuses on the quality of the jar; it is round, an idea which he compounds by the placement of the jar on a hill, which we would presume to be round. He then emphasizes the *power* of the jar, which is to act on the wilderness in such a way as to order it. We sense that the idea of ordering is going to be a key metaphor in the poem. We are also aware of a humorous contrast between the smallness of the jar and the largeness of the whole state of Tennessee. The anecdote, in other words, begins as a simple narrative of exaggeration.

What we sense in the first stanza as a metaphor of ordering is developed in the second stanza as a metaphor of taming. The power of the jar is such that the wilderness is "no longer wild." Since the power of the jar is such that it tames a whole wilderness, we are aware that the speaker wants us to hold in mind the humorous contrast, or juxtaposition, of the small with the great (and we might be reminded of saxifrage splitting a rock). But why does the speaker see the wilderness as tamed yet *sprawled,* since sprawled naturally suggests untamed? His logical purpose is one of anecdotal wit. By this time in the poem we are perhaps seeing that the taming is a process of becoming civilized, yet what would it mean to be civilized if one could not sprawl? Such an existence would be over-ordered, too tame, and thus sterile. In fact, we are led to the possibility that the ordering accomplished by the jar *is* some kind of violation of nature done by man. But *sprawled,* to pursue the positive purpose of anecdotal wit, is a quietly stated metaphor—of physical posture—for rejoicing, as in his reserved wit the speaker is, or may be, rejoicing.

Line 7 raises the crucial question of structure. Why does the speaker repeat the idea of round? How is it part of the anecdote? The repetition calls us to reflect that round is a conventional symbol of perfection, namely, the circle. The jar, in other words, is perfect form. Perhaps, too, we reflect that a jar would normally be a product of man, in contrast to the wilderness, which in turn is perhaps perfect in its way, never having been touched by man. But what further meaning is suggested for the jar? Is the speaker merely growing abstract and forgetting that we are flesh, or, as Yvor Winters has suggested, is the jar "symbolic of the human intellect"?[6] That the jar as perfect form is symbolic of the human intellect seems clear, but the speaker is not wholly abstract. As with Williams, but more submerged, more wry, there is a witty suggestion of instinctual at-

---

6 *In Defense of Reason* (Denver, University of Denver Press, 1937), p. 437.

traction of the wilderness for the jar. In "rose up" the whole wilderness may be seen as an absurd image of male desire, with a consequent increase in the humor of the taming idea.

The jar in line 8 is a port, or a haven, for the wild passions of man. The natural relation between man and woman becomes part of life's luxuriance, though it ought to be seen from a comic point of view. Then, as a complement to the comic point of view, there is the serious view that to bring a jar into the wilderness is to violate the wilderness. "The poem would appear," Winters writes, "to be primarily an expression of the corrupting effect of the intellect upon natural beauty. . . ."[7] But the corruption, paradoxically, turns into a new beauty as the jar symbol moves from intellect to flesh. One might even recall Milton's use of the paradox of the fortunate fall, the idea that the fall of man was a good thing to have happened.[8]

The third stanza flatly hastens to further the exaggeration of the anecdote. The jar as a manifestation of perfect form (intellect) and of the perfect and ordering comic act of the flesh takes "dominion everywhere." Yet instead of being a splash of color—a trite symbol of carnal luxuriance—it is the reverse, "Gray and bare," an ironic affirmation of even greater luxuriance but combined with a reminder perhaps of death, the "gray." The last two lines are a perfect conclusion to the anecdote. The jar does not create in the sense of generating new life, but rather in the sense of giving composition, order, or meaning to a scene.[9] The speaker's final emphasis is thus on the jar as intellect, but he humorously sees the achievement of intellect— which surely includes the very poem he is writing—as self-limiting. He recognizes in a self-ironic way that the limitless power of the imagination is limited by a jar being just a jar, and perhaps his humor is the final symbol of the paradox that his mind is both made up and not made up.

What begins, then, as a simple anecdote of exaggeration becomes a complex statement of the value of radical individuality, the poem's speaker as creator. We have said that, in contrast to Williams, Stevens speaks in a voice that is relatively impersonal. Yet the impersonal voice, as we would expect, is implicitly personal. It is the voice of a thoughtful man. The reserve of his analogy suggests a certain self-conscious intellectuality. Rather than the outgoing, hortatory "Let the snake," or let the jar, Stevens' speaker seems in his impersonality to be meditative, an impression which his concern for form, a good subject for meditation, confirms. Moreover, his anecdote in its total character is a flat statement rather than an onrushing piece of drama. The poem is a picture; on the whole it is static. We thus move into the speaker's mind and discover that his humorous anecdote is a brief meditation on the nature of reality, a meditation which discovers that in the final analysis reality is his own consciousness, his own anec-

---

7 *In Defense of Reason,* p. 437.

8 See Arthur O. Lovejoy, "Milton and the Paradox of the Fortunate Fall," in *Essays in the History of Ideas* (Baltimore, The Johns Hopkins Press, 1948).

9 See Roy Harvey Pearce, *The Continuity of American Poetry* (Princeton, Princeton University Press, 1961), pp. 381-382.

dote as a contrivance of mind, as imagination, which is the thing he values and which, incidentally, the poem as a whole must demonstrate. And in his meditative quality the Stevens of no formal religion recalls the Anglican Eliot. Indeed, twenty-four years after *Harmonium* he achieved in *Transport to Summer* (1947) a great volume of meditative poetry, comparable in quality to the sensuous, luxuriant, hedonistic poems of *Harmonium*.[10]

In turning from Stevens to Robert Frost, we turn from an impersonal voice to a highly personal one. In fact, so individual is the voice of Robert Frost that it is typically described in regional terms as the voice of a New England Yankee. Yet the voice of Robert Frost is not personal in the same sense that the voice of William Carlos Williams is a personal one. Frost's regional voice wastes no time in becoming universal, as does Williams' voice, but the difference is that Frost is creating a consistent fictional character, a *persona*.[11] To be sure, there may be times when we cannot tell the difference between the real life Robert Frost and his fictional Yankee, but it is well to remember that he is playing the game of creating character. Perhaps this is one thing he had in mind when he wrote, "It takes all sorts of in and outdoor schooling/To get adapted to my kind of fooling." His New England Yankee is well revealed in the famous short poem *Fire and Ice:*

> Some say the world will end in fire,
> Some say in ice.
> From what I've tasted of desire
> I hold with those who favor fire.
> 5　But if it had to perish twice,
> I think I know enough of hate
> To say that for destruction ice
> Is also great
> And would suffice.

Following our reading of *A Sort of a Song* and *Anecdote of the Jar,* we might first notice that *Fire and Ice* is *not* an analogy, and this instantly raises the question: What is it? Clearly it is an explicit statement, or commentary, on the subject of the end of the world. The overall manner in which the commentary is delivered—a manner that is perfectly obvious—is easy or casual. This manner may be understood by an examination of differences. The opening "Some say" is disarming as a voice of casualness and also of vagueness. When it is repeated in line 2, we know that the speaker is meditating on his subject, impartially recording two possibilities in order, as we soon learn, to choose one of them. To reduce his subject to basic possibilities is, moreover, a casual simplification, however sanctified by tradition,

10 See Louis L. Martz, "Wallace Stevens: The World as Meditation," in *Literature and Belief: The English Institute Essays for 1957,* ed. M. H. Abrams (New York, Columbia University Press, 1958); reprinted in *Wallace Stevens: A Collection of Critical Essays* (Englewood Cliffs, N.J., Spectrum Book, 1963), p. 136.

11 See John F. Lynen, *The Pastoral Art of Robert Frost* (New Haven, Yale University Press, 1960). An excellent study of Frost. See particularly pp. 98-101 for his perceptive analysis of *Fire and Ice* to which I am much indebted.

particularly by the Bible. Drop "Some say" and you have a voice of alarmed or angry conviction: "The world will end in fire."

Thus the basic device of the poem is to create a discrepancy between the thing said and the manner in which it is said, a discrepancy between the destruction of the world by fire as a real possibility and the casual manner of the speaker. It is a device of speaking lightly about a serious subject. Humorists do it all the time, but so do we, as, for example, in our calm calculations of kill and overkill in the event of nuclear war. The discrepancy, so natural in our everyday conversation, is an ironic one, and so is Frost's speaker ironic; his casual voice is a form of understatement. He means to use his casualness as a vehicle for his seriousness. Imagine now the possibility of a deadly serious speaker opening with "Some say." Casualness, though normal to the phrase, is not absolute in it. The dramatic situation could be such as to suggest an angry speaker. What at first is a disarmingly regular iambic tetrameter could also function as ferocious emphasis of the literal content of the line. What Frost is doing, in other words, is counterpointing meanings in order to suggest the complexity of his emotion.

In lines 3 and 4 the wry voice of the New England Yankee is revealed with particular emphasis by the verbs *tasted* and *hold*. *Tasted* implies a relish for life, a sampling, and a full experience too. *I hold with* is an idiom that an essentially sophisticated speaker would have to use with at least a touch of self-irony. By the end of line 4 we should, in fact, be laughing at or with the self-ironic, mildly spoofing tone of the speaker, but somewhere in the dark background is the counterpointed meaning—for example, *tasted* used in the sense of grimly burned by desire or in the sense of something on the tongue that makes one recoil. The speaker is, moreover, differentiating himself from those who lightheadedly "favor" fire; he is too aware to be among the superficial, and he regards most of mankind as foolish to incline toward the great destructive force fire with the light impartiality of *favor*, though perhaps he ironically envies them since they are not called upon to suffer as he must.

In line 5 he turns to the device of hyperbole, the absurd, the contradictory idea of perishing twice. The hyperbole functions to modulate his tone from wryly self-ironic to what John Lynen perceptively calls "jocular." But, again, the jocularity is counterpointed; the speaker is anguished to the point of bitterness—the hyperbole which relieves his suffering serves also to intensify it. In line 6 we wonder just how much is *enough*—was it just enough hate or too much which the speaker has experienced? The remaining lines of the poem complete his joke about the relation between fire and ice as metaphors for two aspects of human passion; ice, or hate, he is saying ironically, is a good competitor for the end of destruction, which, of course, is also to say self-ironically that as human beings we easily confuse means and ends or, more accurately, that we get so involved in discussing means that we forget about ends. The wry understatement of *suffice* is a perfect ending for the poem; hate will do as a means to end the world if we do not have any better vision of an end, which by implication the speaker has, though he does not reveal it explicitly. One concludes that his voice is wry and self-ironic and that his value—simple, age-old, and ludicrous to say—is love.

In the preceding commentaries the intent has been to suggest the quality of the poetic achievements of four major American poets. I confess, frankly, a desire to avoid the unavoidable, what one thinks of as "anthology" generalizations, which is to say, generalizations not adequately substantiated or qualified. The student of poetry should have a large body of reading behind him before he attempts to generalize. Above all, his reading should *not* be a mere confirming of this or that scholar's summary conclusions about a poet. While some might see a risk of ignorance in this position, the actual inclination is to avoid a certain kind of ignorance: belief in generalizations that have not been experienced or personally confirmed in some way, an ignorance which is inexcusable in the study of poetry because it denies the very function of poetry itself, which is to provide the reader with an experience of life that is tremendously exciting and uniquely available in language as it comes to be known as poetry. Thus at this point, rather than offering further generalizations on the range of the several achievements of Frost, Stevens, Williams, and Eliot, I refer the student to the bibliography included for each poet. I would, moreover, suggest that a good way to use the bibliography is to use the index in any book equipped with one. *After* reading a poem, the student will naturally want to know more about it, to know what has been said about it; that is the time to make use of an index or a table of contents. Or after reading a number of poems, the student will naturally want to know more about the early Eliot, so different and yet so like the later Eliot, or the later Stevens, so different yet so like the earlier Stevens, or the later Williams, the Williams of *Paterson*, or the marvelously homogeneous Robert Frost at any time in his development. Each poet has the stature to draw one on to a lifetime interest in his work.

Selected Contemporaries of Frost, Stevens, Williams, and Eliot

Space limitations and a choice to give emphasis to poets of today preclude an extensive discussion of even a selection of the many contemporaries of Frost, Stevens, Williams, and Eliot, deserving as those contemporaries may be. This brief sketch (with, of course, some risk of hurried generalization) of the seven selected contemporaries is intended to serve as a stimulus to further reading of the seven and as a transition to the poets of today; the emphasis is on the quality of their voices, with a suggestion of their values. The overall assumption is that the reader of modern poetry will better enjoy any individual poet by reading him with awareness of other poets or of other possibilities. In this connection, rather than treating them chronologically in order of their birth, I have elected to arrange them in what I hope is an interesting continuity.

Although it is usually futile to try to separate good poets according to whether they are simple or complex, or according to their degree of complexity, E. E. Cummings invites, nevertheless, the comment that he tends to be a voice of simplicity. His main concern is persistently with the miracle of being alive. He is a lover of the individual and of the possibilities of individual growth toward the end of joy. His values are, in simple and trite summary, joy, love, life, the self. It is not surprising, then, that his voice is an unoriginal one made original. One can assume that any poet who will use such phrases or sentences as "the magnificent honesty of space," "the humble proud," or "skies now are skies" is in trouble. It is almost inconceivable that, without some original language or some kind of original characterization, such a voice could hold our attention. Thus such phrases or sentences as "the courage to receive time's mightiest dream" or the pungently colloquial "If you can't eat you got to smoke" are refreshing to our ears. So, too, is his most famous trademark, wrenched syntax or the Cummings twist, as in "You fall in hate with love" or the last stanza of *Rosetree, Rosetree:*

> lovetree! least the
> rose alive must three, must
> four and (to quite become
> nothing) five times, proclaim
> fate isn't fatal
> —a heart her each petal

No period at the end of the poem, of course. The stanza also illustrates Cummings' intense, and self-consciously intense, lyricism. He is, as it were, a voice that is super-lyric. In fact, a common and quite fair accusation made against him is that his technique calls so much attention to itself that it often gets in the way of the experience with which he is dealing—in this he will compare with John Ciardi, who is discussed subsequently. But each reader must judge for himself to what extent technique interferes with meaning, since continued reading of a poet simply leads one to become accustomed to the poet's technique and therefore to accept it without objection *if* other aspects of the poem interrelate well. It could, moreover, be argued that Cummings' technique is so self-conscious that it tends to parody itself and thus helps create a redeeming humor in his voice—not to mention that he does have a good sense of humor anyway, which may be seen, interestingly, in the grim *Thanksgiving 1956*. But the simple voice of E. E. Cummings in its central quality is that of a joyous celebrant of life, of a man who can thank God for a most amazing day, which he twists to "for most this amazing day," "for everything/which is natural which is infinite which is yes."

Whereas Cummings is essentially an unoriginal voice made original, the voice of Hart Crane seems to be original almost from beginning to end. It is, for example, rare for Crane to speak like this: "We can evade you, and all else but the heart" (*Chaplinesque*), that is, to voice his meaning explicitly, flatly. Much more typical is the originality of

"Soft sleeves of sound/Attend the darkling harbor, the pillowed bay," or "the sky,/Cool feathery fold," or such an hyperbole as "*a forest shudders in your hair*"—phrases (from *The Harbor Dawn*) which anticipate, incidentally, the discussion of James Dickey and Richard Eberhart which follows. Like the voice of Cummings, the voice of Hart Crane is a voice of lyric joy, of such exclamation as "O blue-eyed Mary with the claret scarf,/Saturday Mary, mine!" Like the voice of Cummings, Crane's voice is anti-rational, visionary, prayerful, but it is also a voice of the yearning self, a voice of creative effort in contrast to the more assured voice of Cummings. One would guess from reading the two poets that if one of them were to commit suicide it would be, as it was, Crane and not Cummings. The intense lyricism of Crane becomes, as it were, its own value, as does his intense metaphor, for example:

> but we have seen
> The moon in lonely alleys make
> A grail of laughter of an empty ash can,
> CHAPLINESQUE

In other words, language for Crane is creativity, a fact which recalls the achievement and the view of poetry of Wallace Stevens and of William Carlos Williams.

The voice of Robinson Jeffers is violent and rhetorical, angry and bitter. He has a simplicity which links him to Cummings, but he is not so much a voice that is anti-intellectual as a voice that just isn't intellectual, a fact manifested in the triteness of perhaps too much of his language—for example, the statement "In pleasant peace and security/How suddenly the soul in a man begins to die" (*The Cruel Falcon*). But, unlike Cummings, Jeffers does not resort to radical technique in order to secure a quality of originality. His voice has a power of its own, the power of original language, original metaphor. Here are some samples from his narrative of violence *Roan Stallion*: "a drift of coyotes by the river cried bitterly against moonrise," "in the white lake of moonlight," "nothing conscious/But the possible God and the cropped grass," "two figures, woman and stallion,/Came down the silent emptiness of the dome of the hill." Speaking in a personal voice, Jeffers asserts that he would rather be a worm in a wild apple than be a son of man (*Original Sin*). His value, finally, may be summed up as "the sanity of field and mountain/And the cold ocean glittering stars" (*May-June, 1940*). But if his voice is prayerful, it is also hard-bitten in a way that contrasts with Hart Crane's.

Musicality, or intense lyricism, links the voice of Conrad Aiken to the voices of E. E. Cummings and Hart Crane. But Aiken's musicality may be either quite conventional or highly original. Here, for example, is the opening stanza of the conventional *All Lovely Things*:

> All lovely things will have an ending,
> All lovely things will fade and die,

And youth, that's now so bravely spending,
Will beg a penny by and by.

The lines could have been written by A. E. Housman. But here is
the opening of "Changing Mind," the sixth part of *The Divine Pilgrim*,
which Housman likely could not have written:

The room filled with the sound of voices,
The voices weaving like vines or voices of viols,
And the voices mixed, filling the warm room
From wall to vibrant wall. It was then I saw
5   The talk itself, the fourfold torrent of talk
(Below the candles and above the fire)
Moving like golden water!

Like Crane, Aiken is a poet absorbed in language. He is constantly
busy "measuring words against each other," though he also com-
ments, "I grow tired of measuring words against each other" (*Improvisations: Lights and Snow*). His is a voice full of pensiveness.
"Forgotten sadness" takes possession of his heart, which he compares
to an old dark house. He is preoccupied with the passage of time and,
like Jeffers, with death, though he does not speak with the anger and
bitterness typical of Jeffers when responding to the disintegration of
the world. Aiken's voice is a questioning voice—"Many things perplex
and leave me troubled" (*Improvisations: Lights and Snow*). He is searching for identity, which is, of course, his value. He seeks to discover
self; to echo his own title, he is a man on a divine pilgrimage.

The voice of Marianne Moore is a voice of energetic movement,
with the naturalness of speech yet in a highly original idiom:

your hair, the tails of two
fighting-cocks head to head in stone—like sculptured scimitars re-
peating the curve of your ears in reverse order: your
eyes, flowers of ice

and
5   snow sown by tearing winds on the cordage of disabled ships;
your raised hand,
an ambiguous signature:

THOSE VARIOUS SCALPELS,

Clearly her energy is strongly a descriptive energy. In a voice that is
metrically unpredictable, she revels in objects. And she revels in them
consciously, suggesting, for example, in a poem called *Values in Use*,
that if we are abstract we shall wish we had been specific. Thus precision, the sheer quality of living, is one of her signal values. Like Cummings', her voice is exceedingly affirmative, but she has a way of
looking into herself by looking outward, whereas Cummings tends
to draw us to his own personality. She is, in short, detached, but,

paradoxically, in her detachment she is involved. Hers is also a voice of wit, often wry, as in the opening of her famous poem *Poetry:* "I, too, dislike it: there are things that are important beyond all this fiddle," Or in the question: "But/why dissect destiny with instruments which/are more highly specialized than the tissues of destiny itself?" *(Those Various Scalpels,).* Yet her question is an intellectual's question. Although she does not share Aiken's pensiveness, she is with him as a deliberately probing mind.

Another deliberately probing mind is that of John Crowe Ransom, whose voice is persistently, perhaps narrowly, the voice of traditional forms, quatrains and sestets in rhymed iambic meter, yet with the originality of rhythm and metaphor suggested by his description of fingers as "Ten frozen parsnips hanging in the weather" *(Winter Remembered).* His voice is also original in his persistent wit, humor, and self-irony. Consider, for example, the good-humored balladry of *Captain Carpenter,* which opens:

> Captain Carpenter rose up in his prime
> Put on his pistols and went riding out
> But had got wellnigh nowhere at that time
> Till he fell in with ladies in a rout.

Or the fact that in *Old Mansion* his general reference to "the tired historian" is also a witty reference to himself. He has, moreover, like Marianne Moore, a quality of detachment while yet being involved. His voice can be restrained and at the same time passionate:

> for I must
> Weep for your nakedness and no retinue,
> And leap up as of old to follow you;
> But what I wear is flesh; it weighs like stone.
> Hilda

There is no simple summary of what Ransom values except to say that he values life as a humanist would. One thinks of him in contrast to Cummings exulting in that "which is natural which is infinite which is yes." The flesh which Ransom wears seems to say "maybe" to the infinite, to ponder it, to ponder the fact of mortality.

If it is fair to say that the voice of E. E. Cummings is relatively simple, then it would seem also fair to say that the voice of Ezra Pound is relatively complex, a fact occasioned by his great learning and his use of all kinds of allusions. So complex does he at least *seem* that a definitive exegesis of his poetical works simply does not exist, though of course much interesting and penetrating work has been done. His voice is thus obviously a voice of culture, a voice of the intellectual, unabashed in his love of and his defense of culture. Yet his voice is not that of the highbrow, since his allusions are made to seem altogether natural to what he is saying, to his personality and to the way he is searching out the meaning of human experience. His involvement in words is enormous. Like Aiken and more so, Pound is intense about the necessity of knowing words. His voice takes on a dual quality, that of knowledge in the sense of study and knowledge in the sense of the experience perceived. It is probably fair to say that, with him, image is never very far from idea, idea never very far from image.

Pound's voice, moreover, is typically passionate, often with the colloquial vigor of the opening of *Cino:* "Bah! I have sung women in three cities." Or we may glance at a random selection of some of the words which Pound uses without apology but which are not usually associated with the speech of an intellectual: *botched* (referring to civilization), *new-fangled, palaver, jab, snout, pus, vermin, arse-belching, dung-flow, louse eggs, belly.* Or we may imagine him offering an ironic salutation to a generation of the thoroughly smug and the thoroughly uncomfortable (*Salutation*). Add to this a cultivated, controlled musicality, and one has what is probably only a beginning of a description of his voice as a poet. Nevertheless, we may see in the opening lines of *Ancient Music* several of his typical qualities as a poetic voice: colloquial vigor; knowledge of older language (that is, immersement in the past, in tradition); literary taste (suggested, for example, by "raineth," the literary form of a word); and the imperative of passion:

> Winter is icummen in,
> Lhude sing Goddamm,
> Raineth drop and staineth slop,
> And how the wind doth ramm!
> Sing: Goddamm.

Clearly enough Pound values the past, tradition, song, culture, the passion of living, intelligence, the individual, and, perhaps dominating them all, what we might hesitantly call an anti-romantic originality.

Six Poets of Today: An Orchestration of Voices

We may turn, then, to six poets of today, orchestrated according to voice. Rather than select a single poem from each for commentary, it seems appropriate to take a wider perspective than commentary on a single poem allows. In this way the discussion of the four major poets will be complemented. Moreover, for these six poets a bibliography can hardly be said to exist. I am led, therefore, to make a tentative critical estimate of each, in the hope that the student will be led to form his own view on the nature of poetry and to decide what his own taste is for particular poets.

A good voice with which to begin is that of William Stafford. His is a voice of quiet affirmation, wry, maturely resigned, and somewhat plain. It is the voice of a conservative man who is searching, as his poem *Vocation* has it, "to find what the world is trying to be." It is the voice of a man whose value is to *belong*—a word he likes. But in belonging he finds true freedom; he is not one of those other-directeds described by David Riesman. There is something of the paradox about him: he seems to lack personality while actually having a great deal of it. If one had to put a label on cause, it might be said that much of his distinctive voice traces to the care with which he develops his speaker's situation. His poems always go somewhere, always give a sense of completeness of experience. No one would ever accuse him of being a phony, though he himself, aware of that universal possibility, has written: "In my sleep a little man cries, 'Faker! Faker!'/ and I tell myself mildly and seriously/that it is well to listen" (*The Title Comes Later*). But his poems often go where they go without memorable phrases, for on the whole he is not a poet of the memorable phrase. If this were said about almost anyone else, it would be tantamount to saying that he was not a poet at all. Then in addition to weakness in diction, which of course is partly *justified* as characterization of the plain-spoken man, he has one other weakness which may also relate to the necessity of characterization, a weakness of dramatic impact, or a quality of flatness as opposed to rising intensity, and this is, incidentally, a weakness of which he himself has expressed awareness.

If in the Stafford voice we hear weaknesses in diction, his poems should be rife with examples. They are. But it is at the risk of wrenching phrases from context, of ignoring the crucial importance of placement, of not looking at the poem as a whole, that I offer the following as intrinsically flat, vague, or somehow wrong. Following each phrase or sentence is a page reference to *Traveling Through the Dark* (1962) and a comment on the nature of the flatness:

with terrible things to do (p. 16)	Both *terrible* and *things* are hard words to get away with in a poem.
in dark spells in our little town (p. 23)	*Spells* is not vivid and, like it or no, *in our little town* is typical of the sentimentalist.
ever so strong (p. 24)	Again the unwanted alliance with sentimentality.
ruined but relieved (p. 25)	Strained alliteration in the bad sense of "poetic."
The bitter habit of the forlorn cause (p. 30)	Too abstract.
the edge of some new knowing (p. 48)	Worn romanticism.

cold, natural scenes (p. 51)	As from a freshman theme.
even to the teeth of the wind (p. 68)	Bad metaphor.
the world is waste (p. 69)	Touch of pontification.
And the river there meant something (p. 81)	Better to tell us what.
All countries have their majesties (p. 89)	Too much like a topic sentence.

Here are some phrases and sentences which, like the above, are flat but perhaps more functional in suggesting the character and the voice of the plain-spoken man:

It is usually best (p. 11)

I thought hard (p. 11)

You tell your troubles to it (p. 18)

the world is loaded with places (p. 29)

We live in a terrible season (p. 52)

this instant of what I was (p. 60)

a pretty good world (p. 64)

good things will happen (p. 71)

It is all right to be simply the way you have to be (p. 75)

it is well to listen (p. 80)

Such examples immediately raise the question, is Stafford's originality in the strict structure of his poems, or does he balance flat diction with more original combinations? He does, and very well. Note how the following examples invite us to want to know more about who is speaking:

to be as afraid as the teeth are big (p. 20)

translating the vast versions of the wind (p. 23)

gray shirt for me (p. 33)

the taxes of Rome were at your feet (p. 49)

Suicidal gestures of nobility driven to the wrist (p. 57)

Love the Butcher Bird Lurks Everywhere (p. 62)

food spiced by the neon light (p. 72)

fish in the lake leap arcs of realization (p. 75)

Since the examples extend the invitation, it is appropriate to look at a representative Stafford poem. Here is *Lake Chelan:*

> They call it regional, this relevance—
> the deepest place we have: in this pool forms
> the model of our land, a lonely one,
> responsive to the wind. Everything we own
> 5 has brought us here: from here we speak.
>
> The sun stalks among these peaks to sight
> the lake down aisles, long like a gun;
> a ferryboat, lost by a century, toots
> for trappers, the pelt of the mountains
> 10 rinsed in the sun and that sound.
>
> Suppose a person far off to whom this lake
> occurs: told a problem, he might hear a word
> so dark he drowns an instant, and stands dumb
> for the centuries of his country and the suave
> 15 hills beyond the stranger's sight.
>
> Is this man dumb, then, for whom Chelan lives
> in the wilderness? On the street you've seen
> someone like a trapper's child pause,
> and fill his eyes with some irrelevant flood—
> 20 a tide stops him, delayed in his job.
>
> Permissive as a beach, he turns inland,
> harks like a fire, glances through the dark
> like an animal drinking, and arrives along that line
> a lake has found far back in the hills
> 25 where what comes finds a brim gravity exactly requires.

The poem moves inexorably to its last phrase, which is thematically and dramatically a triumph of original awareness—what man is in relation to nature, to history, to himself, or to what we *own* (line 4) both in the sense of possess, as objects, or admit, as ideas. The first stanza sets up the relationship between the speaker and the lake; it helps, incidentally, if we know that *deepest* refers to a lake in north-central Washington 1419 feet deep; it is also a spectacular sixty-five miles long and one-half mile wide. The speaker is reflective, but in a double-edged way: "They call it regional" is both a casual observation and an ironic differentiation of himself or the *we* from the *they*, since the speaker seeks the lake's supraregional meaning. In the second stanza he seeks to comprehend the larger scene, the *sun* suggesting the source of life and the *ferryboat* life's inevitable change and yet its continuity in an individuality so strong that its toot claims a place in history.

In the third stanza the speaker draws us to individuality and, paradoxically, to universality, the fact of the lake in a human consciousness; more specifically, he sees the lake as a symbol of how love of country becomes a reality. In its claim on our awareness the lake as a whole is thus not unlike the toot of the ferryboat, though Chelan is part of a much larger history. In the fourth stanza the speaker, searching the meaning of human consciousness, takes up the theme of being *dumb*, in the sense of "speechless," an effect of the lake on us, and, wryly, in the sense of "stupid." But *this man* is no more stupid than the *trapper's child* who speaks *through* his pause and makes relevance out of seeming irrelevance, not unlike the lake itself, which speaks in its silence, fills our eyes, stops us, forces us into an awareness, a relationship. In the fifth stanza we move with the *he* to the end of a somewhat breathless journey and to the discovery of the lake's meaning or value, which, abstractly, is order in the universe in which man finds himself with the gift of consciousness.

The poem moves well despite the fact that the identity of the stranger in stanza three, the man in stanza four, and the *he* in stanza five could be more distinct and in clearer relationship, and despite the fact that there is a certain vagueness in the diction; what, for example, is meant by "in this pool *forms*/the model of our land"? The following stanzas do not give us precise dramatic definition of this key idea, although their general relationship to it is clear. Why in the second stanza is the sun personified and made a rinsing agent? In stanza three what makes "a word/so dark he drowns an instant"? In the last stanza what is the geography, why does the *he* turn *inland?* But a poem is supposed to provoke us to ask questions—it is difficult to draw the line on which of them it assumes full responsibility to answer.

We move from the quiet power of William Stafford to the flashy rhetoric and tough wit of John Ciardi, with the caution that *rhetoric* is not meant as a pejorative term. Although both poets know how to build a poem so that we have a sense of going somewhere, they make an interesting contrast. One of Stafford's strengths is that he builds *slowly* to a last line of considerable impact. Ciardi, on the other hand, has a strong propensity to begin a poem with shock and thus to challenge himself to hold his reader; in other words, if you begin with a bang, where do you go from there? For example, the radical humor of *In Place of a Curse*, which begins:

At the next vacancy for God, if I am elected,

In this poem he ends by abolishing Hell and letting everyone into Heaven, but not without having this climactic reminder read over "the meek by trade" that they might suffer for not being human: "'Beware the calculations of the meek, who gambled nothing,/gave nothing, and could never receive enough.'" Ciardi thus takes the voice of a strong, rough-and-tumble man and makes his values explicit. In our example he chooses a radical situation, and while a radical situation need not involve a radical diction, a radical diction is nevertheless typical Ciardi. He likes particularly the radicality of the colloquial, as in the title *After Sunday Dinner We Uncles Snooze*. Or the colloquial can become witty, figurative language as in this opening:

> Of all her appalling virtues, none
> leaves more crumbs in my bed, nor
> more gravel in my tub
> than the hunch of her patience
>   at its mouseholes.
>
> DAMN HER

In his radicality, Ciardi rather deliberately provokes the fastidious, but this is part of the character he is creating. It is impossible that this character will be universally liked, whereas William Stafford's character is almost sure to be. Consider, for example, the following, which some Frenchmen will surely dislike, as well as some Americans who really don't care about Clemenceau. But the wit works to a truth, or at least to the rhetorician's partial truth:[12]

> He [Clemenceau] made war
> As if he strangled a mistress—tenderly
> But with a certain competence.
>
> THE BABOON AND THE STATE

In his character of a manly man, Ciardi in his overstatement reminds one of Hemingway in his understatement, tough on the outside as a necessary shield for truly valid emotion that could easily drift into what he knows would be a detestable sentimentality. Consider the sympathy in the following, again an opening:

> Waking outside his Babylonian binge
>   in the wet and cramp of morningstone, the sot
> begins his daily death.
>
> A THOUSANDTH POEM FOR DYLAN THOMAS

The comic alliteration of *Babylonian binge* is a particularly good shield against sentimentality because it suggests a deliberate control of language, which in turn suggests a knowing of the self. Self-knowledge is, moreover, valued by Ciardi because one of his central concerns is the limit of reason, which, as a rational man, he emphasizes. "Mystery? What child is born explained?" (*Showing a Foreigner Through His Studio, Leonardo Answers a Question*). Or, "an intellect beyond rea-

---

12 For an example of Ciardi's consciousness of his own technique see the not particularly successful poem *'Nothing Is Really Hard but to be Real'* in *Person to Person* (1964).

son/hungers for the peace of your spent body" (*A Voice Said*). There is self-searching in this biographical echo:

> I was born
> free to my own confusions, though in hock
> to Mother and Father Sweatshop's original stock
> in Boston, Mass., four families to a john.
>
> Bedlam Revisited

"A man can survive anything except not caring," he writes in *Joshua on Eighth Avenue,* and, above all, his rhetoric is meant to reflect his caring. In his caring he is like a graceful bulldozer. But his gracefully bulldozing rhetoric carries with it the danger of all rhetoric, namely, that it may call an attention to itself which gets in the way of the poem as drama. Ciardi's poems typically exist in a perilous balance, and thus one's reaction to them is likely to be an extreme, the judgment that his rhetoric either works or fails.

Although a brief description cannot do justice to a good poet, it would be particularly unfair to Ciardi not to recognize his gifts as a lyric poet, specifically his capacity to speak in a voice as tender as it can be tough, to be graceful without bulldozing. Here, for example, is the love poem *In Pity as We Kiss and Lie.* It has the trademarks of the classicist, balances, repetitions, rhymed quatrains, for example— a total feeling for form—but it does not have the Ciardi trademarks we have been emphasizing:

> Softly wrong, we lie and kiss,
> heart to heart and thigh to thigh.
> Like man and woman. As if this
> were how and who and when and why.
>
> 5   Some two in the time of man
> and woman found it sweet
> to trade what such half-bodies can
> that both be made complete.
>
> Some two in a place that was
> 10 hardly right but softly true
> found themselves and founded us—
> he to her and I to you.
>
> Softly wrong and hardly right,
> heart to heart and thigh to thigh,
> 15 in each others arms tonight
> we lie and kiss and kiss and lie.
>
> If he by her and I by you,
> like man and woman, now and then
> find each other softly true—
> 20 what of how, who, why, and when?

Till hardly wrong, as mercy is—
when and how and who and why—
softly right we lie and kiss
in pity as we kiss and lie.

Both William Stafford and John Ciardi speak in voices that suggest strong rational control, or a rational examination of the meaning of human experience. Though each has, of course, his own kind of passion, neither speaks with the passionate intensity of James Dickey, whom we perhaps ally with Shelley and whom we find it difficult not to dub a romantic. In this he both compares and contrasts with Stafford, who in temperament and values has an affinity with Wordsworth: in *Lake Chelan* the concern is to set up a relationship of exchange between man and nature, one of Wordsworth's great concerns in *The Prelude* and altogether typical of him. But whereas Wordsworth is a conservative romantic, Shelley is a radical one. Ciardi might be reasonably called a radical classicist. Ciardi and Dickey both have a radicality about them that distinguishes their voices from the voice of Stafford. But although Dickey is highly imaginative, it would be alien to him to use anything like the Ciardi rhetoric because he typically wants to move quickly and directly to the quality of his experience, which is to say that he is not terribly concerned to draw attention to his language as language. In this sense, like Stafford's, his diction is characterized by much plain, literal speech, but it is much less a dominant characteristic than in Stafford's case. The characteristic which is dominant is steady intensity, as when "A moment tries to come in/Through the windows, when one must go/Beyond what there is in the room" (*Approaching Prayer*). James Dickey is a voice usually in the act of going beyond.

He typically, for the sake of immediacy, treats his subject in the first person and in the present tense, the now. And as if to emphasize the nowness of that now, he often uses a regular accent, a kind of pounding rhythm which, though anapestic, echoes the accentual and alliterative Old English poetry. Here are some examples, numbered for convenience:

1. The leap of a fish from its shadow
   Makes the whole lake instantly tremble.
   THE LIFEGUARD

2. I set my broad sole upon silver,
   On the skin of the sky, on the moonlight.
   THE LIFEGUARD

3. I breathe on my thumbs, and am blowing
   A horn that encircles the forest.
   THE SUMMONS

4. When I give up my hold on my breath
   I long to dress deeply at last
   In the gold of my waiting brother

Who shall wake and shine on my limbs
As I walk, made whole, into Heaven.

ARMOR

5. I am hearing the shape of the rain
   Taking the shape of the tent and believe it,
   Laying down all around where I lie
   A profound, unspeakable law.

IN THE MOUNTAIN TENT

6. While the world fades, it is *becoming.*
   As the trees shut away all seeing,
   In my mouth I mix it with sunlight.
   Here, in the dark, it is *being.*

ON THE COOSAWATTEE

7. I popped with sweat as I thought
   I heard Doris Holbrook scrape
   Like a mouse in the southern-state sun
   That was eating the paint in blisters
   From a hundred car tops and hoods.

CHERRYLOG ROAD

8. My nearly dead power to pray
   Like an army increased and assembled,
   As when, in a harvest of sparks,
   The helmet leapt from the furnace
   And clamped itself
   On the heads of a billion men.

DRINKING FROM A HELMET

Dickey's fantastic aural dexterity is surely crucial in giving the quality of intensity to his verse. Rhythmically the examples speak or sing for themselves. The alliteration is easy to identify and, once identified, to enjoy by letting the voice perform it, as surely the Old English scop once did, strumming his harp in accompaniment. But Dickey's sound sensitivity comprehends much more than the relatively obvious device of alliteration. What it comprehends is extremely difficult to evaluate and, in its final effect, subjective, though we know that poets do it all the time and that it cannot be faked. The best word for it is *assonance,* or sound resemblance, but of course sound resemblance is sound variation.

Consider the pleasing sound relationships Dickey has offered: in example 1, *tant* and *tremb;* in example 2, *sky,* an emphasized word, and the unaccented *light* in *moonlight;* in example 3, *horn* and *forest;* in example 4, *hold* in one line and *long* in the next, *breath* at the end of one line and *last* at the end of the next, *gold* and *brother, wake* and *walk;* in example 5, the phrase *down all around;* in example 6, the skillfully separated *becoming* and *being;* in example 7, the way *thought* sound balances the line with *popped;* in example 8, the sound weave of *harvest, helmet,* and *heads.* Such a discriminating ear is the kind that sometimes gets a poet dubbed the poet's poet, it being assumed that a poet revels in sound and looks up to the superior reveler. Neither Stafford nor Ciardi, both of whom have an accomplished ear, make quite such a tour de force of sound as James Dickey.

Other qualities of Dickey's distinctive voice are suggested by our examples. Whereas Stafford is wry, and Ciardi a vigorous wit, Dickey does not lean to humor. With his intensity, generally, goes a seriousness, which is not the same as to say that he is humorless or solemn or lugubrious. But any poet who values strongly the relationship between becoming and being, by now easily viewed as threadbare romantic motifs, has to make a decision either to engage in some kind of self-irony or to shoot for a new romantic originality. Put another way, such intensity invites parody—to chat about Dickey's unspeakable law, or how it would feel if that horn happened to encircle your neck rather than the forest.

The only answer to such a built-in threat is originality, which is one reason why Dickey's sound dexterity is crucial to his success. A second crucial reason is that he does not use cliché metaphors, which would only be legitimate if used in an ironic context, but rather shows his power to create original metaphor, or original variation of the old, and thus cannot be hurt by parody. Consider the daring and aptness of "the skin of the sky," "hearing the shape of the rain / Take the shape of the tent," "In my mouth I mix it with sunlight," the sun eating the paint (not so original) "in blisters" (the common metaphor rescued to originality), or the helmets leaping from the furnace and the hyperbole of a billion men. Dickey's power, which is strongly visual, strongly metaphoric, is the power to animate just about anything.

He also has the necessary power of wholeness. He is not a poet whose original metaphors or aural dexterity becomes merely decorative in poems fundamentally lacking in structure. He develops situation with care, and the reader will discover in examining some of the poems from which our examples are taken that his original language seems to spring naturally from the facts of experience. That he is concerned with careful development is mildly suggested by the fact that he leans to poems of over thirty lines, although I suspect that another reason for this preference is that he has some difficulty creating credibility, needs, in other words, to draw his reader into his world with fullness of detail. Nevertheless, here is a short Dickey poem, *A Birth,* which except for its shortness is typical and which shows that he is not a decorator but a builder:

> Inventing a story with grass
> I find a young horse deep inside it.
> I cannot nail wires around him;
> My fence posts fail to be solid,
>
> 5 And he is free, strangely, without me.
> With his head still browsing the greenness,

He walks slowly out of the pasture
To enter the sun of his story.

My mind freed of its own creature,
10   I find myself deep in my life
In a room with my child and my mother,
When I feel the sun climbing my shoulder

Change, to include a new horse.

The poem is essentially a brief, suggestive exploration of the relation between invention, or imagination, and another kind of reality, the everyday. The grass motif of stanza one becomes greenness in stanza two, which introduces the sun into the speaker's story. The sun reappears in stanza three, animated and intimately connected to the resolution of the speaker's experience. The *new horse* of the last line is a symbolic understatement of the power and the value of the imagination, an understatement which can be seen in balance to the overstatement of the sun cooperating, as it were, in the expanded or analogical meaning of the speaker's experience. *Deep* in line 2 and again in line 10 serves obliquely to insist that the imaginative birth is very real. The *new horse* finally becomes a symbol of any new poem which once created is *free,* stanza two, and *freed,* stanza three, from the mind of its creator. This idea, in contemporary poetry at least, is much overworked—magazine editors abhor it—yet *A Birth* is fresh.

If it has perhaps been implied that James Dickey is a perfect poet, the implication should be strongly qualified. For one thing, he has the great problem of any poet in the romantic tradition, how to vary the single central experience of *being.* We recall, perhaps, that Shelley and Keats both died young and that Wordsworth ran out of steam early in his career, producing little poetry of consequence in the last four decades of his life. It is, then, not surprising that James Dickey writes some weak poetry; again at the risk of seeing things out of context, with a comment on each example:

Impossible, brighter than sunlight. THE CHANGE	Trite metaphor.
Let flowing create A new, inner being: INSIDE THE RIVER	Explicit romantic theme, flat.
A middle-aged, softening man Grinning and shaking his head In amazement to last him forever. SPRINGER MOUNTAIN	Not vivid and some- what prosy.
Four held me stretching against The chalked red boards, Spreading my hands and feet,	

And nailed me to the boxcar
With twenty-penny nails.
A FOLK SINGER OF THE THIRTIES

Christ symbol too obvious.

He lies laughing silently
In the dark of utter delight.
THE BEING

Utter delight is a worn phrase; probably makes the alliteration fail.

It should be said, to qualify the qualification, that James Dickey seldom lets a poem run very long with soft diction and that he invariably has an integrity of seeing that minimizes the bad effect of some weak language.

Neither Stafford, Ciardi, nor Dickey has a reputation as a poet equal to that of Richard Eberhart, who is widely anthologized and is doubtless known to more college students than any other poet of today here considered. In fact, some of his poems, such as *The Groundhog, The Fury of Aerial Bombardment,* and *The Horse Chestnut Tree,* have become anthology fixtures and favorites. I am thus led to emphasize the more recent Eberhart, the Eberhart of *The Quarry* (1964) rather than of *Collected Poems, 1930-1960.* Eberhart, old or new, is an explicit romantic who would "in true sensuality/Discover the nativity/And history/Of the soul among its immortalities" (*The Record*). No one could be more aware than he of the difficulty of doing this old work in a new way, but he takes up the challenge well equipped with a delicate ear and an original hold on language. His skill is such that he can hardly write a bad poem, though he has the habit of including some vapid language in nearly every poem he writes and is thus in this sense a weaker poet than James Dickey. More rational, more reflective than Dickey, he can be described as a rational romantic.

Following are examples of some language fairly typical of Eberhart, lame phrases, clichés, poor abstractions, and prosiness, with page references to *The Quarry:*

A whole day of sailing is delight (p. 13)

Fullfold in fond, filial devotion (p. 36)

the rich meaning of necessity (p. 45)

The fantastic reality of the human condition (p. 56)

I thought man had an honesty/Precluding malice (p. 59)

Yet their power over life always fascinated me (p. 65)

The world is rocking that most stable was (p. 72)

I should late/Make some final statement/About man's fate (p. 95)

But again to play the risky matching game which is not a seeing of whole poems, here are some typical examples of Eberhart originality:

> It [a kite] is the sperm searching the great womb of the sky
> (p. 5)

> Now to expatiate and temporize/This artful brag (p. 16)

> Individuation is the way to the universal (p. 30)

> Bluebells, bluebells, how frail and Spring-like,
> Another world all fragile and intact,
> O bluebells of the early memories and life,
> A fair elixir before the killing facts. (p. 51)

> He defeated evil, death, and battle
> In love redeeming the human flesh,
> Reddest love, innocent and experiential,
> Which grows and fructifies the human wish. (p. 62)

The last two examples, which are stanzas, should suggest that the phrase can be absorbed into the larger unit of the poem. There is little power in such phrases as "frail and Spring-like," yet the larger whole, the total voice, is not spoiled.

If the question then becomes, what makes Richard Eberhart whole as a poet, I would say two qualities of his voice. One is a verbal playfulness which the short poem *Clocks* nicely illustrates:

> I opened a delicate, French metal box
> Careful lest I should give nicks or knocks
> To one of the most cheerful looking of clocks—
>
> Wondering what was the nature of time,
> 5 What it had to do with the nature of rhyme—
>
> When out of this metal case stepped a fairy
> As milky white as if out of a dairy
> And looked me straight in the eye, very airy.

But more important, I would say, is his singing voice—he is accurately described as incantatory. *Sea-Ruck,* which recalls the musicality of Tennyson, hardly needs comment:

> Washback of the waters, swirl of time,
> Flashback of time, swirl of the waters,
>
> *Loll and stroke, loll and stroke,*
>
> The world remade, the world broken,
> 5 Knocked rhythm, make of the slime,

The surge and control, stroke of the time,
Heartbreaking healing in the grime, and groaner

Holding its power, holding its hurl,
Loll and hurl, power to gain and destroy,

10   *The tall destruction not to undo*

A saffron inevitable sun, far and near,
Some vast control, beyond tear and fear,

Where the blood flows, and nights go,
Man in his makeshift, there is home,

15   And the dark swells, the everlasting toll,
And being like this sea, the unrolling scroll,

       Stroke and loll, loll and stroke, stroke, loll

The voice of W. D. Snodgrass, like that of Richard Eberhart, is
distinctly musical, but, unlike Eberhart, Snodgrass is not so much
concerned with the mystery of being as with an immediate actuality,
a here and now valued as a here and now. Snodgrass, who writes
often in rhymed stanzas, follows the poets of form, the classicists.
There is, for example, a little of Ben Jonson in him, or A. E. Housman, or perhaps it would be better to say that they have something
in common. Snodgrass in any case is a poet whose diction is usually
simple, with much of the quality of everyday speech, yet his ear is
so discriminating that he manages to avoid the worst qualities of
everyday speech, particularly the use of clichés. In fact, the observation that his diction is often plain is *not* accompanied by the complaint
that he offends the ear with tired phrases. Consider the delicacy and
control of the fourth section of his title poem *Heart's Needle;* the *you*
is a little girl who will be child of a broken home:

       No one can tell you why
    the season will not wait;
       the night I told you I
    must leave, you wept a fearful rate
5   to stay up late.

       Now that it's turning Fall,
    we go to take our walk
       among municipal
    flowers, to steal one off its stalk
10   to try and talk.

       We huff like windy giants
    scattering with our breath
       gray-headed dandelions;

Spring is the cold wind's aftermath.
15   The poet saith.

But the asters, too, are gray,
ghost-gray. Last night's cold
is sending on their way
petunias and dwarf marigold
20   hunched sick and old.

Like nerves caught in a graph
the morning-glory vines
frost has erased by half
still scrawl across their rigid twines.
25   Like broken lines

of verses I can't make.
In its unraveling loom
we find a flower to take,
with some late buds that might still bloom,
30   back to your room.

Night comes and the stiff dew.
I'm told a friend's child cried
because a cricket, who
had minstreled every night outside
35   her window, died.

The control, recalling Frost, is that of understatement, intensifying emotion by holding it back, so appropriate here to the speaker and his situation.

Snodgrass' control is typically seen as the biting wit of a man both accepting and protesting. The war experience seems to have left him, or his speaker, knowing "what authoritative lies / Would plan us as our old lives had been planned" or "Free to choose just what they meant we should" (*Returned to Frisco, 1946*). His voice combines bitterness with ambivalence:

Those war years, many a wife
wandered the fields after such pods to fill life
preservers so another man might not be lost.
                    WINTER BOUQUET

Not even nature offers a ready rescue:

while you walk
the sun bobs and is snarled
in the enclosing weir
of trees, in their dead stalks.
                    THE MARSH

If anything, there is self-rescue, the rescue of a man who values good humor and wit, as in the lines following the above, also the last lines of the poem:

> Stick in the mud, old heart,
>   what are you doing here?

In effect, the grim content of what he is saying is played off against a lightness of manner. It is a way of avoiding sentimentality, a way of being mature. But Snodgrass does not, like Ciardi, give the sense that sentimentality might lurk dangerously near. *These Trees Stand . . .,* representative in its final effect of the brighter Snodgrass, is worth quoting in full for its delightful view of man as a comic character:

> These trees stand very tall under the heavens.
> While *they* stand, if I walk, all stars traverse
> This steep celestial gulf their branches chart.
> Though lovers stand at sixes and at sevens
> 5   While civilizations come down with the curse,
> Snodgrass is walking through the universe.
>
> I can make any world go around *your* house.
> But note this moon. Recall how the night nurse
> Goes ward-rounds, by the mild, reflective art
> 10   Of focusing her flashlight on her blouse.
> Your name's safe conduct into love or verse;
> Snodgrass is walking through the universe.
>
> Your name's absurd, miraculous as sperm
> And as decisive. If you can't coerce
> 15   One thing outside yourself, why you're the poet!
> What irrefrangible atoms whirl, affirm
> Their destiny and form Lucinda's skirts!
> She can't make up your mind. Soon as you know it,
> Your firmament grows touchable and firm.
> 20   If all this world runs battlefield or worse,
> Come, let us wipe our glasses on our shirts:
> Snodgrass is walking through the universe.

The last poet of the distinctive voice whom I have chosen to examine is James Wright, who is something like two poets in one, since after the publication of *Saint Judas* (1959), he turned to a new style which he explicitly announced with the publication of *The Branch Will Not Break* (1963). The early style is strongly a style of form, much like that of Snodgrass, and there is a temperamental affinity between the two, particularly in their contrast to the romantic affirmative view of life we see in Stafford, Dickey, and Eberhart. This is not to say that Snodgrass and Wright are all pessimism or do not love life, but they are what we frequently think of as modern in their values, living on the whole without the comfort of strong religious conviction—which is not to challenge the integrity of the romantic view or to see it as easy to come by or to live by. But James Wright has about him the fascination of a man who has been to hell and back; in literary terms, we associate him with the naturalistic tradition, life known in rawness and cruelty. Out of such experience he shapes a symbolic art. He has power rare in American poetry, rare in any poetry. For example, his elegiac love poem *The Accusation*, which exemplifies his first style:

> I kissed you in the dead of dark,
> And no one knew, or wished to know,
> You bore, across your face, a mark
> From birth, those shattered years ago.
> 5 Now I can never keep in mind
> The memory of your ugliness
> At a clear moment. Now my blind
> Fingers alone can read your face.
>
> Often enough I had seen that slash
> 10 Of fire you quickly hid in shame;
> You flung your scarf across the flesh,
> And turned away, and said my name.
> Thus I remember daylight and
> The scar that made me pity you.
> 15 God damn them both, you understand.
> Pity can scar love's face, I know.
>
> I loved your face because your face
> Was broken. When my hands were heavy,
> You kissed me only in a darkness
> 20 To make me daydream you were lovely.
> All the lovely emptiness
> On earth is easy enough to find.
> You had no right to turn your face
> From me. Only the truth is kind.
>
> 25 I cannot dream of you by night.
> I half-remember what you were.
> And I remember the cold daylight,
> And pity your disgusting scar
> As any light-eyed fool could pity,
> 30 Who sees you walking down the street.
> I lose your stark essential beauty.
> I dream some face I read about.
>
> If I were given a blind god's power
> To turn your daylight on again,
> 35 I would not raise you smooth and pure:
> I would bare to heaven your uncommon pain,
> Your scar I had a right to hold,
> To look on, for the pain was yours.

Now you are dead, and I grow old,
40   And the doves cackle out of doors.

And lovers, flicking on the lights,
Turn to behold each lovely other.
Let them remember fair delights.
How can I ever love another?
45   You had no right to banish me
From that scarred truth of wretchedness,
Your face, that I shall never see
Again, though I search every place.

His use of dark and light, sight and blindness, ugliness and beauty, the relation of pity and love, emptiness and fullness of life, death and life, face and hands, dream and reality, heaven and hell, youth and age, permanency and impermanency, guilt and innocence are carefully controlled, subordinated to the drama of the situation, fitted to a structure. Of course, all poets who have a distinctive voice show such control, but Wright takes us where few, in the nature of things, can venture.

Wright's second or later style is essentially a movement to free form in which description and image do their own dramatizing. It recalls the French poets of the symbolist movement, who were a strong influence on T. S. Eliot (see Edmund Wilson's *Axel's Castle*), and a distinct modern Continental influence is also present. Yet what is important is not influences but results. In Wright's case, the result is, not unexpectedly, mixed. The style is one which tends either cleanly to succeed or cleanly to fail. It fails when too much is asked of object or image, an asking readily seen in the short poem *In the Cold House:*

I slept a few minutes ago,
Even though the stove has been out for hours.
I am growing old.
A bird cries in bare elder trees.

This is the kind of poem that elicits a quietly resigned *so what?* But here in *Autumn Begins in Martins Ferry, Ohio* is an example of the style when it succeeds:

In the Shreve High football stadium,
I think of Polacks nursing long beers in Tiltonsville,
And gray faces of Negroes in the blast furnace at Benwood,
And the ruptured night watchman of Wheeling Steel,
5   Dreaming of heroes.

All the proud fathers are ashamed to go home.
Their women cluck like starved pullets,
Dying for love.

Therefore,
10   Their sons grow suicidally beautiful
     At the beginning of October,
     And gallop terribly against each other's bodies.

To specify why one succeeds and one fails is difficult. One might be tempted to say that the language of the second has greater vividness, which it has, and that this is a reason for its success, which it is, or that, being longer, the second gives a sense of development impossible in the shorter poem, which it does. But try striking out the word *therefore*. Does not the poem then fail? If this observation is accurate, it has an obvious moral—that the artist's control of whatever style he writes in is more important than the style itself or that the control is, ultimately, the style. Or, his voice is his own despite the fact that we may have heard *some* of its qualities before. It is hard to see James Wright as better in one style than in the other, just as it is hard not to see him as effective in both, speaking, that is, in his own distinctive voice.

The Poet as Individual

The preceding description of the distinctive voices of seventeen poets ought to suggest a final emphasis on the individuality of the poet. Yet it should quickly be said that this individuality does not prevent us from normally recognizing close or contrasting relationships between one poet and other poets—other individuals—nor from consciously or unconsciously attempting to classify the poets whom we read and like or dislike—liking and disliking being themselves further examples of classification. To like or to dislike, moreover, is usually to work from certain norms. Broadly speaking, we are our own norm; liking or disliking a poem expresses our taste. But more specifically, and to take a problem of modern literary criticism, we tend in our judgments of poems to proceed from certain biases, such as a bias in favor of dramatic over expository or argumentative power, though the fact that poets today are not much interested in writing a poem such as Pope's *Essay on Man* tells us as much about ourselves as about the nature of poetry. As one would expect, the problem quickly complicates itself with paradox, the dramatically powerful poem expositing, the expository poem being in its way dramatic.[13]

Such complication with regard to our use of norms suggests in turn the necessity of describing *what* a poet does *before* we judge him,

---

13 See Maynard Mack's discussion of Pope's poetry as poetry of statement in "'Wit and Poetry and Pope': Some Observations on his Imagery," in *Pope and His Contemporaries: Essays Presented to George Sherburn* (Oxford, Oxford University Press, Inc., 1949). Reprinted in *Eighteenth Century English Literature: Modern Essays in Criticism,* ed. James L. Clifford (New York, Oxford University Press, Inc., 1959).

which is not quite to say that the two processes, description and judgment, are wholly or easily separable, the fact being that to describe implies a choice or a judgment of what to describe. For this reason there was no attempt in the preceding commentary to make a clean separation of description and judgment. The distinction itself, however, is a useful one, likely to prevent us from rejecting a poet who does something, such as use a harsh colloquial idiom, to which we are not tuned or, contrarily, to accept a poet as good merely because he writes in some familiar style to which we are favorably disposed. In the reading of poetry, catholicity of taste should be an important aim. When we come to classify a poet, and by implication to express a like or a dislike, it is well to keep in mind Shakespeare's spoof of labels when he has Polonius describe the various kinds of drama:

> The best actors in the world, either for tragedy,
> comedy, history, pastoral, pastoral-comical, historical-
> pastoral, tragical-historical, tragical-comical-historical-
> pastoral; scene individable, or poem unlimited.
> (HAMLET: II, ii, 387-390)

Having described poets as classical, romantic, and modern, secular and devotional, personal and impersonal, radical, wry, witty, rational, and so on, we ought, without losing sight of the value of such description, to reflect also on its limitations, perhaps imagining the best poets in the world, either for classical, romantic, modern, classical-modern, romantic-modern, romantic-classical-modern, rational-romantic-classical-modern, poem analyzable or poem unlimited.[14] With the kind of perspective suggested by Shakespeare, we may find a satisfying personal proportion while enjoying the poets of the twentieth century both as men of their age and as individuals.

---

14 The idea of the limitation of a term is, of course, anything but new. See, for example, Eliot's discussion of the danger of using such terms as "romantic" and "classic" in Part I of *After Strange Gods*, a danger which, he adds, does not give us permission to avoid them altogether.

A Note on the Selection

I hope that the following collection of thirty poets will be seen as rich not only in the unity of a period but also in variety. It contains poems that vary in length from a few lines to several hundred, from moment to narrative. Although none of the poets submits to a label, it contains poets of tight form and ranges to such loose form as the prose-poetry of Karl Shapiro's *Bourgeois Poet.* It contains poems of intense lyric quality—by Cummings, Crane, and Roethke, for example —and poems of reason and wit, such as many passages by Eliot and poems by Kunitz and Ciardi, not that passion and reason are by any scheme mutually exclusive. It contains poems as deeply personal as those from Lowell's *Life Studies* and poems whose author is more or less unseen, as in the narrative *Roan Stallion,* though the relation between personal and impersonal end in both cases, it seems to me, as a paradox. It contains tempers which are conservative, such as William Stafford, and tempers which are radical, such as Allen Ginsberg, though I think that history will find a great deal of paradox here too. It contains poems by poets from a variety of geographical locations, coast to coast, North and South, and, of course, Eliot in England. It contains the heirs of Whitman and the heirs of other traditions. It contains poets so concerned with Self that they could hardly come from any century but the twentieth, and poets much less easily identified by the easy labels of an era. And, possibly as a corollary to form—and vital to the whole experience of poetry—it contains poets of varied language, from the elegance of Stevens and the neatness of Ransom to the colloquial fury of Pound, Dugan, and Ginsberg. Taken together these thirty poets embody much of the quality of life in twentieth-century America—its mind and its geography—and become, as it were, one voice for us to experience.

FOUR MAJOR POETS

Robert Frost (1874-1963)

Robert Frost was born in San Francisco but moved to Massachusetts when he was eleven. He married Elinor Miriam White in 1895, attended Harvard from 1897 to 1899, and farmed at Derry, New Hampshire, from 1900 to 1910 while writing and teaching. In 1912 he moved to England with his wife and four children, returning to New Hampshire in 1915 and moving to Vermont in 1919. His first book of poems, *A Boy's Will,* was published in England in 1913, and his second, *North of Boston,* in 1914. His subsequent career was concentrated in writing and in teaching at such places as Amherst College, the University of Michigan, and Harvard, though he lectured and read his poetry all over the country. He was Consultant in Poetry at the Library of Congress in 1958. In 1961 he brought his poem *The Gift Outright* to read at the inauguration of President John F. Kennedy, but a glaring sun forced him to recite from memory. He died in Boston two months before his eighty-ninth birthday. Four times he won the Pulitzer Prize, in 1924 for *Selected Poems; New Hampshire,* in 1931 for *Collected Poems,* in 1937 for *A Further Range,* and in 1943 for *A Witness Tree.* His extensive honors include a United States Senate Resolution citing his achievement (March 24, 1950) and honorary degrees from both Oxford and Cambridge in 1958.

The Pasture

I'm going out to clean the pasture spring;
I'll only stop to rake the leaves away
(And wait to watch the water clear, I may):
I sha'n't be gone long.—You come too.

5   I'm going out to fetch the little calf
That's standing by the mother. It's so young,
It totters when she licks it with her tongue.
I sha'n't be gone long.—You come too.

MOWING

There was never a sound beside the wood but one,
And that was my long scythe whispering to the ground.
What was it it whispered? I knew not well myself;
Perhaps it was something about the heat of the sun,
5   Something, perhaps, about the lack of sound—
And that was why it whispered and did not speak.
It was no dream of the gift of idle hours,
Or easy gold at the hand of fay or elf:
Anything more than the truth would have seemed too weak
10 To the earnest love that laid the swale in rows,
Not without feeble-pointed spikes of flowers
(Pale orchises), and scared a bright green snake.
The fact is the sweetest dream that labor knows.
My long scythe whispered and left the hay to make.

A LINE-STORM SONG

The line-storm clouds fly tattered and swift,
    The road is forlorn all day,
Where a myriad snowy quartz stones lift,
    And the hoof-prints vanish away.
5   The roadside flowers, too wet for the bee,
    Expend their bloom in vain.
Come over the hills and far with me,
    And be my love in the rain.

The birds have less to say for themselves
10   In the wood-world's torn despair
Than now these numberless years the elves,
    Although they are no less there:
All song of the woods is crushed like some
    Wild, easily shattered rose.
15   Come, be my love in the wet woods, come,
    Where the boughs rain when it blows.

There is the gale to urge behind
    And bruit our singing down,
And the shallow waters aflutter with wind
20   From which to gather your gown.
What matter if we go clear to the west,
    And come not through dry-shod?
For wilding brooch shall wet your breast
    The rain-fresh goldenrod.

25   Oh, never this whelming east wind swells
    But it seems like the sea's return
To the ancient lands where it left the shells
    Before the age of the fern;

And it seems like the time when after doubt
30   Our love came back amain.
Oh, come forth into the storm and rout
      And be my love in the rain.

BIRCHES

When I see birches bend to left and right
Across the lines of straighter darker trees,
I like to think some boy's been swinging them.
But swinging doesn't bend them down to stay
5   As ice-storms do. Often you must have seen them
Loaded with ice a sunny winter morning
After a rain. They click upon themselves
As the breeze rises, and turn many-colored
As the stir cracks and crazes their enamel.
10   Soon the sun's warmth makes them shed crystal shells
Shattering and avalanching on the snow-crust—
Such heaps of broken glass to sweep away
You'd think the inner dome of heaven had fallen.
They are dragged to the withered bracken by the load,
15   And they seem not to break; though once they are bowed
So low for long, they never right themselves:
You may see their trunks arching in the woods
Years afterwards, trailing their leaves on the ground
Like girls on hands and knees that throw their hair
20   Before them over their heads to dry in the sun.
But I was going to say when Truth broke in
With all her matter-of-fact about the ice-storm
I should prefer to have some boy bend them
As he went out and in to fetch the cows—
25   Some boy too far from town to learn baseball,
Whose only play was what he found himself,
Summer or winter, and could play alone.
One by one he subdued his father's trees
By riding them down over and over again
30   Until he took the stiffness out of them,
And not one but hung limp, not one was left
For him to conquer. He learned all there was
To learn about not launching out too soon
And so not carrying the tree away
35   Clear to the ground. He always kept his poise
To the top branches, climbing carefully
With the same pains you use to fill a cup
Up to the brim, and even above the brim.
Then he flung outward, feet first, with a swish,
40   Kicking his way down through the air to the ground.
So was I once myself a swinger of birches.
And so I dream of going back to be.

It's when I'm weary of considerations,
And life is too much like a pathless wood
45   Where your face burns and tickles with the' cobwebs
Broken across it, and one eye is weeping
From a twig's having lashed across it open.
I'd like to get away from earth awhile
And then come back to it and begin over.
50   May no fate willfully misunderstand me
And half grant what I wish and snatch me away
Not to return. Earth's the right place for love:
I don't know where it's likely to go better.
I'd like to go by climbing a birch tree,
55   And climb black branches up a snow-white trunk
Toward heaven, till the tree could bear no more,
But dipped its top and set me down again.
That would be good both going and coming back.
One could do worse than be a swinger of birches.

PUTTING IN THE SEED

You come to fetch me from my work tonight
When supper's on the table, and we'll see
If I can leave off burying the white
Soft petals fallen from the apple tree
5   (Soft petals, yes, but not so barren quite,
Mingled with these, smooth bean and wrinkled pea;)
And go along with you ere you lose sight
Of what you came for and become like me,
Slave to a springtime passion for the earth.
10   How Love burns through the Putting in the Seed
On through the watching for that early birth
When, just as the soil tarnishes with weed,
The sturdy seedling with arched body comes
Shouldering its way and shedding the earth crumbs.

FOR ONCE, THEN, SOMETHING

Others taunt me with having knelt at well-curbs
Always wrong to the light, so never seeing
Deeper down in the well than where the water
Gives me back in a shining surface picture
5   Me myself in the summer heaven godlike
Looking out of a wreath of fern and cloud puffs.
Once, when trying with chin against a well-curb,
I discerned, as I thought, beyond the picture,
Through the picture, a something white, uncertain,
10   Something more of the depths—and then I lost it.
Water came to rebuke the too clear water.

One drop fell from a fern, and lo, a ripple
Shook whatever it was lay there at bottom,
Blurred it, blotted it out. What was that whiteness?
Truth? A pebble of quartz? For once, then, something.

15

The Rose Family

The rose is a rose,
And was always a rose.
But the theory now goes
That the apple's a rose,
And the pear is, and so's
The plum, I suppose.
The dear only knows
What will next prove a rose.
You, of course, are a rose—
But were always a rose.

5

10

Two Tramps in Mud Time

Out of the mud two strangers came
And caught me splitting wood in the yard.
And one of them put me off my aim
By hailing cheerily 'Hit them hard!'
I knew pretty well why he dropped behind
And let the other go on a way.
I knew pretty well what he had in mind:
He wanted to take my job for pay.

5

Good blocks of beech it was I split,
As large around as the chopping block;
And every piece I squarely hit
Fell splinterless as a cloven rock.
The blows that a life of self-control
Spares to strike for the common good
That day, giving a loose to my soul,
I spent on the unimportant wood.

10

15

The sun was warm but the wind was chill.
You know how it is with an April day
When the sun is out and the wind is still,
You're one month on in the middle of May.
But if you so much as dare to speak,
A cloud comes over the sunlit arch,
A wind comes off a frozen peak,
And you're two months back in the middle of March.

20

25 A bluebird comes tenderly up to alight
And fronts the wind to unruffle a plume
His song so pitched as not to excite
A single flower as yet to bloom.
It is snowing a flake: and he half knew
30 Winter was only playing possum.
Except in color he isn't blue,
But he wouldn't advise a thing to blossom.

The water for which we may have to look
In summertime with a witching-wand,
35 In every wheelrut's now a brook,
In every print of a hoof a pond.
Be glad of water, but don't forget
The lurking frost in the earth beneath
That will steal forth after the sun is set
40 And show on the water its crystal teeth.

The time when most I loved my task
These two must make me love it more
By coming with what they came to ask.
You'd think I never had felt before
45 The weight of an ax-head poised aloft,
The grip on earth of outspread feet.
The life of muscles rocking soft
And smooth and moist in vernal heat.

Out of the woods two hulking tramps
50 (From sleeping God knows where last night,
But not long since in the lumber camps).
They thought all chopping was theirs of right.
Men of the woods and lumberjacks,
They judged me by their appropriate tool.
55 Except as a fellow handled an ax,
They had no way of knowing a fool.

Nothing on either side was said.
They knew they had but to stay their stay
And all their logic would fill my head:
60 As that I had no right to play
With what was another man's work for gain.
My right might be love but theirs was need.
And where the two exist in twain
Theirs was the better right—agreed.

65 But yield who will to their separation,
My object in living is to unite
My avocation and my vocation
As my two eyes make one in sight.
Only where love and need are one,

And the work is play for mortal stakes,
Is the deed ever really done
For Heaven and the future's sakes.

THE STRONG ARE SAYING NOTHING

The soil now gets a rumpling soft and damp,
And small regard to the future of any weed.
The final flat of the hoe's approval stamp
Is reserved for the bed of a few selected seed.

5   There is seldom more than a man to a harrowed piece.
Men work alone, their lots plowed far apart,
One stringing a chain of seed in an open crease,
And another stumbling after a halting cart.

To the fresh and black of the squares of early mould
10   The leafless bloom of a plum is fresh and white;
Though there's more than a doubt if the weather is not too cold
For the bees to come and serve its beauty aright.

Wind goes from farm to farm in wave on wave,
But carries no cry of what is hoped to be.
15   There may be little or much beyond the grave,
But the strong are saying nothing until they see.

DESIGN

I found a dimpled spider, fat and white,
On a white heal-all, holding up a moth
Like a white piece of rigid satin cloth—
Assorted characters of death and blight
5   Mixed ready to begin the morning right,
Like the ingredients of a witches' broth—
A snow-drop spider, a flower like froth,
And dead wings carried like a paper kite.
What had that flower to do with being white,
10   The wayside blue and innocent heal-all?
What brought the kindred spider to that height,
Then steered the white moth thither in the night?
What but design of darkness to appall?—
If design govern in a thing so small.

BUT GOD'S OWN DESCENT

But God's own descent
Into flesh was meant
As a demonstration

That the supreme merit
5 Lay in risking spirit
In substantiation.
Spirit enters flesh
And for all it's worth
Charges into earth
10 In birth after birth
Ever fresh and fresh.
We may take the view
That its derring-do
Thought of in the large
15 Is one mighty charge
On our human part
Of the soul's ethereal
Into the material.

FOR JOHN F. KENNEDY HIS INAUGURATION

Gift Outright of "The Gift Outright"

WITH SOME PRELIMINARY HISTORY IN RHYME

Summoning artists to participate
In the august occasions of the state
Seems something artists ought to celebrate.
Today is for my cause a day of days.
5 And his be poetry's old-fashioned praise
Who was the first to think of such a thing.
This verse that in acknowledgment I bring
Goes back to the beginning of the end
Of what had been for centuries the trend;
10 A turning point in modern history.
Colonial had been the thing to be
As long as the great issue was to see
What country'd be the one to dominate
By character, by tongue, by native trait,
15 The new world Christopher Columbus found.
The French, the Spanish, and the Dutch were downed
And counted out. Heroic deeds were done.
Elizabeth the First and England won.
Now came on a new order of the ages
20 That in the Latin of our founding sages
(Is it not written on the dollar bill
We carry in our purse and pocket still?)
God nodded his approval of as good.
So much those heroes knew and understood,
25 I mean the great four, Washington,
John Adams, Jefferson, and Madison,—
So much they knew as consecrated seers

They must have seen ahead what now appears,
They would bring empires down about our ears
30 And by the example of our Declaration
Make everybody want to be a nation.
And this is no aristocratic joke
At the expense of negligible folk.
We see how seriously the races swarm
35 In their attempts at sovereignty and form.
They are our wards we think to some extent
For the time being and with their consent,
To teach them how Democracy is meant.
"New order of the ages" did we say?
40 If it looks none too orderly today,
'Tis a confusion it was ours to start
So in it have to take courageous part.
No one of honest feeling would approve
A ruler who pretended not to love
45 A turbulence he had the better of.
Everyone knows the glory of the twain
Who gave America the aeroplane
To ride the whirlwind and the hurricane.
Some poor fool has been saying in his heart
50 Glory is out of date in life and art.
Our venture in revolution and outlawry
Has justified itself in freedom's story
Right down to now in glory upon glory.
Come fresh from an election like the last,
55 The greatest vote a people ever cast,
So close yet sure to be abided by,
It is no miracle our mood is high.
Courage is in the air in bracing whiffs
Better than all the stalemate an's and ifs.
60 There was the book of profile tales declaring
For the emboldened politicians daring
To break with followers when in the wrong,
A healthy independence of the throng,
A democratic form of right divine
65 To rule first answerable to high design.
There is a call to life a little sterner,
And braver for the earner, learner, yearner.
Less criticism of the field and court
And more preoccupation with the sport.
70 It makes the prophet in us all presage
The glory of a next Augustan age
Of a power leading from its strength and pride,
Of young ambition eager to be tried,
Firm in our free beliefs without dismay,
75 In any game the nations want to play.
A golden age of poetry and power
Of which this noonday's the beginning hour.

"The Gift Outright"

The land was ours before we were the land's.
She was our land more than a hundred years
Before we were her people. She was ours
In Massachusetts, in Virginia,
5   But we were England's, still colonials,
Possessing what we still were unpossessed by,
Possessed by what we now no more possessed.
Something we were withholding made us weak
Until we found out that it was ourselves
10   We were withholding from our land of living,
And forthwith found salvation in surrender.
Such as we were we gave ourselves outright
(The deed of gift was many deeds of war)
To the land vaguely realizing westward,
15   But still unstoried, artless, unenhanced,
Such as she was, such as she would become.

Wallace Stevens (1879-1955)

Wallace Stevens was born in Reading, Pennsylvania, educated at
Harvard, and admitted to the New York bar in 1904. He practiced
law in New York until 1916. From that year until his death he lived
in Hartford, Connecticut, becoming vice-president of the Hartford
Accident and Indemnity Company in 1934. He married in 1909 and
had one child, a daughter. His first book of poems, *Harmonium,* was
published in 1923 when he was forty-four. His awards include the
Bollingen Prize in 1949, the National Book Award in 1951 for *Auroras
of Autumn,* and the National Book Award and the Pulitzer Prize in
1955 for *Collected Poems.* He was a member of the National Institute
of Arts and Letters.

The Paltry Nude Starts on a Spring Voyage

But not on a shell, she starts,
Archaic, for the sea.
But on the first-found weed
She scuds the glitters,
5   Noiselessly, like one more wave.

She too is discontent
And would have purple stuff upon her arms,

The Paltry Nude Starts on a Spring Voyage. **1.** *on a shell:* In Botticelli's "The
Birth of Venus" the goddess stands in a shell carried to shore by the four winds. Cf.
William Carlos Williams, *Paterson,* IV, iii (New Directions paperbook ed., p. 236).

Tired of the salty harbors,
Eager for the brine and bellowing
10   Of the high interiors of the sea.

The wind speeds her,
Blowing upon her hands
And watery back.
She touches the clouds, where she goes
15   In the circle of her traverse of the sea.

Yet this is meagre play
In the scurry and water-shine,
As her heels foam—
Not as when the goldener nude
20   Of a later day

Will go, like the centre of sea-green pomp,
In an intenser calm,
Scullion of fate,
Across the spick torrent, ceaselessly,
25   Upon her irretrievable way.

DOMINATION OF BLACK

At night, by the fire,
The colors of the bushes
And of the fallen leaves,
Repeating themselves,
5   Turned in the room,
Like the leaves themselves
Turning in the wind.
Yes: but the color of the heavy hemlocks
Came striding.
10   And I remembered the cry of the peacocks.

The colors of their tails
Were like the leaves themselves
Turning in the wind,
In the twilight wind.
15   They swept over the room,
Just as they flew from the boughs of the hemlocks
Down to the ground.
I heard them cry—the peacocks.
Was it a cry against the twilight
20   Or against the leaves themselves
Turning in the wind,
Turning as the flames
Turned in the fire,
Turning as the tails of the peacocks

25   Turned in the loud fire,
     Loud as the hemlocks
     Full of the cry of the peacocks?
     Or was it a cry against the hemlocks?

     Out of the window,
30   I saw how the planets gathered
     Like the leaves themselves
     Turning in the wind.
     I saw how the night came,
     Came striding like the color of the heavy hemlocks.
35   I felt afraid.
     And I remembered the cry of the peacocks.

The Snow Man

     One must have a mind of winter
     To regard the frost and the boughs
     Of the pine-trees crusted with snow;

     And have been cold a long time
5   To behold the junipers shagged with ice,
     The spruces rough in the distant glitter

     Of the January sun; and not to think
     Of any misery in the sound of the wind,
     In the sound of a few leaves,

10   Which is the sound of the land
     Full of the same wind
     That is blowing in the same bare place

     For the listener, who listens in the snow,
     And, nothing himself, beholds
15   Nothing that is not there and the nothing that is.

Nuances of a Theme by Williams

It's a strange courage
you give me, ancient star:

Shine alone in the sunrise
toward which you lend no part!

            I
Shine alone, shine nakedly, shine like bronze,
that reflects neither my face nor any inner part
of my being, shine like fire, that mirrors nothing.

Lend no part to any humanity that suffuses
5   you in its own light.
Be not chimera of morning,
Half-man, half-star.
Be not an intelligence,
Like a widow's bird
10   Or an old horse.

A HIGH-TONED OLD CHRISTIAN WOMAN

Poetry is the supreme fiction, madame.
Take the moral law and make a nave of it
And from the nave build haunted heaven. Thus,
The conscience is converted into palms,
5   Like windy citherns hankering for hymns.
We agree in principle. That's clear. But take
The opposing law and make a peristyle,
And from the peristyle project a masque
Beyond the planets. Thus, our bawdiness,
10   Unpurged by epitaph, indulged at last,
Is equally converted into palms,
Squiggling like saxophones. And palm for palm,
Madame, we are where we began. Allow,
Therefore, that in the planetary scene
15   Your disaffected flagellants, well-stuffed,
Smacking their muzzy bellies in parade,
Proud of such novelties of the sublime,
Such tink and tank and tunk-a-tunk-tunk,
May, merely may, madame, whip from themselves
20   A jovial hullabaloo among the spheres.
This will make widows wince. But fictive things
Wink as they will. Wink most when widows wince.

SUNDAY MORNING

Complacencies of the peignoir, and late
Coffee and oranges in a sunny chair,
And the green freedom of a cockatoo
Upon a rug mingle to dissipate
5   The holy hush of ancient sacrifice.
She dreams a little, and she feels the dark
Encroachment of that old catastrophe,
As a calm darkens among water-lights.
The pungent oranges and bright, green wings
10   Seem things in some procession of the dead,
Winding across wide water, without sound.
The day is like wide water, without sound,

Stilled for the passing of her dreaming feet
Over the seas, to silent Palestine,
15   Dominion of the blood and sepulchre.

Why should she give her bounty to the dead?
What is divinity if it can come
Only in silent shadows and in dreams?
Shall she not find in comforts of the sun,
20   In pungent fruit and bright, green wings, or else
In any balm or beauty of the earth,
Things to be cherished like the thought of heaven?
Divinity must live within herself:
Passions of rain, or moods in falling snow;
25   Grievings in loneliness, or unsubdued
Elations when the forest blooms; gusty
Emotions on wet roads on autumn nights;
All pleasures and all pains, remembering
The bough of summer and the winter branch.
30   These are the measures destined for her soul.

Jove in the clouds had his inhuman birth.
No mother suckled him, no sweet land gave
Large-mannered motions to his mythy mind.
He moved among us, as a muttering king,
35   Magnificent, would move among his hinds,
Until our blood, commingling, virginal,
With heaven, brought such requital to desire
The very hinds discerned it, in a star.
Shall our blood fail? Or shall it come to be
40   The blood of paradise? And shall the earth
Seem all of paradise that we shall know?
The sky will be much friendlier then than now,
A part of labor and a part of pain,
And next in glory to enduring love,
45   Not this dividing and indifferent blue.

She says, "I am content when wakened birds,
Before they fly, test the reality
Of misty fields, by their sweet questionings;
But when the birds are gone, and their warm fields
50   Return no more, where, then, is paradise?"
There is not any haunt of prophecy,
Nor any old chimera of the grave,
Neither the golden underground, nor isle
Melodious, where spirits gat them home,
55   Nor visionary south, nor cloudy palm
Remote on heaven's hill, that has endured
As April's green endures; or will endure
Like her remembrance of awakened birds,
Or her desire for June and evening, tipped
60   By the consummation of the swallow's wings.

She says, "But in contentment I still feel
The need of some imperishable bliss."
Death is the mother of beauty; hence from her,
Alone, shall come fulfilment of our dreams
65 And our desires. Although she strews the leaves
Of sure obliteration on our paths,
The path sick sorrow took, the many paths
Where triumph rang its brassy phrase, or love
Whispered a little out of tenderness,
70 She makes the willow shiver in the sun
For maidens who were wont to sit and gaze
Upon the grass, relinquished to their feet.
She causes boys to pile new plums and pears
On disregarded plate. The maidens taste
75 And stray impassioned in the littering leaves.

Is there no change of death in paradise?
Does ripe fruit never fall? Or do the boughs
Hang always heavy in that perfect sky,
Unchanging, yet so like our perishing earth,
80 With rivers like our own that seek for seas
They never find, the same receding shores
That never touch with inarticulate pang?
Why set the pear upon those river-banks
Or spice the shores with odors of the plum?
85 Alas, that they should wear our colors there,
The silken weavings of our afternoons,
And pick the strings of our insipid lutes!
Death is the mother of beauty, mystical,
Within whose burning bosom we devise
90 Our earthly mothers waiting, sleeplessly.

Supple and turbulent, a ring of men
Shall chant in orgy on a summer morn
Their boisterous devotion to the sun,
Not as a god, but as a god might be,
95 Naked among them, like a savage source.
Their chant shall be a chant of paradise,
Out of their blood, returning to the sky;
And in their chant shall enter, voice by voice,
The windy lake wherein their lord delights,
100 The trees, like serafin, and echoing hills,
That choir among themselves long afterward.
They shall know well the heavenly fellowship
Of men that perish and of summer morn.
And whence they came and whither they shall go
105 The dew upon their feet shall manifest.

She hears, upon that water without sound,
A voice that cries, "The tomb in Palestine

Is not the porch of spirits lingering.
It is the grave of Jesus, where He lay."
110 We live in an old chaos of the sun,
Or old dependency of day and night,
Or island solitude, unsponsored, free,
Of that wide water, inescapable.
Deer walk upon our mountains, and the quail
115 Whistle about us their spontaneous cries;
Sweet berries ripen in the wilderness;
And, in the isolation of the sky,
At evening, casual flocks of pigeons make
Ambiguous undulations as they sink,
120 Downward to darkness, on extended wings.

To the One of Fictive Music

Sister and mother and diviner love,
And of the sisterhood of the living dead
Most near, most clear, and of the clearest bloom,
And of the fragrant mothers the most dear
5 And queen, and of diviner love the day
And flame and summer and sweet fire, no thread
Of cloudy silver sprinkles in your gown
Its venom of renown, and on your head
No crown is simpler than the simple hair.

10 Now, of the music summoned by the birth
That separates us from the wind and sea,
Yet leaves us in them, until earth becomes,
By being so much of the things we are,
Gross effigy and simulacrum, none
15 Gives motion to perfection more serene
Than yours, out of our imperfections wrought,
Most rare, or ever of more kindred air
In the laborious weaving that you wear.

For so retentive of themselves are men
20 That music is intensest which proclaims
The near, the clear, and vaunts the clearest bloom,
And of all vigils musing the obscure,
That apprehends the most which sees and names,
As in your name, an image that is sure,
25 Among the arrant spices of the sun,
O bough and bush and scented vine, in whom
We give ourselves our likest issuance.

Yet not too like, yet not so like to be
Too near, too clear, saving a little to endow
30 Our feigning with the strange unlike, whence springs

The difference that heavenly pity brings.
For this, musician, in your girdle fixed
Bear other perfumes. On your pale head wear
A band entwining, set with fatal stones.
35 Unreal, give back to us what once you gave:
The imagination that we spurned and crave.

EVENING WITHOUT ANGELS

the great interests of man: air
and light, the joy of having a
body, the voluptuousness of
looking.
MARIO ROSSI

Why seraphim like lutanists arranged
Above the trees? And why the poet as
Eternal *chef d'orchestre?*

        Air is air,
5 Its vacancy glitters round us everywhere.
Its sounds are not angelic syllables
But our unfashioned spirits realized
More sharply in more furious selves.

        And light
10 That fosters seraphim and is to them
Coiffeur of haloes, fecund jeweller—
Was the sun concoct for angels or for men?
Sad men made angels of the sun, and of
The moon they made their own attendant ghosts,
15 Which led them back to angels, after death.

Let this be clear that we are men of sun
And men of day and never of pointed night,
Men that repeat antiquest sounds of air
In an accord of repetitions. Yet,
20 If we repeat, it is because the wind
Encircling us, speaks always with our speech.

Light, too, encrusts us making visible
The motions of the mind and giving form
To moodiest nothings, as, desire for day
25 Accomplished in the immensely flashing East,
Desire for rest, in that descending sea
Of dark, which in its very darkening
Is rest and silence spreading into sleep.

. . . Evening, when the measure skips a beat
30 And then another, one by one, and all

To a seething minor swiftly modulate.
Bare night is best. Bare earth is best. Bare, bare,
Except for our own houses, huddled low
Beneath the arches and their spangled air,
35 Beneath the rhapsodies of fire and fire,
Where the voice that is in us makes a true response,
Where the voice that is great within us rises up,
As we stand gazing at the rounded moon.

NUDITY IN THE COLONIES

Black man, bright nouveautés leave one, at best, pseudonymous.
Thus one is most disclosed when one is most anonymous.

CONNOISSEUR OF CHAOS

I
A. A violent order is disorder; and
B. A great disorder is an order. These
Two things are one. (Pages of illustrations.)

II
If all the green of spring was blue, and it is;
5 If the flowers of South Africa were bright
On the tables of Connecticut, and they are;
If Englishmen lived without tea in Ceylon, and they do;
And if it all went on in an orderly way,
And it does; a law of inherent opposites,
10 Of essential unity, is as pleasant as port,
As pleasant as the brush-strokes of a bough,
An upper, particular bough in, say, Marchand.

III
After all the pretty contrast of life and death
Proves that these opposite things partake of one,
15 At least that was the theory, when bishops' books
Resolved the world. We cannot go back to that.
The squirming facts exceed the squamous mind,
If one may say so. And yet relation appears,
A small relation expanding like the shade
20 Of a cloud on sand, a shape on the side of a hill.

IV
A. Well, an old order is a violent one.
This proves nothing. Just one more truth, one more
Element in the immense disorder of truths.

CONNOISSEUR OF CHAOS. 12. *Marchand:* Jean Hippolyte Marchand (1883-1941),
French painter whose landscapes and still lifes suggest intense melancholy.

B. It is April as I write. The wind
25   Is blowing after days of constant rain.
All this, of course, will come to summer soon.
But suppose the disorder of truths should ever come
To an order, most Plantagenet, most fixed . . .
A great disorder is an order. Now, A
30   And B are not like statuary, posed
For a vista in the Louvre. They are things chalked
On the sidewalk so that the pensive man may see.

V

The pensive man . . . He sees that eagle float
For which the intricate Alps are a single nest.

SO-AND-SO RECLINING ON HER COUCH

On her side, reclining on her elbow.
This mechanism, this apparition,
Suppose we call it Projection A.

She floats in air at the level of
5   The eye, completely anonymous,
Born, as she was, at twenty-one,

Without lineage or language, only
The curving of her hip, as motionless gesture,
Eyes dripping blue, so much to learn.

10   If just above her head there hung,
Suspended in air, the slightest crown
Of Gothic prong and practick bright,

The suspension, as in solid space,
The suspending hand withdrawn, would be
15   An invisible gesture. Let this be called

Projection B. To get at the thing
Without gestures is to get at it as
Idea. She floats in the contention, the flux

Between the thing as idea and
20   The idea as thing. She is half who made her.
This is the final Projection, C.

The arrangement contains the desire of
The artist. But one confides in what has no
Concealed creator. One walks easily

25   The unpainted shore, accepts the world
As anything but sculpture. Good-bye,
Mrs. Pappadopoulos, and thanks.

The Lack of Repose

A young man seated at his table
Holds in his hand a book you have never written
Staring at the secretions of the words as
They reveal themselves.

5 It is not midnight. It is mid-day,
The young man is well-disclosed, one of the gang,
Andrew Jackson Something. But this book
Is a cloud in which a voice mumbles.

It is a ghost that inhabits a cloud,
10 But a ghost for Andrew, not lean, catarrhal
And pallid. It is the grandfather he liked,
With an understanding compounded by death

And the associations beyond death, even if only
Time. What a thing it is to believe that
15 One understands, in the intense disclosures
Of a parent in the French sense.

And not yet to have written a book in which
One is already a grandfather and to have put there
A few sounds of meaning, a momentary end
20 To the complication, is good, is a good.

Sketch of the Ultimate Politician

He is the final builder of the total building,
The final dreamer of the total dream,
Or will be. Building and dream are one.

There is a total building and there is
5 A total dream. There are words of this,
Words, in a storm, that beat around the shapes.

There is a storm much like the crying of the wind,
Words that come out of us like words within,
That have rankled for many lives and made no sound.

10 He can hear them, like people on the walls,
Running in the rises of common speech,
Crying as that speech falls as if to fail.

There is a building stands in a ruinous storm,
A dream interrupted out of the past,
15 From beside us, from where we have yet to live.

THE WOMAN IN SUNSHINE

It is only that this warmth and movement are like
The warmth and movement of a woman.

It is not that there is any image in the air
Nor the beginning nor end of a form:

5   It is empty. But a woman in threadless gold
Burns us with brushings of her dress

And a dissociated abundance of being,
More definite for what she is—

Because she is disembodied,
10   Bearing the odors of the summer fields,

Confessing the taciturn and yet indifferent,
Invisibly clear, the only love.

LEBENSWEISHEITSPIELEREI

Weaker and weaker, the sunlight falls
In the afternoon. The proud and the strong
Have departed.

Those that are left are the unaccomplished,
5   The finally human,
Natives of a dwindled sphere.

Their indigence is an indigence
That is an indigence of the light,
A stellar pallor that hangs on the threads.

10   Little by little, the poverty
Of autumnal space becomes
A look, a few words spoken.

Each person completely touches us
With what he is and as he is,
15   In the stale grandeur of annihilation.

ARCHITECTURE

I
What manner of building shall we build?
Let us design a chastel de chasteté.
De pensée. . . .

Never cease to deploy the structure.
5   Keep the laborers shouldering plinths.
Pass the whole of life earing the clink of the
Chisels of the stone-cutters cutting the stones.

II

In this house, what manner of utterance shall there be?
What heavenly dithyramb
10   And cantilene?
What niggling forms of gargoyle patter?
Of what shall the speech be,
In that splay of marble
And of obedient pillars?

III

15   And how shall those come vested that come there?
In their ugly reminders?
Or gaudy as tulips?
As they climb the stairs
To the group of Flora Coddling Hecuba?
20   As they climb the flights
To the closes
Overlooking whole seasons?

IV

Let us build the building of light.
Push up the towers
25   To the cock-tops.
These are the pointings of our edifice,
Which, like a gorgeous palm,
Shall tuft the commonplace.
These are the window-sill
30   On which the quiet moonlight lies.

V

How shall we hew the sun,
Split it and make blocks,
To build a ruddy palace?
How carve the violet moon
35   To set in nicks?
Let us fix portals, east and west,
Abhorring green-blue north and blue-green south.
Our chiefest dome a demoiselle of gold.
Pierce the interior with pouring shafts,
40   In diverse chambers.
Pierce, too, with buttresses of coral air
And purple timbers,
Various argentines,
Embossings of the sky.

45 And, finally, set guardians in the grounds,
Gray, gruesome grumblers.
For no one proud, nor stiff,
No solemn one, nor pale,
No chafferer, may come
50 To sully the begonias, nor vex
With holy or sublime ado
The kremlin of kermess.

VII

Only the lusty and the plenteous
Shall walk
55 The bronze-filled plazas
And the nut-shell esplanades.

LYTTON STRACHEY, ALSO, ENTERS INTO HEAVEN

I care for neither fugues nor feathers.
What interests me most is the people
Who have always interested me most,
To see them without their passions
5 And to understand them.

Perhaps, without their passions, they will be
Men of memories explaining what they meant.
One man opposing a society
If properly misunderstood becomes a myth.
10 I fear the understanding.

Death ought to spare their passions.
Memory without passion would be better lost.
But memory and passion, and with these
The understanding of heaven, would be bliss,
15 If anything would be bliss.

How strange a thing it was to understand
And how strange it ought to be again, this time
Without the distortions of the theatre,
Without the revolutions' ruin,
20 In the presence of the barefoot ghosts!

Perception as an act of intelligence
And perception as an act of grace
Are two quite different things, in particular
When applied to the mythical.
25 As for myself, I feel a doubt:

I am uncertain whether the perception
Applied on earth to those that were myths
In every various sense, ought not to be preferred
To an untried perception applied
30 In heaven. But I have no choice.

In this apologetic air, one well
Might muff the mighty spirit of Lenin.
That sort of thing was always rather stiff.
Let's hope for Mademoiselle de Lespinasse,
35 Instead, or Horace Walpole or Mrs. Thrale.

He is nothing, I know, to me nor I to him.
I had looked forward to understanding. Yet
An understanding may be troublesome.
I'd rather not. No doubt there's a quarter here,
40 Dixhuitième and Georgian and serene.

William Carlos Williams (1883-1963)

William Carlos Williams was born in Rutherford, New Jersey, where
he settled permanently in 1909 to practice pediatrics. His first book,
Poems, was published in the same year. A graduate of the University
of Pennsylvania Medical School, he also went to school in Geneva,
Switzerland, and, after his internship in New York, to the University
of Leipzig. He married in 1912 and had two sons. His prizes and
awards include the *Dial* Award in 1926 for service to American literature, *Poetry* magazine's Guarantor's Prize in 1931, the Loines
Award for *Paterson, Book II* in 1948, the National Book Award in
1949 for *Paterson, Book III,* and the Bollingen Prize in 1953. He was
a member of the American Academy of Arts and Letters, the National
Institute of Arts and Letters, and the Academy of American Poets.

FIRST PRAISE

Lady of dusk-wood fastnesses,
    Thou art my Lady.
I have known the crisp, splintering leaf-tread with thee on before,
White, slender through green saplings;
5 I have lain by thee on the brown forest floor
    Beside thee, my Lady.

Lady of rivers strewn with stones,
    Only thou art my Lady.
Where thousand the freshets are crowded like peasants to a fair;

10 Clear-skinned, wild from seclusion
They jostle white-armed down the tent-bordered thoroughfare
    Praising my Lady.

MEZZO FORTE

Take that, damn you; and that!
    And here's a rose
  To make it right again!
    God knows
5   I'm sorry, Grace; but then,
It's not my fault if you will be a cat.

CON BRIO

Miserly, is the best description of that poor fool
Who holds Lancelot to have been a morose fellow,
Dolefully brooding over the events which had naturally to follow
The high time of his deed with Guinevere.
5 He has a sick historical sight, if I judge rightly,
To believe any such thing as that ever occurred.
But, by the god of blood, what else is it that has deterred
Us all from an out and out defiance of fear
But this same perdamnable miserliness,
10 Which cries about our necks how we shall have less and less
Than we have now if we spend too wantonly?
Bah, this sort of slither is below contempt!
In the same vein we should have apple trees exempt
From bearing anything but pink blossoms all the year,
15 Fixed permanent lest their bellies wax unseemly, and the dear
Innocent days of them be wasted quite.
How can we have less? Have we not the deed?
Lancelot thought little, spent his gold and rode to fight
Mounted, if God was willing, on a good steed.

PORTRAIT OF A LADY

Your thighs are appletrees
whose blossoms touch the sky.
Which sky? The sky
where Watteau hung a lady's
5 slipper. Your knees
are a southern breeze—or
a gust of snow. Agh! what
sort of man was Fragonard?
—as if that answered
10 anything. Ah, yes—below

the knees, since the tune
drops that way, it is
one of those white summer days,
the tall grass of your ankles
15   flickers upon the shore—
Which shore?—
the sand clings to my lips—
Which shore?
Agh, petals maybe. How
20   should I know?
Which shore? Which shore?
I said petals from an appletree.

THE YACHTS

contend in a sea which the land partly encloses
shielding them from the too heavy blows
of an ungoverned ocean which when it chooses

tortures the biggest hulls, the best man knows
5   to pit against its beating, and sinks them pitilessly.
Mothlike in mists, scintillant in the minute

brilliance of cloudless days, with broad bellying sails
they glide to the wind tossing green water
from their sharp prows while over them the crew crawls

10   ant-like, solicitously grooming them, releasing,
making fast as they turn, lean far over and having
caught the wind again, side by side, head for the mark.

In a well guarded arena of open water surrounded by
lesser and greater craft which, sycophant, lumbering
15   and flittering follow them, they appear youthful, rare

as the light of a happy eye, live with the grace
of all that in the mind is fleckless, free and
naturally to be desired. Now the sea which holds them

is moody, lapping their glossy sides, as if feeling
20   for some slightest flaw but fails completely.
Today no race. Then the wind comes again. The yachts

move, jockeying for a start, the signal is set and they
are off. Now the waves strike at them but they are too
well made, they slip through, though they take in canvas.

25   Arms with hands grasping seek to clutch at the prows.
Bodies thrown recklessly in the way are cut aside.
It is a sea of faces about them in agony, in despair ·

until the horror of the race dawns staggering the mind,
the whole sea become an entanglement of watery bodies
30   lost to the world bearing what they cannot hold. Broken,

beaten, desolate, reaching from the dead to be taken up
they cry out, failing, failing! their cries rising
in waves still as the skillful yachts pass over.

SMELL

Oh strong ridged and deeply hollowed
nose of mine! what will you not be smelling?
What tactless asses we are, you and I, boney nose,
always indiscriminate, always unashamed,
5   and now it is the souring flowers of the bedraggled
poplars: a festering pulp on the wet earth
beneath them. With what deep thirst
we quicken our desires
to that rank odor of a passing springtime!
10   Can you not be decent? Can you not reserve your ardors
for something less unlovely? What girl will care
for us, do you think, if we continue in these ways?
Must you taste everything? Must you know everything?
Must you have a part in everything?

IMPROMPTU: THE SUCKERS

Take it out in vile whisky, take it out
in lifting your skirts to show your silken
crotches; it is this that is intended.
You are it. Your pleas will always be denied.
5   You too will always go up with the two guys,
scapegoats to save the Republic and
especially the State of Massachusetts. The
Governor says so and you ain't supposed
to ask for details—

10   Your case has been reviewed by high-minded
and unprejudiced observers (like hell
they were!) the president of a great

IMPROMPTU: THE SUCKERS. **5.** *the two guys:* Sacco and Vanzetti, tried for murder
and convicted in a jury trial in Massachusetts: executed August 23, 1927. Despite the
confession of Celestino Madeiros that he had participated in the crime with the Joe
Morelli gang, the state supreme court refused to upset the verdict, and the governor
refused to exercise his power of clemency. In 1959 the Massachusetts legislature de-
clined a proposal by one of its members to recommend a retroactive pardon to the
governor.

university, the president of a noteworthy
technical school and a judge too old to sit
on the bench, men already rewarded for
their services to pedagogy and the enforcement
of arbitrary statutes. In other words
pimps to tradition—

Why in hell didn't they choose some other
kind of "unprejudiced adviser" for their
death council? instead of sticking to that
autocratic strain of Boston backwash, except
that the council was far from unprejudiced
but the product of a rejected, discredited
class long since outgrown except for use in
courts and school, and that they
wanted it so—

Why didn't they choose at least one decent
Jew or some fair-minded Negro or anybody
but such a triumvirate of inversion, the
New England aristocracy, bent on working off
a grudge against you, Americans, you
are the suckers, you are the ones who will
be going up on the eleventh to get the current
shot into you, for the glory of the state
and the perpetuation of abstract justice—

And all this in the face of the facts: that
the man who swore, and deceived the jury
wilfully by so doing, that the bullets found
in the bodies of the deceased could be
identified as having been fired from the pistol
of one of the accused—later
acknowledged that he could not so identify
them; that the jurors now seven years after
the crime do not remember the details and
have wanted to forget them; that the
prosecution has never succeeded in
apprehending the accomplices nor in connecting
the prisoners with any of the loot stolen—

The case is perfect against you, all the
documents say so—in spite of the fact that
it is reasonably certain that you were not
at the scene of the crime, shown, quite as
convincingly as the accusing facts in the
court evidence, by better reasoning to have
been committed by someone else with whom
the loot can be connected and among whom the
accomplices can be found—

It's no use, you are Americans, just the dregs.
It's all you deserve. You've got the cash,
what the hell do you care? You've got
nothing to lose. You are inheritors of a great
tradition. My country right or wrong!
You do what you're told to do. You don't
answer back the way Tommy Jeff did or Ben
Frank or Georgie Washing. I'll say you
don't. You're civilized. You let your
betters tell you where you get off. Go ahead—

But after all, the thing that swung heaviest
against you was that you were scared when
they copped you. Explain that you
nature's nobleman! For you know that every
American is innocent and at peace in his
own heart. He hasn't a damned thing to be
afraid of. He knows the government is for
him. Why, when a cop steps up and grabs
you at night you just laugh and think it's
a hell of a good joke—

This is what was intended from the first.
So take it out in your rotten whisky and
silk underwear. That's what you get out of
it. But put it down in your memory that this
is the kind of stuff that they can't get away
with. It is there and it's loaded. No one
can understand what makes the present age
what it is. They are mystified by certain
insistences.

THE LAST TURN

Then see it! in distressing
detail—from behind a red light
at 53rd and 8th
of a November evening, the jazz
of the cross lights echoing the
crazy weave of the breaking mind:
splash of a half purple, half
naked woman's body whose jeweled
guts the cars drag up and down—
No house but has its brains
blown off by the dark!
Nothing recognizable, the whole one
jittering direction made of all
directions spelling the inexplicable:
pigment upon flesh and flesh

the pigment the genius of a world,
against which rages the fury of
our concepts, artless but supreme.

When Structure Fails Rhyme Attempts to Come to the Rescue

The old horse dies slow.
By gradual degrees
the fervor of his veins
matches the leaves'

5   stretch, day by day. But
the pace that his
mind keeps is the pace
of his dreams. He

does what he can, with
10   unabated phlegm,
ahem! but the pace that
his flesh keeps—

leaning, leaning upon
the bars—beggars
15   by far all pace and every
refuge of his dreams.

The Mind's Games

If a man can say of his life or
any moment of his life, There is
nothing more to be desired! his state
becomes like that told in the famous
5   double sonnet—but without the
sonnet's restrictions. Let him go look
at the river flowing or the bank
of late flowers, there will be one
small fly still among the petals
10   in whose gauzy wings raised above
its back a rainbow shines. The world
to him is radiant and even the fact
of poverty is wholly without despair.

So it seems until there rouse
15   to him pictures of the systematically
starved—for a purpose, at the mind's
proposal. What good then the
light winged fly, the flower or
the river—too foul to drink of or

even to bathe in? The 90 storey building
beyond the ocean that a rocket
will span for destruction in a matter
of minutes but will not
bring him, in a century, food or
relief of any sort from his suffering.

The world too much with us? Rot!
the world is not half enough with us—
the rot of a potato with
a healthy skin, a rot that is
never revealed till we are about to
eat—and it revolts us. Beauty?
Beauty should make us paupers,
should blind us, rob us—for it
does not feed the sufferer but makes
his suffering a fly-blown putrescence
and ourselves decay—unless
the ecstasy be general.

April Is the Saddest Month

There they were
stuck
dog and bitch
halving the compass

Then when
with his yip
they parted
oh how frolicsome

she grew before him
playful
dancing and
how disconsolate

he retreated
hang-dog
she following
through the shrubbery

The Sound of Waves

A quatrain? Is that
the end I envision?
Rather the pace
which travel chooses.

Female? Rather the end
of giving and receiving
—of love: love surmounted
is the incentive.

Hardly. The incentive
is nothing surmounted,
the challenge lying
            elsewhere.

No end but among words
looking to the past,
plaintive and unschooled,
wanting a discipline

But wanting
more than discipline
a rock to blow upon
as a mist blows

or rain is driven
against some
headland jutting into
a sea—with small boats

perhaps riding under it
while the men fish
there, words blowing in
taking the shape of stone

           .   .   .   .

Past that, past the image:
a voice!
out of the mist
above the waves and

the sound of waves, a
voice   .   speaking!

DEEP RELIGIOUS FAITH

Past death
        past rainy days
               or the distraction
of lady's-smocks all silver-white;
           beyond the remote borders
               of poetry itself
if it does not drive us,
       it is vain.

Yet it is
10 that which made El Greco
                    paint his green and distorted saints
                    and live
lean.
                    It is what in life drives us
15   to praise music
and the old
                    or sit by a friend
                    in his last hours.

All that which makes the pear ripen
20   or the poet's line
                    come true!
Invention is the heart of it.

Without the quirks
                    and oddnesses of invention
25   the paralytic is confirmed
in his paralysis,
                    it is from a northern
                    and half-savage country
where the religion
30   is hate.

                    There
the citizens are imprisoned.
                    The rose
                    may not be worshipped
35 or the poet look to it
                    for benefit.

In the night a
                    storm of gale proportions came
                    up.
40   No one was there to envisage
a field of daisies!
                    There were bellowings
                    and roarings
from a child's book
45   of fairy tales,
                    the rumble
of a distant bombing
                    —or of a bee!
                    Shame on our poets,
50 they have caught the prevalent fever:
                    impressed
                    by the "laboratory,"
they have forgot
                    the flower!

55   which goes beyond all
laboratories!
           They have quit the job
               of invention. The
imagination has fallen asleep
60   in a poppy-cup.

WILL YOU GIVE ME A BABY?

Will you give me a baby? asked the young colored woman
in a small voice standing naked by the bed. Refused
she shrank within herself. She too refused. It makes me
too nervous, she said, and pulled the covers round her.

ON THIS MOST VOLUPTUOUS NIGHT OF THE YEAR

On this most voluptuous night of the year
the term of the moon is yellow with no light
the air's soft, the night bird has
only one note, the cherry tree in bloom

5   makes a blur on the woods, its perfume
no more than half guessed moves in the mind.
No insect is yet awake, leaves are few.
In the arching trees there is no sleep.

The blood is still and indifferent, the face
10   does not ache nor sweat soil nor the
mouth thirst. Now love might enjoy its play
and nothing disturb the full octave of its run.

PATERSON, KEEP YOUR PECKER UP

          Paterson,
keep your pecker up
        whatever the detail!
           Anywhere is everywhere:
5 You can learn from poems
        that an empty head tapped on
          sounds hollow
in any language! The figures
        are of heroic size.

PATERSON, KEEP YOUR PECKER UP. *Paterson:* The speaker is now an old man. "His procreant urge stays with him; his powers lessen. In all honesty he can only say to himself, 'Paterson,/keep your pecker up/whatever the detail!'" Roy Harvey Pearce, *The Continuity of American Poetry* (Princeton, Princeton University Press, 1961), p. 347. Compare Williams' humor here with *A Sort of a Song*, discussed in Introduction.

T. S. Eliot (1888-1965)

T. S. Eliot was born in St. Louis but settled in London and in 1927 became a British subject. He was educated at Harvard, where he received his B.A. in 1910, his M.A. in 1911, and worked on a Ph.D. in philosophy but chose not to take the degree. He also attended the Sorbonne in 1910-1911 and Merton College, Oxford, in 1914-1915. In 1923 he founded the literary magazine *The Criterion*, which he edited until 1939. In 1925 he joined the London publishing house of Faber and Faber, with which he was associated until his death. His first wife, Vivian Haigh, died in 1947. Ten years later he married Esmé Valerie Fletcher. He was awarded the Nobel Prize for Literature in 1948.

SWEENEY ERECT

> *And the trees about me,*
> *Let them be dry and leafless; let the rocks*
> *Groan with continual surges; and behind me*
> *Make all a desolation. Look, look, wenches!*

Paint me a cavernous waste shore
   Cast in the unstilled Cyclades,
Paint me the bold anfractuous rocks
   Faced by the snarled and yelping seas.

5 Display me Aeolus above
   Reviewing the insurgent gales
Which tangle Ariadne's hair
   And swell with haste the perjured sails.

Morning stirs the feet and hands
10   (Nausicaa and Polypheme).
Gesture of orang-outang
   Rises from the sheets in steam.

This withered root of knots of hair
   Slitted below and gashed with eyes,
15 This oval O cropped out with teeth:
   The sickle motion from the thighs

Jackknifes upward at the knees
   Then straightens out from heel to hip

SWEENEY ERECT. *Epigraph:* from Beaumont and Fletcher's *The Maid's Tragedy* (1608-1611). The speaker is a girl, Aspatia, looking at a tapestry of Ariadne, who was deserted by Theseus, to whom she had given the thread to guide himself out of the Labyrinth after he slew the Minotaur. *Erect:* The pun on the sexual meaning here is obvious, but Sweeney is also man as an ape who walks erect—in *Sweeney Among the Nightingales,* "Apeneck Sweeney." Cf. Polypheme (10) and "orang-outang" (11).

Pushing the framework of the bed
20   And clawing at the pillow slip.

Sweeney addressed full length to shave
   Broadbottomed, pink from nape to base,
Knows the female temperament
   And wipes the suds around his face.

25 (The lengthened shadow of a man
   Is history, said Emerson
Who had not seen the silhouette
   Of Sweeney straddled in the sun.)

Tests the razor on his leg
30   Waiting until the shriek subsides.
The epileptic on the bed
   Curves backward, clutching at her sides.

The ladies of the corridor
   Find themselves involved, disgraced,
35 Call witness to their principles
   And deprecate the lack of taste

Observing that hysteria
   Might easily be misunderstood;
Mrs. Turner intimates
40   It does the house no sort of good.

But Doris, towelled from the bath,
   Enters padding on broad feet,
Bringing sal volatile
   And a glass of brandy neat.

A GAME OF CHESS
from THE WASTELAND: PART II

The Chair she sat in, like a burnished throne,
Glowed on the marble, where the glass
Held up by standards wrought with fruited vines
From which a golden Cupidon peeped out

A GAME OF CHESS *from* THE WASTELAND: PART II. *A Game of Chess:* The title refers to
Act II scene 2 of Middleton's *Women Beware Women* (c. 1626), in which a game of chess
distracts attention from a seduction. **1.** *The Chair she sat in:* The *she* is a neurotic high-
society woman sitting before her vanity table. The description parodies (yet with ironic
seriousness) Enobarbus' description of Cleopatra in Shakespeare's *Antony and Cleopatra* (II, ii, 195-223): "The barge she sat in, like a burnish'd throne, / Burned on the
water: the poop was beaten gold; / Purple the sails, and so perfumed that / The winds
were love-sick with them. . . ." The Chair suggests Cassiopeia, character from Greek
myth condemned for eternity to look at her face in a mirror; the constellation Cassiopeia roughly resembles a chair.

(Another hid his eyes behind his wing)
Doubled the flames of sevenbranched candelabra
Reflecting light upon the table as
The glitter of her jewels rose to meet it,
From satin cases poured in rich profusion;
10 In vials of ivory and coloured glass
Unstoppered, lurked her strange synthetic perfumes,
Unguent, powdered, or liquid—troubled, confused
And drowned the sense in odours; stirred by the air
That freshened from the window, these ascended
15 In fattening the prolonged candle-flames,
Flung their smoke into the laquearia,
Stirring the pattern on the coffered ceiling.
Huge sea-wood fed with copper
Burned green and orange, framed by the coloured stone,
20 In which sad light a carvèd dolphin swam.
Above the antique mantel was displayed
As though a window gave upon the sylvan scene
The change of Philomel, by the barbarous king
So rudely forced; yet there the nightingale
25 Filled all the desert with inviolable voice
And still she cried, and still the world pursues,
"Jug Jug" to dirty ears.
And other withered stumps of time
Were told upon the walls; staring forms
30 Leaned out, leaning, hushing the room enclosed.
Footsteps shuffled on the stair.
Under the firelight, under the brush, her hair
Spread out in fiery points
Glowed into words, then would be savagely still.

35 "My nerves are bad to-night. Yes, bad. Stay with me.
"Speak to me. Why do you never speak. Speak.
    "What are you thinking of? What thinking? What?
"I never know what you are thinking. Think."

    I think we are in rats' alley
40 Where the dead men lost their bones.

    "What is that noise?"
                The wind under the door.

---

16. *laquearia*: gilded areas between crossbeams of a ceiling, here a reference to the banquet which Dido gives in honor of Aeneas (*Aeneid*, I, 726); more generally, a reference to illicit love. **22.** *sylvan scene*: *Paradise Lost*, IV, 140, Satan viewing the garden of Eden for the first time. **23.** *The change of Philomel*: Ovid, *Metamorphoses*, VI, 412-674. Philomela, raped by King Tereus of Thrace, who also cut off her tongue, is changed into a nightingale; that is, having been violated, she sings with voice inviolable. **27.** *"Jug Jug"*: Elizabethan songs describe Philomela's song in this rather anti-onomatopoetic way; that is, the holy is made unholy. **42.** *The wind under the door*: In Webster's play *The Devil's Law Case* (1619-1620) the line "Is the wind in that door still?" is used in the sense of Is the person dead or alive?

"What is that noise now? What is the wind doing?"
        Nothing again nothing.

45
                  "Do
"You know nothing? Do you see nothing? Do you remember
"Nothing?"

I remember
Those are pearls that were his eyes.
50 "Are you alive, or not? Is there nothing in your head?"
                     But
O O O O that Shakespeherian Rag—
It's so elegant
So intelligent
55 "What shall I do now? What shall I do?"
"I shall rush out as I am, and walk the street
"With my hair down, so. What shall we do to-morrow?
"What shall we ever do?"
             The hot water at ten.
60 And if it rains, a closed car at four.
And we shall play a game of chess,
Pressing lidless eyes and waiting for a knock upon the door.

When Lil's husband got demobbed, I said—
I didn't mince my words, I said to her myself,
65 HURRY UP PLEASE ITS TIME
Now Albert's coming back, make yourself a bit smart.
He'll want to know what you done with that money he gave you
To get yourself some teeth. He did, I was there.
You have them all out, Lil, and get a nice set,
70 He said, I swear, I can't bear to look at you.
And no more can't I, I said, and think of poor Albert,
He's been in the army four years, he wants a good time,
And if you don't give it him, there's others will, I said.
Oh is there, she said. Something o' that, I said.
75 Then I'll know who to thank, she said, and give me a straight look.
HURRY UP PLEASE ITS TIME
If you don't like it you can get on with it, I said.
Others can pick and choose if you can't.
But if Albert makes off, it won't be for lack of telling.
80 You ought to be ashamed, I said, to look so antique.
(And her only thirty-one.)
I can't help it, she said, pulling a long face,
It's them pills I took, to bring it off, she said.
(She's had five already, and nearly died of young George.)
85 The chemist said it would be all right, but I've never been the same.

---

52. *that Shakespeherian Rag:* note spelling—Shakespeare is given a jazz treatment, that is, is debased. **63.** *demobbed:* demobilized. The speaker is now a cockney woman. **65.** HURRY UP PLEASE ITS TIME: traditional way in English pubs to announce closing time.

You are a proper fool, I said.
Well, if Albert won't leave you alone, there it is, I said,
What you get married for if you don't want children?
HURRY UP PLEASE ITS TIME
90   Well, that Sunday Albert was home, they had a hot gammon,
And they asked me in to dinner, to get the beauty of it hot—
HURRY UP PLEASE ITS TIME
HURRY UP PLEASE ITS TIME
Goonight Bill. Goonight Lou. Goonight May. Goonight.
95   Ta ta. Goonight. Goonight.
Good night, ladies, good night, sweet ladies, good night, good night.

ASH WEDNESDAY

I

Because I do not hope to turn again
Because I do not hope
Because I do not hope to turn
Desiring this man's gift and that man's scope
5   I no longer strive to strive towards such things
(Why should the agèd eagle stretch its wings?)
Why should I mourn
The vanished power of the usual reign?

Because I do not hope to know again
10   The infirm glory of the positive hour
Because I do not think
Because I know I shall not know
The one veritable transitory power
Because I cannot drink
15   There, where trees flower, and springs flow, for there is nothing again

Because I know that time is always time
And place is always and only place
And what is actual is actual only for one time
And only for one place
20   I rejoice that things are as they are and
I renounce the blessèd face

---

96. *Good night, ladies: Hamlet*, IV, v, 72. Spoken by the mad Ophelia: "Come, my coach! Good night, ladies; good night, sweet ladies; good night, good night." Here an ironic expression of the speaker's disgust.

ASH WEDNESDAY. **1.** *Because I do not hope to turn again:* translation of the first line of *In Exile at Sarzana* by the exiled Italian poet Guido Cavalcanti (c. 1255-1300). Eliot's speaker is a penitent who, like Guido, turns to his Lady. The goal of the penitent is a mystical union with God. See the treatment of penitence in the works of the Spanish mystic St. John of the Cross (1542-1591). **4.** *Desiring . . .:* Shakespeare, sonnet 29: "When in disgrace with fortune and men's eyes,/I all alone beweep my outcast state,/ . . . Desiring this man's art, and that man's scope" (1,2,7). **6.** *agèd eagle:* symbol of the grace of baptism and an image used by St. John of the Cross. See also the dream of the Eagle, Dante, *Purgatorio*, IX.

And renounce the voice
Because I cannot hope to turn again
Consequently I rejoice, having to construct something
25 Upon which to rejoice

And pray to God to have mercy upon us
And I pray that I may forget
These matters that with myself I too much discuss
Too much explain
30 Because I do not hope to turn again
Let these words answer
For what is done, not to be done again
May the judgement not be too heavy upon us

Because these wings are no longer wings to fly
35 But merely vans to beat the air
The air which is now thoroughly small and dry
Smaller and dryer than the will
Teach us to care and not to care
Teach us to sit still.

40 Pray for us sinners now and at the hour of our death
Pray for us now and at the hour of our death

II

Lady, three white leopards sat under a juniper-tree
In the cool of the day, having fed to satiety
On my legs my heart my liver and that which had been contained
45 In the hollow round of my skull. And God said
Shall these bones live? shall these
Bones live? And that which had been contained
In the bones (which were already dry) said chirping:
Because of the goodness of this Lady
50 And because of her loveliness, and because
She honours the Virgin in meditation,
We shine with brightness. And I who am here dissembled
Proffer my deeds to oblivion, and my love
To the posterity of the desert and the fruit of the gourd.
55 It is this which recovers
My guts the strings of my eyes and the indigestible portions

40. *Pray for us . . . .:* from the "Hail Mary": "Holy Mary, mother of God, pray for us sinners now and at the hour of our death." **42.** *three white leopards:* The symbolism here has not been pinpointed, and Eliot's associative technique suggests that it cannot be. *juniper-tree:* See I Kings, 19:1-12. Elijah, despairing, sat down under a juniper-tree. See also Grimm's fairy tale *The Juniper Tree.* **46.** *Shall these bones:* Ezekiel, 37:3. "And he said unto me, Son of man, can these bones live? And I answered, O Lord God, thou knowest." **54.** *fruit of the gourd:* Jonah, 4:10-11. "Then said the Lord, Thou has had pity on the gourd, for the which thou has not labored, neither madest it grow; which came up in a night, and perished in a night. And should I not spare Nineveh that great city, wherein are more than six score thousand persons that cannot discern between their right hand and their left hand; and also much cattle?"

Which the leopards reject. The Lady is withdrawn
In a white gown, to contemplation, in a white gown.
Let the whiteness of bones atone to forgetfulness.
60 There is no life in them. As I am forgotten
And would be forgotten, so I would forget
Thus devoted, concentrated in purpose. And God said
Prophesy to the wind, to the wind only for only
The wind will listen. And the bones sang chirping
65 With the burden of the grasshopper, saying

    Lady of silences
Calm and distressed
Torn and most whole
Rose of memory
70 Rose of forgetfulness
Exhausted and life-giving
Worried reposeful
The single Rose
Is now the Garden
75 Where all loves end
Terminate torment
Of love unsatisfied
The greater torment
Of love satisfied
80 End of the endless
Journey to no end
Conclusion of all that
Is inconclusible
Speech without word and
85 Word of no speech
Grace to the Mother
For the Garden
Where all love ends.

    Under a juniper-tree the bones sang, scattered and shining
90 We are glad to be scattered, we did little good to each other,
Under a tree in the cool of the day, with the blessing of sand,
Forgetting themselves and each other, united
In the quiet of the desert. This is the land which ye
Shall divide by lot. And neither division nor unity
95 Matters. This is the land. We have our inheritance.

            III
At the first turning of the second stair
I turned and saw below
The same shape twisted on the banister
Under the vapour in the fetid air

---

96. *stair:* See Dante and St. John of the Cross. Dante ascends to God in spiraling
circles. St. John describes the Ten Degrees of the Mystical Ladder of Divine Love;
the tenth is the mystical union of the soul with God, the beatific vision.

100 Struggling with the devil of the stairs who wears
The deceitful face of hope and of despair.

At the second turning of the second stair
I left them twisting, turning below;
There were no more faces and the stair was dark,
105 Damp, jaggèd, like an old man's mouth drivelling, beyond repair,
Or the toothed gullet of an agèd shark.

At the first turning of the third stair
Was a slotted window bellied like the fig's fruit
And beyond the hawthorn blossom and a pasture scene
110 The broadbacked figure drest in blue and green
Enchanted the maytime with an antique flute.
Blown hair is sweet, brown hair over the mouth blown,
Lilac and brown hair;
Distraction, music of the flute, stops and steps of the mind over
the third stair,
115 Fading, fading; strength beyond hope and despair
Climbing the third stair.

Lord, I am not worthy
Lord, I am not worthy

but speak the word only.

IV
120 Who walked between the violet and the violet
Who walked between
The various ranks of varied green
Going in white and blue, in Mary's colour,
Talking of trivial things
125 In ignorance and in knowledge of eternal dolour
Who moved among the others as they walked,
Who then made strong the fountains and made fresh the springs

Made cool the dry rock and made firm the sand
In blue of larkspur, blue of Mary's colour,
130 Sovegna vos

Here are the years that walk between, bearing
Away the fiddles and the flutes, restoring
One who moves in the time between sleep and waking, wearing

---

108. *fig's fruit:* symbol, generally, of lust; more specifically, of the female sexual organ. **117.** *Lord, I am not worthy:* Matthew, 8:8. "The centurion answered and said, Lord, I am not worthy that thou shouldest come under my roof: but speak the word only, and my servant shall be healed." At Mass before communion the penitent says, "Lord, I am not worthy that thou shouldest enter under my roof. But speak the word only, and my soul shall be healed." **130.** *Sovegna vos:* "Be mindful." The words are spoken by Arnaut Daniel to Dante, "Be mindful in due season of my pain." See *Purgatorio,* XXVI, 142-148.

White light folded, sheathed about her, folded.
135 The new years walk, restoring
Through a bright cloud of tears, the years, restoring
With a new verse the ancient rhyme. Redeem
The time. Redeem
The unread vision in the higher dream
140 While jewelled unicorns draw by the gilded hearse.

The silent sister veiled in white and blue
Between the yews, behind the garden god,
Whose flute is breathless, bent her head and signed but spoke no word

But the fountain sprang up and the bird sang down
145 Redeem the time, redeem the dream
The token of the word unheard, unspoken

Till the wind shake a thousand whispers from the yew

And after this our exile

V
If the lost word is lost, if the spent word is spent
150 If the unheard, unspoken
Word is unspoken, unheard;
Still is the unspoken word, the Word unheard,
The Word without a word, the Word within
The world and for the world;
155 And the light shone in darkness and
Against the Word the unstilled world still whirled
About the centre of the silent Word.

O my people, what have I done unto thee.

Where shall the word be found, where will the word
160 Resound? Not here, there is not enough silence
Not on the sea or on the islands, not
On the mainland, in the desert or the rain land,
For those who walk in darkness
Both in the day time and in the night time

137-138. *Redeem the time:* Ephesians, 5:14-16. "Awake thou that sleepest, and arise from the dead, and Christ shall give thee light. See that ye walk circumspectly, not as fools, but as wise, Redeeming the time, because the days are evil." **142.** *the yews:* The yew tree is traditionally planted in English churchyards as a symbolic promise of eternal life. **148.** *And after this our exile:* From the prayer following celebration of the Mass. "Turn then, most gracious advocate, thine eyes of mercy toward us. And after this our exile, show unto us the blessed fruit of thy womb, Jesus." **152.** *the Word:* John, 1: 1, 14. "In the beginning was the Word, and the Word was with God, and the Word was God. And the Word was made flesh, and dwelt among us (and we beheld his glory, the glory as of the only begotten of the Father), full of grace and truth." **158.** *O my people:* Micah, 6:3, God pleading with Israel, "O my people, what have I done unto thee? and wherein have I wearied thee? testify against me." Note that Eliot's speaker does not ask a question.

165 The right time and the right place are not here
No place of grace for those who avoid the face
No time to rejoice for those who walk among noise and deny the voice

Will the veiled sister pray for
Those who walk in darkness, who chose thee and oppose thee,
170 Those who are torn on the horn between season and season, time and
time, between
Hour and hour, word and word, power and power, those who wait
In darkness? Will the veiled sister pray
For children at the gate
Who will not go away and cannot pray:
175 Pray for those who chose and oppose

O my people, what have I done unto thee.

Will the veiled sister between the slender
Yew trees pray for those who offend her
And are terrified and cannot surrender
180 And affirm before the world and deny between the rocks
In the last desert between the last blue rocks
The desert in the garden the garden in the desert
Of drouth, spitting from the mouth the withered apple-seed.

O my people.

VI
185 Although I do not hope to turn again
Although I do not hope
Although I do not hope to turn

Wavering between the profit and the loss
In this brief transit where the dreams cross
190 The dreamcrossed twilight between birth and dying
(Bless me father) though I do not wish to wish these things
From the wide window towards the granite shore
The white sails still fly seaward, seaward flying
Unbroken wings

195 And the lost heart stiffens and rejoices
In the lost lilac and the lost sea voices
And the weak spirit quickens to rebel
For the bent golden-rod and the lost sea smell
Quickens to recover
200 The cry of quail and the whirling plover

---

182. *The desert in the garden:* Isaiah, 51:3. "For the Lord shall comfort Zion: he will comfort all her waste places: and he will make her wilderness like Eden, and her desert like the garden of the Lord: joy and gladness shall be found therein, thanksgiving, and the voice of melody." **191.** *Bless me father:* opening used by Catholic in making his confession.

And the blind eye creates
The empty forms between the ivory gates
And smell renews the salt savour of the sandy earth

This is the time of tension between dying and birth
205　The place of solitude where three dreams cross
Between blue rocks
But when the voices shaken from the yew-tree drift away
Let the other yew be shaken and reply.

Blessèd sister, holy mother, spirit of the fountain, spirit of the
　　garden,
210　Suffer us not to mock ourselves with falsehood
Teach us to care and not to care
Teach us to sit still
Even among these rocks,
Our peace in His will
215　And even among these rocks
Sister, mother
And spirit of the river, spirit of the sea,
Suffer me not to be separated

And let my cry come unto Thee.

---

214. *Our peace in His will:* In the *Paradiso* (III, 85) a spirit tells Dante that God's
will is our peace. **218.** *Suffer me not:* from the prayer *Anima Christi,* "Suffer me not to
be separated from Thee." **219.** *And let my cry come unto Thee:* in the Mass a response
to "O Lord, hear my prayer."

SELECTED CONTEMPORARIES
OF FROST, STEVENS,
WILLIAMS, AND ELIOT

Ezra Pound (1885-   )

Ezra Pound was born in Hailey, Idaho, graduated from Hamilton
College in 1905, studied at the University of Pennsylvania in 1905-
1906, and taught for four months at Wabash College in 1907-1908.
He lived in London from 1908 to 1920. His first book of poems,
A Lume Spento was published in 1908, and from 1917 to 1919 he edited
The Little Review. In 1924 he went to live in Italy, where in time he
became a propagandist for the Fascist government. Brought back to
the United States in 1945 on a charge of wartime treason, Pound
was declared mentally incompetent to stand trial and was committed
to St. Elizabeth's Hospital in Washington. He remained there until
1958. After his release he returned to Italy, where he lives with his
wife, the former Dorothy Shakespeare, whom he married in 1914.
In 1949 he was awarded the Bollingen Prize for *The Pisan Cantos*.

CINO

Italian Campagna 1309, the open road

Bah! I have sung women in three cities,
But it is all the same;
And I will sing of the sun.

Lips, words, and you snare them,
5   Dreams, words, and they are as jewels,
Strange spells of old deity,
Ravens, nights, allurement:
And they are not;
Having become the souls of song.

10   Eyes, dreams, lips, and the night goes.
Being upon the road once more,
They are not.
Forgetful in their towers of our tuneing

Once for Wind-runeing
15 They dream us-toward and
Sighing, say, "Would Cino,
Passionate Cino, of the wrinkling eyes,
Gay Cino, of quick laughter,
Cino, of the dare, the jibe,
20 Frail Cino, strongest of his tribe
That tramp old ways beneath the sun-light,
Would Cino of the Luth were here!"

Once, twice, a year—
Vaguely thus word they:

25   "Cino?" "Oh, eh, Cino Polnesi
The singer is't you mean?"
"Ah yes, passed once our way,
A saucy fellow, but . . .
(Oh they are all one these vagabonds),
30   Peste! 'tis his own songs?
Or some other's that he sings?
But *you*, My Lord, how with your city?"

But you "My Lord," God's pity!
And all I knew were out, My Lord, you
35 Were Lack-land Cino, e'en as I am,
O Sinistro.

I have sung women in three cities.
But it is all one.
I will sing of the sun.
40 . . . eh? . . . they mostly had grey eyes,
But it is all one, I will sing of the sun.

        "'Pollo Phoibee, old tin pan, you
Glory to Zeus' aegis-day,
Shield o' steel-blue, th' heaven o'er us
45   Hath for boss thy lustre gay!

'Pollo Phoibee, to our way-fare
Make thy laugh our wander-lied;
Bid thy 'fulgence bear away care.
Cloud and rain-tears pass they fleet!

50   Seeking e'er the new-laid rast-way
To the gardens of the sun . . .

            .   .   .   .   .
I have sung women in three cities
But it is all one.

I will sing of the white birds
55   In the blue waters of heaven,
The clouds that are spray to its sea.

ΔΩΡΙΑ

Be in me as the eternal moods
    of the bleak wind, and not
As transient things are—
    gayety of flowers.
5 Have me in the strong loneliness
    of sunless cliffs
And of gray waters.
    Let the gods speak softly of us
In days hereafter,
10   the shadowy flowers of Orcus
Remember thee.

THE GARDEN

En robe de parade.

SAMAIN

Like a skein of loose silk blown against a wall
She walks by the railing of a path in Kensington Gardens,
And she is dying piece-meal
    of a sort of emotional anaemia.

5 And round about there is a rabble
Of the filthy, sturdy, unkillable infants of the very poor.
They shall inherit the earth.

In her is the end of breeding.
Her boredom is exquisite and excessive.
10 She would like some one to speak to her,
And is almost afraid that I
    will commit that indiscretion.

ANCIENT MUSIC

Winter is icummen in,
Lhude sing Goddamm,
Raineth drop and staineth slop,
And how the wind doth ramm!
5   Sing: Goddamm.
Skiddeth bus and sloppeth us,
An ague hath my ham.

ΔΩΡΙΑ. ΔΩΡΙΑ : *Doria:* Dorian, a Doric girl, or small gifts.

ANCIENT MUSIC. This is not folk music, but Dr. Ker writes that the tune is to be found under the Latin words of a very ancient canon.

Freezeth river, turneth liver,
　　　Damn you, sing: Goddamm.
10　Goddamm, Goddamm, 'tis why I am, Goddamm,
　　　So 'gainst the winter's balm.
Sing goddamm, damm, sing Goddamm.
Sing goddamm, sing goddamm, DAMM.

CANTO 15

The saccharescent, lying in glucose,
the pompous in cotton wool
　　　with a stench like the fats at Grasse,
the great scabrous arse-hole, sh-tting flies,
5　　　rumbling with imperialism,
ultimate urinal, middan, pisswallow without a cloaca,
. . . . . . r less rowdy, ... Episcopus
　　　. . . . . sis,
　　　head down, screwed into the swill,
10　his legs waving and pustular,
　　　a clerical jock strap hanging back over the navel
his condom full of black beetles,
　　　tattoo marks round the anus,
and a circle of lady golfers about him.

15　the courageous violent
　　　slashing themselves with knives,
the cowardly inciters to violence
. . . . . n and . . . . h eaten by weevils,
. . . . ll like a swollen fœtus,
20　·　　　the beast with a hundred legs, USURIA
and the swill full of respecters,
　　　bowing to the lords of the place,
explaining its advantages,
　　　and the laudatores temporis acti
25　claiming that the sh-t used to be blacker and richer
and the fabians crying for the petrification of putrefaction,
for a new dung-flow cut in lozenges,
the conservatives chatting,
　　　distinguished by gaiters of slum-flesh,
30　and the back-scratchers in a great circle,
　　　complaining of insufficient attention,
the search without end, counterclaim for the missing scratch
the litigious,
a green bile-sweat, the news owners, ... s
35　　　the anonymous
. . . . ffe, broken
　　　his head shot like a cannon-ball toward the glass gate,

CANTO 15. **7.** *Episcopus:* bishop.

peering through it an instant,
       falling back to the trunk, epileptic,
40 et nulla fidentia inter eos,
       all with their twitching backs,
with daggers, and bottle ends, waiting an
       unguarded moment;

a stench, stuck in the nostrils;
45 beneath one
       nothing that might not move,
mobile earth, a dung hatching obscenities,
       inchoate error,
boredom born out of boredom,
50 british weeklies, copies of the . . . . c,
a multiple . . . . . . nn,
and I said, "How is it done?"
       and my guide:
This sort breeds by scission,
55 This is the fourmillionth tumour.
In this *bolge* bores are gathered,
Infinite pus flakes, scabs of a lasting pox.

skin-flakes, repetitions, erosions,
endless rain from the arse-hairs,
60 as the earth moves, the centre
       passes over all parts in succession,
a continual bum-belch
       distributing its productions.
Andiamo!
65   One's feet sunk,
the welsh of mud gripped one, no hand-rail,
the bog-suck like a whirl-pool,
and he said:
       Close the pores of your feet!
70 And my eyes clung to the horizon,
       oil mixing with soot;
and again Plotinus:
       To the door,
Keep your eyes on the mirror.
75 Prayed we to the Medusa,
       petrifying the soil by the shield,
Holding it downward
       he hardened the track
Inch before us, by inch,
80   the matter resisting,
The heads rose from the shield,
       hissing, held downwards.

---

40. *et nulla fidentia inter eos:* and no confidence among them. **56.** *bolge:* infernal circle. **64.** *Andiamo!:* Let's go.

Devouring maggots,
　　　the face only half potent,
85　The serpents' tongues
　　　grazing the swill top,
Hammering the souse into hardness,
　　　the narrow rast,
Half the width of a sword's edge.
90　　　　By this through the dern evil,
now sinking, now clinging,
　　　Holding the unsinkable shield.
Oblivion,
　　　forget how long,
95　sleep, fainting nausea.
　　　"Whether in Naishapur or Babylon"
I heard in the dream.
　　　Plotinus gone,
And the shield tied under me, woke;
100　The gate swung on its hinges;
Panting like a sick dog, staggered,
Bathed in alkali, and in acid.
'Ηέλιον τ' 'Ηέλιον
　　　blind with the sunlight,
105　Swollen-eyed, rested,
　　　lids sinking, darkness unconscious.

Canto 47

Who even dead, yet hath his mind entire!
This sound came in the dark
First must thou go the road
　　　　　　　　to hell
5　And to the bower of Ceres' daughter Proserpine,
Through overhanging dark, to see Tiresias,
Eyeless that was, a shade, that is in hell
So full of knowing that the beefy men know less than he,
Ere thou come to thy road's end.
10　　　Knowledge the shade of a shade,
Yet must thou sail after knowledge
Knowing less than drugged beasts. *phtheggometha*
thasson
φθεγγώμεθα θᾶσσου
　　　The small lamps drift in the bay
15　And the sea's claw gathers them.

---

96. *Whether in Naishapur or Babylon: Rubáiyát of Omar Khayyám.* 8. "Whether at Naishápúr or Babylon,/Whether the Cup with sweet or bitter run,/The wine of Life keeps oozing drop by drop,/The Leaves of Life keep falling one by one." Naishapur was Khayyám's birthplace. **103.** 'Ηέλιον τ' 'Ηέλιον "Sun, the Sun."

CANTO 47. **12-14.** *phtheggometha thasson:* Odyssey, X, 228, Polites referring to Circe, "Let us raise our voices without delay."

Neptunus drinks after neap-tide.
Tamuz! Tamuz!!
The red flame going seaward.
    By this gate art thou measured.
20 From the long boats they have set lights in the water,
The sea's claw gathers them outward.
Scilla's dogs snarl at the cliff's base,
The white teeth gnaw in under the crag,
But in the pale night the small lamps float seaward
25   Τυ Διώνα,
                                   TU DIONA

Και Μοῖραι' ᾿Αδονιν
KAI MOIRAI' ADONIN
The sea is streaked red with Adonis,
30 The lights flicker red in small jars.
Wheat shoots rise new by the altar,
    flower from the swift seed.
Two span, two span to a woman,
Beyond that she believes not. Nothing is of any importance.
35 To that is she bent, her intention
To that art thou called ever turning intention
Whether by night the owl-call, whether by sap in shoot,
Never idle, by no means by no wiles intermittent
Moth is called over mountain
40 The bull runs blind on the sword, *naturans*
To the cave art thou called, Odysseus,
By Molü hast thou respite for a little,
By Molü art thou freed from the one bed
    that thou may'st return to another
45 The stars are not in her counting,
    To her they are but wandering holes.
Begin thy plowing
When the Pleiades go down to their rest,
Begin thy plowing
50 40 days are they under seabord,
Thus do in fields by seabord
And in valleys winding down toward the sea.
When the cranes fly high
    think of plowing.
55 By this gate art thou measured
Thy day is between a door and a door
Two oxen are yoked for plowing
Or six in the hill field
White bulk under olives, a score for drawing down stone,
60 Here the mules are gabled with slate on the hill road.

26-28. *TU DIONA KAI MOIRAI' ADONIN:* Bion, Idyl I, "The Lament for Adonis," 93-94.
"You, Dione, and the Fates (weep for) Adonis." Dione was the mother of Aphrodite,
goddess who loved Adonis, who was slain by a wild boar; but in this context Dione
designates Aphrodite herself. **42.** *Molü:* the magic herb which Hermes gave to Odysseus to protect him from Circe.

Thus was it in time.
And the small stars now fall from the olive branch,
Forked shadow falls dark on the terrace
More black than the floating martin
65   that has no care for your presence,
His wing-print is black on the roof tiles
And the print is gone with his cry.
So light is thy weight on Tellus
Thy notch no deeper indented
70 Thy weight less than the shadow
Yet hast thou gnawed through the mountain,
        Scylla's white teeth less sharp.
Hast thou found a nest softer than cunnus
Or hast thou found better rest
75 Hast'ou a deeper planting, doth thy death year
Bring swifter shoot?
Hast thou entered more deeply the mountain?

The light has entered the cave. Io! Io!
The light has gone down into the cave,
80 Splendour on splendour!
By prong have I entered these hills:
That the grass grow from my body,
That I hear the roots speaking together,
The air is new on my leaf,
85 The forked boughs shake with the wind.
Is Zephyrus more light on the bough, Apeliota
more light on the almond branch?
By this door have I entered the hill.
Falleth,
90 Adonis falleth.
Fruit cometh after. The small lights drift out with the tide,
sea's claw has gathered them outward,
Four banners to every flower
The sea's claw draws the lamps outward.
95 Think thus of thy plowing
When the seven stars go down to their rest
Forty days for their rest, by seabord
And in valleys that wind down toward the sea
        Καὶ Μοῖραι' Ἄδονιν
100   KAI MOIRAI' ADONIN
When the almond bough puts forth its flame,
When the new shoots are brought to the altar,
        Τυ Διώνα, Καὶ Μοῖραι'
        TU DIONA, KAI MOIRAI
105 Καὶ Μοῖραι' Ἄδονιν
KAI MOIRAI' ADONIN
        that hath the gift of healing,
that hath the power over wild beasts.

---

73. *cunnus:* Latin word for female sexual organ. **86.** *Apeliota:* the East Wind.

Marianne Moore was born in St. Louis, Missouri, graduated from Bryn Mawr in 1909, taught at the United States Indian School in Carlisle, Pennsylvania, from 1911 to 1915, was a librarian in the New York Public Library system, and from 1925 to 1929 was editor of the literary magazine *The Dial.* She began publishing poetry in the 1920's and in 1952 received the Pulitzer Prize and other awards for her *Collected Poems.* In 1965 she was awarded a fellowship of $5000 by the Academy of American Poets. Miss Moore never married. After living in Brooklyn for many years, Miss Moore moved to Greenwich Village in Manhattan in 1966. Asked to comment on the voice of the poet, she replied:

Obliged to be recently at several colleges, the students all seem to ask, "What *is* poetry?" I have come to this conclusion (for the most in others' words): Poetry is

A special extension of the power of seeing. Howard Nemerov

A thing may be expressed in perhaps seven different ways as prose. In poetry, the words are not replaceable. Stephen Spender

For me, in a poem, the words charm the ear, as much as what is said charms the mind.

One does not seek themes to write about. A book, an incident, a person, a deed comes into the mind so inescapably, one can only be at peace in trying to depict it or express something of it. And this, I've said it before: People are quick to say, "I don't understand." I say, "Be as clear as your natural reticence allows you to be."

To a Chameleon

Hid by the august foliage and fruit
  of the grape-vine
    twine
      your anatomy
        round the pruned and polished stem,
5
          Chameleon.
        Fire laid upon
      an emerald as long as
    the Dark King's massy
10
  one,
could not snap the spectrum up for food
  as you have done.

POETRY

I, too, dislike it: there are things that are important beyond all this
        fiddle.
    Reading it, however, with a perfect contempt for it, one discovers in
    it, after all, a place for the genuine.
        Hands that can grasp, eyes
5   that can dilate, hair that can rise
            if it must, these things are important not because a

high-sounding interpretation can be put upon them but because they
        are
    useful. When they become so derivative as to become unintelligible,
10   the same thing may be said for all of us, that we do not admire what
    we cannot understand: the bat
        holding on upside down or in quest of something to

eat, elephants pushing, a wild horse taking a roll, a tireless wolf under
    a tree, the immovable critic twitching his skin like a horse that feels
    a flea, the base-
15   ball fan, the statistician—
        nor is it valid
            to discriminate against 'business documents and

school-books'; all these phenomena are important. One must make a
        distinction
    however: when dragged into prominence by half poets, the result
    is not poetry,
20   nor till the poets among us can be
        'literalists of
        the imagination'—above
            insolence and triviality and can present

for inspection, imaginary gardens with real toads in them, shall we
        have
25   it. In the meantime, if you demand on the one hand,
    the raw material of poetry in
        all its rawness and
        that which is on the other hand
            genuine, then you are interested in poetry.

THOSE VARIOUS SCALPELS,

those
various sounds consistently indistinct, like intermingled echoes
    struck from thin glasses successively at random—the
        inflection disguised: your hair, the tails of two
5   fighting-cocks head to head in stone—like sculptured scimitars re-
            peating the curve of your ears in reverse order: your eyes, flowers
                of ice

and
snow sown by tearing winds on the cordage of disabled ships; your
    raised hand,
    an ambiguous signature: your cheeks, those rosettes
10   of blood on the stone floors of French châteaux, with
    regard to which the guides are so affirmative—those regrets
        of the retoucher on the contemporary stone: your other hand,

a
bundle of lances all alike, partly hid by emeralds from Persia
15   and the fractional magnificence of Florentine
        goldwork—a collection of little objects—
    sapphires set with emeralds, and pearls with a moonstone, made
        fine
        with enamel in grey, yellow, and dragon-fly blue; a lemon, a

pear
20 and three bunches of grapes, tied with silver: your dress, a magnif-
        icent square
    cathedral tower of uniform
        and at the same time, diverse appearance—a
    species of vertical vineyard rustling in the storm
        of conventional opinion. Are they weapons or scalpels? Whetted

25 to
brilliance by the hard majesty of that sophistication which is su-
    perior to opportunity, these things are rich
        instruments with which to experiment; naturally. But
    why dissect destiny with instruments which
30   are more highly specialized than the tissues of destiny itself?

'KEEPING THEIR WORLD LARGE'[1]

All too literally, their flesh
and their spirit are our shield
                New York Times, 7th June, 1944

        I should like to see that country's tiles, bedrooms,
stone patios
            and ancient wells: Rinaldo
Caramonica's the cobbler's, Frank Sblendorio's
5   and Dominick Angelastro's country—
        the grocer's, the iceman's, the dancer's—the
    beautiful Miss Damiano's; wisdom's

        and all angels' Italy, this Christmas Day
this Christmas year.
10   A noiseless piano, an
innocent war, the heart that can act against itself. Here,

---

[1]The Reverend James Gordon Gilkey.

each unlike and all alike, could
so many—stumbling, falling, multiplied
till bodies lay as ground to walk on—say

15   'If Christ and the apostles died in vain, I'll
die in vain with them'?
When the very heart was a prayer
against this way of victory. Stem after stem
of what we call the tree—set, row
20   on row; that forest of white crosses; the
vision makes us faint. My eyes won't close to it. While

the knife was lifted, Isaac the offering
lay mute.
These, laid like animals for sacrifice,
25 like Isaac on the mount, were their own substitute.
And must they all be harmed by those
whom they have saved. Tears that don't fall are what
they wanted. Belief in belief marching

marching marching—all alone, all similar,
30 spurning pathos,
clothed in fear—marching to death
marching to life; it was like the cross, is like the cross.
Keeping their world large, that silent
marching marching marching and this silence
35 for which there is no description, are

the voices of fighters with no rests between,
who would not yield;
whose spirits and whose bodies
all too literally were our shield, are still our shield.
40   They fought the enemy, we fight
fat living and self-pity. Shine, O shine
unfalsifying sun, on this sick scene.

RESCUE WITH YUL BRYNNER

(Appointed special consultant to the United Nations High Commissioner for Refugees, 1959-1960)

"Recital? 'Concert' is the word,"
and stunning, by the Budapest Symphony—
displaced but not deterred—
listened to by me,
5   though with detachment then,
like a grasshopper that did not
know it missed the mower, a pygmy citizen;
a case, I'd say, of too slow a grower.

There were thirty million; there are thirteen still—
10　healthy to begin with, kept waiting till they're ill.
History judges. It will
salute Winnipeg's incredible
conditions: "Ill; no sponsor; and no kind of skill."
　　Odd—a reporter with guitar—a puzzle.
15　Mysterious Yul did not come to dazzle.

　　Magic bird with multiple tongue—
five tongues—equipped for a crazy twelve-month tramp
(a plod), he flew among
the damned, found each camp
20　　where hope had slowly died
　　　(some had never seen a plane).
　　Instead of feathering himself, he exemplified
　　　the rule that, self-applied, omits the gold.
He said, "You may feel strange; nothing matters less.
25　Nobody notices; you'll find some happiness.
No new 'big fear'; no distress."
Yul can sing—twin of an enchantress—
elephant-borne dancer in silver-spangled dress,
　　swirled aloft by trunk, with star-tipped wand, Tamara,
30　　as true to the beat as *Symphonia Hungarica*.

　　Head bent down over the guitar,
he barely seemed to hum; ended "all come home";
　　did not smile; came by air;
did not have to come.
35　　The guitar's an event.
　　　Guests of honor can't dance; don't smile.
　　"Have a home?" a boy asks. "Shall we live in a tent?"
　　　"In a house," Yul answers. His neat cloth hat
has nothing like the glitter reflected on the face
40　of milkweed-witch seed-brown dominating a palace
that was nothing like the place
where he is now. His deliberate pace
is a king's, however. "You'll have plenty of space."
　　Yule—Yul log for the Christmas-fire tale-spinner—
45　　of fairy tales that can come true: Yul Brynner.

Robinson Jeffers (1887-1962)

Born in Pittsburgh, Pennsylvania, Robinson Jeffers was a frequent
visitor to Europe in the 1890's and attended boarding schools in
Switzerland and Germany from 1899 to 1903. He moved to California
in 1903, graduated from Occidental College two years later, and did

graduate work in various subjects until 1911. He married in 1913 and had two children. After receiving a legacy in 1912, he settled at Tor House on Carmel Bay, south of Monterey, California, in 1914, building himself a stone tower in which he did much of his writing. He was a member of the National Institute of Arts and Letters and of the American Academy of Arts and Letters and in 1958 received the Academy of American Poets award.

ROAN STALLION

The dog barked; then the woman stood in the doorway, and hearing
    iron strike stone down the steep road
Covered her head with a black shawl and entered the light rain; she
    stood at the turn of the road.
A nobly formed woman; erect and strong as a new tower; the features
    stolid and dark
But sculptured into a strong grace; straight nose with a high bridge,
    firm and wide eyes, full chin,
5   Red lips; she was only a fourth part Indian; a Scottish sailor had
    planted her in young native earth,
Spanish and Indian, twenty-one years before. He had named her
    California when she was born;
That was her name; and had gone north.
                      She heard the hooves
    and wheels come nearer, up the steep road.
The buckskin mare, leaning against the breastpiece, plodded into
    sight round the wet bank.
10   The pale face of the driver followed; the burnt-out eyes; they had
    fortune in them. He sat twisted
On the seat of the old buggy, leading a second horse by a long
    halter, a roan, a big one,
That stepped daintily; by the swell of the neck, a stallion. "What
    have you got, Johnny?" "Maskerel's stallion.
Mine now. I won him last night, I had very good luck." He was
    quite drunk. "They bring their mares up here now.
I keep this fellow. I got money besides, but I'll not show you." "Did
    you buy something, Johnny,
15   For our Christine? Christmas comes in two days, Johnny." "By
    God, forgot," he answered laughing.
"Don't tell Christine it's Christmas; after while I get her something,
    maybe." But California:
"I shared your luck when you lost: you lost *me* once, Johnny, remem-
    ber? Tom Dell had me two nights
Here in the house: other times we've gone hungry: now that you've
    won, Christine will have her Christmas.
We share your luck, Johnny. You give me money, I go down to
    Monterey to-morrow,

ROAN STALLION. **100.** *a noise of wing-feathers:* cf. myth of Zeus descending on Leda in the form of a swan. See William Butler Yeats' poem *Leda and the Swan.*

20   Buy presents for Christine, come back in the evening. Next day
         Christmas." "You have wet ride," he answered
     Giggling. "Here money. Five dollar; ten; twelve dollar. You buy two
         bottles of rye whisky for Johnny."
     "All right. I go to-morrow."
                                He was an outcast Hollander; not
     old, but shriveled with bad living.
     The child Christine inherited from his race blue eyes, from his life
     a wizened forehead; she watched
25   From the house-door her father lurch out of the buggy and lead with
         due respect the stallion
     To the new corral, the strong one; leaving the wearily breathing
         buckskin mare to his wife to unharness.

     Storm in the night; the rain on the thin shakes of the roof like the
         ocean on rock streamed battering; once thunder
     Walked down the narrow canyon into Carmel valley and wore away
         westward; Christine was wakeful
     With fears and wonders; her father lay too deep for storm to touch
         him.
30   Dawn comes late in the year's dark,
     Later into the crack of a canyon under redwoods; and California
         slipped from bed
     An hour before it; the buckskin would be tired; there was a little
         barley, and why should Johnny
     Feed all the barley to his stallion? That is what he would do. She
         tiptoed out of the room.
     Leaving her clothes, he'd waken if she waited to put them on, and
         passed from the door of the house
35   Into the dark of the rain; the big black drops were cold through
         the thin shift, but the wet earth
     Pleasant under her naked feet. There was a pleasant smell in the
         stable; and moving softly,
     Touching things gently with the supple bend of the unclothed body,
         was pleasant. She found a box,
     Filled it with deep dry barley and took it down to the old corral.
         The little mare sighed deeply
     At the rail in the wet darkness; and California returning between
         two redwoods up to the house
40   Heard the happy jaws grinding the grain. Johnny could mind the
         pigs and chickens. Christine called to her
     When she entered the house, but slept again under her hand. She
         laid the wet night-dress on a chair-back
     And stole into the bedroom to get her clothes. A plank creaked, and
         he wakened. She stood motionless
     Hearing him stir in the bed. When he was quiet she stooped after
         her shoes, and he said softly,
     "What are you doing? Come back to bed." "It's late, I'm going to
         Monterey, I must hitch up."

45   "You come to bed first. I been away three days. I give you money, I
take back the money
And what you do in town then?" She sighed sharply and came to
the bed.
                                  He reaching his hands from it
Felt the cool curve and firmness of her flank, and half rising caught
her by the long wet hair.
She endured, and to hasten the act she feigned desire; she had not
for long, except in dream, felt it.
50 Yesterday's drunkenness made him sluggish and exacting; she saw,
turning her head sadly,
The windows were bright gray with dawn; he embraced her still,
stopping to talk about the stallion.
At length she was permitted to put on her clothes. Clear daylight
over the steep hills;
Gray-shining cloud over the tops of the redwoods; the winter stream
sang loud; the wheels of the buggy
Slipped in deep slime, ground on washed stones at the road-edge.
Down the hill the wrinkled river smothered the ford.
55 You must keep to the bed of stones: she knew the way by willow
and alder: the buckskin halted mid-stream,
Shuddering, the water her own color washing up to the traces; but
California, drawing up
Her feet out of the whirl onto the seat of the buggy swung the whip
over the yellow water
And drove to the road.

                            All morning the clouds were racing north-
ward like a river. At noon they thickened.
60 When California faced the southwind home from Monterey it was
heavy with level rainfall.
She looked seaward from the foot of the valley; red rays cried sunset
from a trumpet of streaming
Cloud over Lobos, the southwest occident of the solstice. Twilight
came soon, but the tired mare
Feared the road more than the whip. Mile after mile of slow gray
twilight.
                        Then, quite suddenly, darkness.
65 "Christine will be asleep. It is Christmas Eve. The ford. That hour
of daylight wasted this morning!"
She could see nothing; she let the reins lie on the dashboard and
knew at length by the cramp of the wheels
And the pitch down, they had reached it. Noise of wheels on stones,
plashing of hooves in water; a world
Of sounds; no sight; the gentle thunder of water; the mare snorting,
dipping her head, one knew,
To look for footing, in the blackness, under the stream. The hushing
and creaking of the sea-wind
70 In the passion of invisible willows.

The mare stood still; the woman shouted to her; spared whip,
For a false leap would lose the track of the ford. She stood. "The baby's things," thought California,
"Under the seat: the water will come over the floor"; and rising in the midst of the water
She tilted the seat; fetched up the doll, the painted wooden chickens, the wooly bear, the book
75 Of many pictures, the box of sweets: she brought them all from under the seat and stored them, trembling,
Under her clothes, about the breasts, under the arms; the corners of the cardboard boxes
Cut into the soft flesh; but with a piece of rope for a girdle and wound about the shoulders
All was made fast. The mare stood still as if asleep in the midst of the water. Then California
Reached out a hand over the stream and fingered her rump; the solid wet convexity of it
80 Shook like the beat of a great heart. "What are you waiting for?" But the feel of the animal surface
Had wakened a dream, obscured real danger with a dream of danger. "What for? for the water-stallion
To break out of the stream, that is what the rump strains for, him to come up flinging foam sidewise,
Fore-hooves in air, crush me and the rig and curl over his woman." She flung out with the whip then;
The mare plunged forward. The buggy drifted sidelong: was she off ground? Swimming? No: by the splashes.
85 The driver, a mere prehensile instinct, clung to the sideirons of the seat and felt the force
But not the coldness of the water, curling over her knees, breaking up to the waist
Over her body. They'd turned. The mare had turned up stream and was wallowing back into shoal water.
Then California dropped her forehead to her knees, having seen nothing, feeling a danger,
And felt the brute weight of a branch of alder, the pendulous light leaves brush her bent neck
90 Like a child's fingers. The mare burst out of water and stopped on the slope to the ford. The woman climbed down
Between the wheels and went to her head. "Poor Dora," she called her by her name, "there, Dora. Quietly,"
And led her around, there was room to turn on the margin, the head to the gentle thunder of the water.
She crawled on hands and knees, felt for the ruts, and shifted the wheels into them. "You can see, Dora.
I can't. But this time you'll go through it." She climbed into the seat and shouted angrily. The mare
95 Stopped her two forefeet in the water. She touched with the whip. The mare plodded ahead and halted.

Then California thought of prayer: "Dear little Jesus,
Dear baby Jesus born to-night, your head was shining
Like silver candles. I've got a baby too, only a girl. You had light
    wherever you walked.
Dear baby Jesus give me light." Light streamed: rose, gold, rich
    purple, hiding the ford like a curtain.
100   The gentle thunder of water was a noise of wing-feathers, the fans
    of paradise lifting softly.
The child afloat on radiance had a baby face, but the angels had
    birds' heads, hawks' heads,
Bending over the baby, weaving a web of wings about him. He held
    in the small fat hand
A little snake with golden eyes, and California could see clearly on
    the under radiance
The mare's pricked ears, a sharp black fork against the shining
    light-fall. But it dropped; the light of heaven
105   Frightened poor Dora. She backed; swung up the water,
And nearly oversetting the buggy turned and scrambled backward;
    the iron wheel-tires rang on boulders.

Then California weeping climbed between the wheels. Her wet
    clothes and the toys packed under
Dragged her down with their weight; she stripped off cloak and dress
    and laid the baby's things in the buggy;
Brought Johnny's whisky out from under the seat; wrapped all in
    the dress, bottles and toys, and tied them
110   Into a bundle that would sling over her back. She unharnessed the
    mare, hurting her fingers
Against the swollen straps and the wet buckles. She tied the pack
    over her shoulders, the cords
Crossing her breasts, and mounted. She drew up her shift about her
    waist and knotted it, naked thighs
Clutching the sides of the mare, bare flesh to the wet withers, and
    caught the mane with her right hand,
The looped-up bridle-reins in the other. "Dora, the baby gives you
    light." The blinding radiance
115   Hovered the ford. "Sweet baby Jesus give us light." Cataracts of
    light and Latin singing
Fell through the willows; the mare snorted and reared: the roar and
    thunder of the invisible water;
The night shaking open like a flag, shot with the flashes; the baby
    face hovering; the water
Beating over her shoes and stockings up to the bare thighs; and over
    them, like a beast
Lapping her belly; the wriggle and pitch of the mare swimming;
    the drift, the sucking water; the blinding
120   Light above and behind with not a gleam before, in the throat of
    darkness; the shock of the fore-hooves
Striking bottom, the struggle and surging lift of the haunches. She
    felt the water streaming off her

From the shoulders down; heard the great strain and sob of the mare's breathing, heard the horseshoes grind on gravel.
When California came home the dog at the door snuffled at her without barking; Christine and Johnny
Both were asleep; she did not sleep for hours, but kindled fire and knelt patiently over it,
125 Shaping and drying the dear-bought gifts for Christmas morning.

She hated (she thought) the proud-necked stallion.
He'd lean the big twin masses of his breast on the rail, his red-brown eyes flash the white crescents,
She admired him then, she hated him for his uselessness, serving nothing
But Johnny's vanity. Horses were too cheap to breed. She thought, if he could range in freedom,
130 Shaking the red-roan mane for a flag on the bare hills.
                                                                        A man brought up a mare in April;
Then California, though she wanted to watch, stayed with Christine indoors. When the child fretted
The mother told her once more about the miracle of the ford; her prayers to the little Jesus
The Christmas Eve when she was bringing the gifts home; the appearance, the lights, the Latin singing,
135 The thunder of wing-feathers and water, the shining child, the cataracts of splendor down the darkness.
"A little baby," Christine asked, "the God is a baby?" "The child of God. That was his birthday.
His mother was named Mary: we pray to her too: God came to her. He was not the child of a man
Like you or me. God was his father: she was the stallion's wife— what did I say—God's wife,"
She said with a cry, lifting Christine aside, pacing the planks of the floor. "She is called more blessed
140 Than any woman. She was so good, she was more loved." "Did God live near her house?" "He lives
Up high, over the stars; he ranges on the bare blue hill of the sky." In her mind a picture
Flashed, of the red-roan mane shaken out for a flag on the bare hills, and she said quickly, "He's more
Like a great man holding the sun in his hand." Her mind giving her words the lie, "But no one
Knows, only the shining and the power. The power, the terror, the burning fire covered her over . . ."
145 "Was she burnt up, mother?" "She was so good and lovely, she was the mother of little Jesus.
If you are good nothing will hurt you." "What did she think?" "She loved, she was not afraid of the hooves—
Hands that had made the hills and sun and moon, and the sea and the great redwoods, the terrible strength,

She gave herself without thinking." "You only saw the baby,
mother?" "Yes, and the angels about him,
The great wild shining over the black river." Three times she had
walked to the door, three times returned,
150 And now the hand that had thrice hung on the knob, full of pre-
vented action, twisted the cloth
Of the child's dress that she had been mending. "Oh, Oh, I've torn
it." She struck at the child and then embraced her
Fiercely, the small blond sickly body.
Johnny came in, his face
reddened as if he had stood
Near fire, his eyes triumphing. "Finished," he said, and looked with
malice at Christine. "I go
155 Down valley with Jim Carrier; owes me five dollar, fifteen I charge
him, he brought ten in his pocket.
Has grapes on the ranch, maybe I take a barrel red wine instead of
money. Be back to-morrow.
To-morrow night I tell you— Eh, Jim," he laughed over his shoulder,
"I say to-morrow evening
I show her how the red fellow act, the big fellow. When I come
home." She answered nothing, but stood
In front of the door, holding the little hand of her daughter, in the
path of sun between the redwoods,
160 While Johnny tied the buckskin mare behind Carrier's buggy, and
bringing saddle and bridle tossed them
Under the seat. Jim Carrier's mare, the bay, stood with drooped
head and started slowly, the men
Laughing and shouting at her; their voices could be heard down the
steep road, after the noise
Of the iron-hooped wheels died from the stone. Then one might
hear the hush of the wind in the tall redwoods,
The tinkle of the April brook, deep in its hollow.
165 Humanity is the
start of the race; I say
Humanity is the mold to break away from, the crust to break through,
the coal to break into fire,
The atom to be split.
Tragedy that breaks man's face and a white
fire flies out of it; vision that fools him
Out of his limits, desire that fools him out of his limits, unnatural
crime, inhuman science,
170 Slit eyes in the mask; wild loves that leap over the walls of nature,
the wild fence-vaulter science,
Useless intelligence of far stars, dim knowledge of the spinning
demons that make an atom,
These break, these pierce, these deify, praising their God shrilly
with fierce voices: not in man's shape
He approves the praise, he that walks lightning-naked on the Pacific,
that laces the suns with planets,

The heart of the atom with electrons: what is humanity in this cosmos? For him, the last
175 Least tint of a trace in the dregs of the solution; for itself, the mold
to break away from, the coal
To break into fire, the atom to be split.

                                                  After the child slept, after
the leopard-footed evening
Had glided oceanward, California turned the lamp to its least flame
and glided from the house.
She moved sighing, like a loose fire, backward and forward on the
smooth ground by the door.
180 She heard the night-wind that draws down the valley like the draught
in a flue under clear weather
Whisper and toss in the tall redwoods; she heard the tinkle of the
April brook deep in its hollow.
Cooled by the night the odors that the horses had left behind were
in her nostrils; the night
Whitened up the bare hill; a drift of coyotes by the river cried bitterly against moonrise;
Then California ran to the old corral, the empty one where they
kept the buckskin mare,
185 And leaned, and bruised her breasts on the rail, feeling the sky
whiten. When the moon stood over the hill
She stole to the house. The child breathed quietly. Herself: to
sleep? She had seen Christ in the night at Christmas.
The hills were shining open to the enormous night of the April
moon: empty and empty,
The vast round backs of the bare hills? If one should ride up high
might not the Father himself
Be seen brooding His night, cross-legged, chin in hand, squatting
on the last dome? More likely
190 Leaping the hills, shaking the red-roan mane for a flag on the bare
hills. She blew out the lamp.
Every fiber of flesh trembled with faintness when she came to the
door; strength lacked, to wander
Afoot into the shining of the hill, high enough, high enough . . .
the hateful face of a man had taken
The strength that might have served her, the corral was empty.
The dog followed her, she caught him by the collar,
Dragged him in fierce silence back to the door of the house, latched
him inside.
195   It was like daylight
Out-doors and she hastened without faltering down the footpath,
through the dark fringe of twisted oak-brush,
To the open place in a bay of the hill. The dark strength of the
stallion had heard her coming; she heard him
Blow the shining air out of his nostrils, she saw him in the white
lake of moonlight

Move like a lion along the timbers of the fence, shaking the nightfall
200 Of the great mane; his fragrance came to her; she leaned on the
fence;
He drew away from it, the hooves making soft thunder in the trodden soil.
Wild love had trodden it, his wrestling with the stranger, the shame
of the day
Had stamped it into mire and powder when the heavy fetlocks
Strained the soft flanks. "Oh, if I could bear you!
205 If I had the strength. O great God that came down to Mary, gently
you came. But I will ride him
Up into the hill, if he throws me, if he tramples me, is it not my
desire
To endure death?" She climbed the fence, pressing her body against
the rail, shaking like fever,
And dropped inside to the soft ground. He neither threatened her
with his teeth nor fled from her coming,
And lifting her hand gently to the upflung head she caught the strap
of the headstall,
210 That hung under the quivering chin. She unlooped the halter from
the high strength of the neck
And the arch the storm-cloud mane hung with live darkness. He
stood; she crushed her breasts
On the hard shoulder, an arm over the withers, the other under the
mass of his throat, and murmuring
Like a mountain dove, "If I could bear you." No way, no help, a
gulf in nature. She murmured, "Come,
We will run on the hill. O beautiful, O beautiful," and led him to
the gate and flung the bars on the ground. He threw his head
downward
215 To snuff at the bars; and while he stood, she catching mane and
withers with all sudden contracture
And strength of her lithe body, leaped, clung hard, and was mounted.
He had been ridden before; he did not
Fight the weight but ran like a stone falling;
Broke down the slope into the moon-glass of the stream, and flat-
tened to his neck
She felt the branches of a buck-eye tree fly over her, saw the wall of
the oak-scrub
220 End her world: but he turned there, the matted branches
Scraped her right knee, the great slant shoulders
Laboring the hill-slope, up, up, the clear hill. Desire had died in her
At the first rush, the falling like death, but now it revived,
She feeling between her thighs the labor of the great engine, the
running muscles, the hard swiftness,
225 She riding the savage and exultant strength of the world. Having
topped the thicket he turned eastward,
Running less wildly; and now at length he felt the halter when she
drew on it; she guided him upward;

He stopped and grazed on the great arch and pride of the hill, the
  silent calvary. A dwarfish oakwood
Climbed the other slope out of the dark of the unknown canyon
  beyond; the last wind-beaten bush of it
Crawled up to the height, and California slipping from her mount
  tethered him to it. She stood then,
230 Shaking. Enormous films of moonlight
Trailed down from the height. Space, anxious whiteness, vastness.
  Distant beyond conception the shining ocean
Lay light like a haze along the ledge and doubtful world's end.
  Little vapors gleaming, and little
Darknesses on the far chart underfoot symbolized wood and valley;
  but the air was the element, the moon-
Saturate arcs and spires of the air.
235   Here is solitude, here on the
  calvary, nothing conscious
But the possible God and the cropped grass, no witness, no eye but
  that misformed one, the moon's past fullness.
Two figures on the shining hill, woman and stallion, she kneeling
  to him, brokenly adoring.
He cropping the grass, shifting his hooves, or lifting the long head
  to gaze over the world,
Tranquil and powerful. She prayed aloud, "O God, I am not good
  enough, O fear, O strength, I am draggled.
240 Johnny and other men have had me, and O clean power! Here am
  I," she said falling before him,
And crawled to his hooves. She lay a long while, as if asleep, in
  reach of the fore-hooves, weeping. He avoided
Her head and the prone body. He backed up first; but later plucked
  the grass that grew by her shoulder.
The small dark head under his nostrils: a small round stone, that
  smelt human, black hair growing from it:
The skull shut the light in it: it was not possible for any eyes
245 To know what throbbed and shone under the sutures of the skull,
  or a shell full of lightning
Had scared the roan strength, and he'd have broken tether, screaming, and run for the valley.
                                    The atom bounds-breaking,
Nucleus to sun, electrons to planets, with recognition
Not praying, self-equaling, the whole to the whole, the micro-
  cosm
250 Not entering nor accepting entrance, more equally, more utterly,
  more incredibly conjugate
With the other extreme and greatness; passionately perceptive of
  identity. . . .
                                    The fire threw up figures
And symbols meanwhile, racial myths formed and dissolved in it,
  the phantom rulers of humanity
That without being are yet more real than what they are born of,
  and without shape, shape that which makes them:

255 The nerves and the flesh go by shadowlike, the limbs and the lives
     shadowlike, these shadows remain, these shadows
To whom temples, to whom churches, to whom labors and wars,
     visions and dreams are dedicate:
Out of the fire in the small round stone that black moss covered,
     a crucified man writhed up in anguish;
A woman covered by a huge beast in whose mane the stars were
     netted, sun and moon were his eyeballs,
Smiled under the unendurable violation, her throat swollen with
     the storm and blood-flecks gleaming
260 On the stretched lips; a woman—no, a dark water, split by jets of
     lightning, and after a season
What floated up out of the furrowed water, a boat, a fish, a fire-
     globe?
                                        It had wings, the creature,
And flew against the fountain of lightning, fell burnt out of the
     cloud back to the bottomless water . . .
Figures and symbols, castlings of the fire, played in her brain; but
     the white fire was the essence,
265 The burning in the small round shell of bone that black hair covered,
     that lay by the hooves on the hilltop.

She rose at length, she unknotted the halter; she walked and led the
     stallion; two figures, woman and stallion,
Came down the silent emptiness of the dome of the hill, under the
     cataract of the moonlight.

The next night there was moon through cloud. Johnny had returned
     half drunk toward evening, and California
Who had known him for years with neither love nor loathing to-
     night hating him had let the child Christine
270 Play in the light of the lamp for hours after her bedtime; who fell
     asleep at length on the floor
Beside the dog; then Johnny: "Put her to bed." She gathered the
     child against her breasts, she laid her
In the next room, and covered her with a blanket. The window was
     white, the moon had risen. The mother
Lay down by the child, but after a moment Johnny stood in the
     doorway. "Come drink." He had brought home
Two jugs of wine slung from the saddle, part payment for the
     stallion's service; a pitcher of it
275 Was on the table, and California sadly came and emptied her glass.
     Whisky, she thought,
Would have erased him till to-morrow; the thin red wine. . . . "We
     have a good evening," he laughed, pouring it.
"One glass yet then I show you what the red fellow did." She moving
     toward the house-door his eyes
Followed her, the glass filled and the red juice ran over the table.
     When it struck the floor-planks

He heard and looked. "Who stuck the pig?" he muttered stupidly,
"here's blood, here's blood," and trailed his fingers

280 In the red lake under the lamplight. While he was looking down
the door creaked, she had slipped out-doors,

And he, his mouth curving like a faun's, imagined the chase under
the solemn redwoods, the panting

And unresistant victim caught in a dark corner. He emptied the
glass and went out-doors

Into the dappled lanes of moonlight. No sound but the April brook's.
"Hey Bruno," he called, "find her.

Bruno, go find her." The dog after a little understood and quested,
the man following.

285 When California crouching by an oak-bush above the house heard
them come near she darted

To the open slope and ran down hill. The dog barked at her heels,
pleased with the game, and Johnny

Followed in silence. She ran down to the new corral, she saw the
stallion

Move like a lion along the timbers of the fence, the dark arched
neck shaking the nightfall

Of the great mane; she threw herself prone and writhed under the
bars, his hooves backing away from her

290 Made muffled thunder in the soft soil. She stood in the midst of the
corral, panting, but Johnny

Paused at the fence. The dog ran under it, and seeing the stallion
move, the woman standing quiet,

Danced after the beast, with white-toothed feints and dashes. When
Johnny saw the formidable dark strength

Recoil from the dog, he climbed up over the fence.

The child Christine waked when her mother left her

295 And lay half-dreaming, in the half-waking dream she saw the ocean
come up out of the west

And cover the world, she looked up through clear water at the tops
of the redwoods. She heard the door creak

And the house empty; her heart shook her body, sitting up on the
bed, and she heard the dog

And crept toward light, where it gleamed under the crack of the
door. She opened the door, the room was empty,

The table-top was a red lake under the lamplight. The color of it
was terrible to her;

300 She had seen the red juice drip from a coyote's muzzle, her father
had shot one day in the hills

And carried him home over the saddle: she looked at the rifle on
the wall-rack: it was not moved:

She ran to the door, the dog was barking and the moon was shining:
she knew wine by the odor

But the color frightened her, the empty house frightened her, she
followed down the hill in the white lane of moonlight

The friendly noise of the dog. She saw in the big horse's corral, on
the level shoulder of the hill,

305   Black on white, the dark strength of the beast, the dancing fury
of the dog, and the two others.

One fled, one followed; the big one charged, rearing; one fell under
his forehooves. She heard her mother

Scream: without thought she ran to the house, she dragged a chair
past the red pool and climbed to the rifle,

Got it down from the wall and lugged it somehow through the door
and down the hillside, under the hard weight

Sobbing. Her mother stood by the rails of the corral, she gave it to
her. On the far side

310   The dog flashed at the plunging stallion; in the midst of the space
the man, slow-moving, like a hurt worm

Crawling, dragged his body by inches toward the fence-line. Then
California, resting the rifle

On the top rail, without doubting, without hesitance,

Aimed for the leaping body of the dog, and when it stood, fired. It
snapped, rolled over, lay quiet.

"O mother, you've hit Bruno!" "I couldn't see the sights in the
moonlight," she answered quietly. She stood

315   And watched, resting the rifle-butt on the ground. The stallion
wheeled, freed from his torment, the man

Lurched up to his knees, wailing a thin and bitter bird's cry, and
the roan thunder

Struck; hooves left nothing alive but teeth tore up the remnant. "O
mother, shoot, shoot!" Yet California

Stood carefully watching, till the beast having fed all his fury stretched
neck to utmost, head high,

And wrinkled back the upper lip from the teeth, yawning obscene
disgust over—not a man—

320   A smear on the moon-lake earth: then California moved by some
obscure human fidelity

Lifted the rifle. Each separate nerve-cell of her brain flaming the
stars fell from their places

Crying in her mind: she fired three times before the haunches
crumpled sidewise, the forelegs stiffening,

And the beautiful strength settled to earth: she turned then on her
little daughter the mask of a woman

Who has killed God. The night-wind veering, the smell of the spilt
wine drifted down hill from the house.

BIRDS

The fierce musical cries of a couple of sparrowhawks hunting on the
headland,

Hovering and darting, their heads northwestward,

Prick like silver arrows shot through a curtain the noise of the ocean

Trampling its granite; their red backs gleam

5   Under my window around the stone corners; nothing gracefuller, nothing
Nimbler in the wind. Westward the wave-gleaners,
The old gray sea-going gulls are gathered together, the northwest wind wakening
Their wings to the wild spirals of the wind-dance.
Fresh as the air, salt as the foam, play birds in the bright wind, fly falcons
10 Forgetting the oak and the pinewood, come gulls
From the Carmel sands and the sands at the river-mouth, from Lobos and out of the limitless
Power of the mass of the sea, for a poem
Needs multitude, multitudes of thoughts, all fierce, all flesh-eaters, musically clamorous
Bright hawks that hover and dart headlong, and ungainly
15 Gray hungers fledged with desire of transgression, salt slimed beaks, from the sharp
Rock-shores of the world and the secret waters.

THE CRUEL FALCON

Contemplation would make a good life, keep it strict, only
The eyes of a desert skull drinking the sun,
Too intense for flesh, lonely
Exultations of white bone;
5   Pure action would make a good life, let it be sharp-
Set between the throat and the knife.
A man who knows death by heart
Is the man for that life.
In pleasant peace and security
10 How suddenly the soul in a man begins to die.
He shall look up above the stalled oxen
Envying the cruel falcon,
And dig under the straw for a stone
To bruise himself on.

MAY-JUNE, 1940

Foreseen for so many years: these evils, this monstrous violence, these massive agonies: no easier to bear.
We saw them with slow stone strides approach, everyone saw them; we closed our eyes against them, we looked
And they had come nearer. We ate and drank and slept, they came nearer. Sometimes we laughed, they were nearer. Now
They are here. And now a blind man foresees what follows them: degradation, famine, recovery and so forth, and the
5   Epidemic manias: but not enough death to serve us, not enough death. It would be better for men

To be few and live far apart, where none could infect another; then
    slowly the sanity of field and mountain
And the cold ocean and glittering stars might enter their minds.

                        Another
    dream, another dream.
We shall have to accept certain limitations
10   In future, and abandon some humane dreams; only hard-minded,
    sleepless and realist, can ride this rock-slide
To new fields down the dark mountain; and we shall have to perceive
    that these insanities are normal;
We shall have to perceive that battle is a burning flower or like a huge
    music, and the dive-bomber's screaming orgasm
As beautiful as other passions; and that death and life are not seri-
    ous alternatives.
    One has known all these things
For many years: there is greater and darker to know
15   In the next hundred.

             And why do you cry, my dear, why do you cry?
It is all in the whirling circles of time.
If millions are born millions must die,
If England goes down and Germany up
20   The stronger dog will still be on top,
All in the turning of time.
If civilization goes down, that
Would be an event to contemplate.
It will not be in our time, alas, my dear,
25   It will not be in our time.

New Year's Dawn, 1947

Two morning stars, Venus and Jupiter,
Walk in the pale and liquid light
Above the color of these dawns; and as the tide of light
Rises higher the great planet vanishes
5   While the nearer still shines. The yellow wave of light
In the east and south reddens, the opaque ocean
Becomes pale purple: O delicate
Earnestness of dawn, the fervor and pallor.
—Stubbornly I think again: The state is a blackmailer,
10   Honest or not, with whom we make (within reason)
Our accommodations. There is no valid authority
In church nor state, custom, scripture nor creed,
But only in one's own conscience and the beauty of things.
Doggedly I think again: One's conscience is a trick oracle,
15   Worked by parents and nurse-maids, the pressure of the people,
And the delusions of dead prophets: trust it not.
Wash it clean to receive the transhuman beauty: then trust it.

John Crowe Ransom was born in Pulaski, Tennessee, graduated from Vanderbilt in 1909, was a Rhodes Scholar at Christ Church College, Oxford, from 1910 to 1913, received a B.A. from Oxford in 1913, and, except for two years in France during World War I, taught at Vanderbilt from 1914 to 1937. He married in 1920 and has three children. From 1922 to 1925 he was editor of the literary magazine *Fugitive* and in 1931-1932 was a Guggenheim Fellow at Exeter, England. From 1937 to 1958 he taught at Kenyon College, editing the *Kenyon Review* from its first issue in 1939 to 1961. In 1962 he held an Academy of American Poets fellowship. He was elected to the National Institute of Arts and Letters in 1947 and received the Bollingen Prize and the Loines Award in 1951 and the Brandeis University Gold Medal in Poetry in 1958. On the voice of the poet he writes:

> Once I made three lectures about three properties I coveted in poems; fabulous, musical, and spirited, I called them. What a mighty voice it requires in the poet, to keep his lines strange, and rolling like waves, and brave like the sun!

WINTER REMEMBERED

Two evils, monstrous either one apart,
Possessed me, and were long and loath at going:
A cry of Absence, Absence, in the heart,
And in the wood the furious winter blowing.

5   Think not, when fire was bright upon my bricks,
And past the tight boards hardly a wind could enter,
I glowed like them, the simple burning sticks,
Far from my cause, my proper heat and center.

Better to walk forth in the murderous air
10 And wash my wound in the snows; that would be healing;
Because my heart would throb less painful there,
Being caked with cold, and past the smart of feeling.

And where I went, the hugest winter blast
Would have this body bowed, these eyeballs streaming,
15 And though I think this heart's blood froze not fast,
It ran too small to spare one drop for dreaming.

Dear love, these fingers that had known your touch,
And tied our separate forces first together,
Were ten poor idiot fingers not worth much,
20 Ten frozen parsnips hanging in the weather.

Captain Carpenter rose up in his prime
Put on his pistols and went riding out
But had got wellnigh nowhere at that time
Till he fell in with ladies in a rout.

5   It was a pretty lady and all her train
That played with him so sweetly but before
An hour she'd taken a sword with all her main
And twined him of his nose for evermore.

Captain Carpenter mounted up one day
10   And rode straightway into a stranger rogue
That looked unchristian but be that as may
The Captain did not wait upon prologue.

But drew upon him out of his great heart
The other swung against him with a club
15   And cracked his two legs at the shinny part
And let him roll and stick like any tub.

Captain Carpenter rode many a time
From male and female took he sundry harms
He met the wife of Satan crying "I'm
20   The she-wolf bids you shall bear no more arms."

Their strokes and counters whistled in the wind
I wish he had delivered half his blows
But where she should have made off like a hind
The bitch bit off his arms at the elbows.

25   And Captain Carpenter parted with his ears
To a black devil that used him in this wise
O Jesus ere his threescore and ten years
Another had plucked out his sweet blue eyes.

Captain Carpenter got up on his roan
30   And sallied from the gate in hell's despite
I heard him asking in the grimmest tone
If any enemy yet there was to fight?

"To any adversary it is fame
If he risk to be wounded by my tongue
35   Or burnt in two beneath my red heart's flame
Such are the perils he is cast among.

"But if he can he has a pretty choice
From an anatomy with little to lose
Whether he cut my tongue and take my voice
40   Or whether it be my round red heart he choose."

It was the neatest knave that ever was seen
Stepping in perfume from his lady's bower
Who at this word put in his merry mien
And fell on Captain Carpenter like a tower.

45 I would not knock old fellows in the dust
But there lay Captain Carpenter on his back
His weapons were the old heart in his bust
And a blade shook between rotten teeth alack.

The rogue in scarlet and grey soon knew his mind
50 He wished to get his trophy and depart
With gentle apology and touch refined
He pierced him and produced the Captain's heart.

God's mercy rest on Captain Carpenter now
I thought him Sirs an honest gentleman
55 Citizen husband soldier and scholar enow
Let jangling kites eat of him if they can.

But God's deep curses follow after those
That shore him of his goodly nose and ears
His legs and strong arms at the two elbows
60 And eyes that had not watered seventy years.

The curse of hell upon the sleek upstart
Who got the Captain finally on his back
And took the red red vitals of his heart
And made the kites to whet their beaks clack clack.

OLD MANSION

As an intruder I trudged with careful innocence
To mask in decency a meddlesome stare,
Passing the old house often on its eminence,
Exhaling my foreign weed on its weighted air.

5 Here age seemed newly imaged for the historian
After his monstrous châteaux on the Loire,
A beauty not for depicting by old vulgarian
Reiterations that gentle readers abhor.

It was a Southern manor. One hardly imagines
10 Towers, arcades, or forbidding fortress walls;
But sufficient state though its peacocks now were pigeons;
Where no courts kept, but grave rites and funerals.

Indeed, not distant, possibly not external
To the property, were tombstones, where the catafalque

15   Had carried their dead; and projected a note too charnel
But for the honeysuckle on its intricate stalk.

Stability was the character of its rectangle
Whose line was seen in part and guessed in part
Through trees. Decay was the tone of old brick and shingle.
20   Green shutters dragging frightened the watchful heart

To assert: Your mansion, long and richly inhabited,
Its porches and bowers suiting the children of men,
Will not for ever be thus, O man, exhibited,
And one had best hurry to enter it if one can.

25   And at last, with my happier angel's own temerity,
Did I clang their brazen knocker against the door,
To beg their dole of a look, in simple charity,
Or crumbs of wisdom dropping from their great store.

But it came to nothing—and may so gross denial
30   Which has been deplored with a beating of the breast
Never shorten the tired historian, loyal
To acknowledge defeat and discover a new quest.

The old mistress was ill, and sent my dismissal
By one even more wrappered and lean and dark
35   Than that warped concierge and imperturbable vassal
Who had bid me begone from her master's Gothic park.

Emphatically, the old house crumbled; the ruins
Would litter, as already the leaves, this petted sward;
And no annalist went in to the lords or the peons;
40   The antiquary would finger the bits of shard.

But on retreating I saw myself in the token,
How loving from my dying weed the feather curled
On the languid air; and I went with courage shaken
To dip, alas, into some unseemlier world.

HILDA

I
The dearest was the one to whom it fell
To walk and wear her beauty as in a play
To be enacted nobly on a great day;
And stormily we approved the bosom-swell,
5   And the tones tinkling. For her touch and smell
I brought bright flowers, till garlanded she stood
Scared with her splendor, as in the sight of God
A pale girl curtsying with an asphodel.

No, No, she answered in the extreme of fear,
10 I cannot. On the dropping of those petals
Rode the Estranger, scorning their sweet mettles,
Blossoms and woman too; him she looked at,
Not me the praiser; she was too honest for that,
I was a clod mumbling, to catch her ear.

II

15 The perished were the fairest. And now uprise
Particular ghosts, who hollow and clamorous
Come as blanched lepers crying, "Do not spurn us,"
Ringing in my ears, wetting my eyes,
Obsequious phantoms and disbodied sighs.
20 Soon they are frightened and go fast; a smoke
Which clung about my quincebushes, then broke,
And while I look is smeared upon the skies.

But Hilda! proudest, lingering last alone,
Wreathing my roses with blue bitter dust,
25 Think not I would reject you, for I must
Weep for your nakedness and no retinue,
And leap up as of old to follow you;
But what I wear is flesh; it weighs like stone.

Conrad Aiken (1889-   )

Born in Savannah, Georgia, Conrad Aiken graduated from Harvard
in 1911, was contributing editor of *The Dial* from 1917 to 1919,
London correspondent for the *New Yorker* from 1934 to 1936, and
Consultant in Poetry at the Library of Congress from 1950 to 1952.
He has been married three times and has three children by his first
marriage. He lives on Stony Brook Road in Brewster, Massachusetts,
a village on Cape Cod. His many prizes and awards include the
Pulitzer Prize in 1930 for his *Selected Poems,* the Shelley Memorial
Award in 1930, a Guggenheim fellowship in 1934, the National Book
Award in 1954 for his *Collected Poems,* the Bollingen Prize in Poetry
in 1956, an Academy of American Poets fellowship in 1957, the Gold
Medal of the National Institute of Arts and Letters in 1958, and the
Huntington Hartford Foundation award of $5000 in 1961. He has
selected the following comment from a radio broadcast called *Poetry
and the Mind of Modern Man,* which he gave for the Voice of America:

Poetry has always kept easily abreast with the utmost man can do
in extending the horizon of his consciousness, whether outward
or inward. It has always been the most flexible, the most comprehensive, the most far-seeing, and hence the most successful, of
the modes by which he has accepted the new in experience, realized

it, and adjusted himself to it. Whether it is a change in his conception of the heavens, or of the law of gravity, or of morality, or of the nature of consciousness, it has always at last been in poetry that man has given his thought its supreme expression—which is to say that most of all, in this, he succeeds in making real for himself the profound myth of personal existence and experience.

ALL LOVELY THINGS

All lovely things will have an ending,
All lovely things will fade and die,
And youth, that's now so bravely spending,
Will beg a penny by and by.

5 Fine ladies all are soon forgotten,
And goldenrod is dust when dead,
The sweetest flesh and flowers are rotten
And cobwebs tent the brightest head.

Come back, true love! Sweet youth, return!—
10 But time goes on, and will, unheeding,
Though hands will reach, and eyes will yearn,
And the wild days set true hearts bleeding.

Come back, true love! Sweet youth, remain!—
But goldenrod and daisies wither,
15 And over them blows autumn rain,
They pass, they pass, and know not whither.

IMPROVISATIONS: LIGHTS AND SNOW

1

The girl in the room beneath
Before going to bed
Strums on a mandolin
The three simple tunes she knows.
5 How inadequate they are to tell what her heart feels!
When she has finished them several times
She thrums the strings aimlessly with her finger-nails
And smiles, and thinks happily of many things.

2

I stood for a long while before the shop-window
10 Looking at the blue butterflies embroidered on tawny silk.
The building was a tower before me,
Time was loud behind me,
Sun went over the housetops and dusty trees;
And there they were, glistening, brilliant, motionless,

15 Stitched in a golden sky
By yellow patient fingers long since turned to dust.

3

The first bell is silver,
And breathing darkness I think only of the long scythe of time.
The second bell is crimson,
20 And I think of a holiday night, with rockets
Furrowing the sky with red, and a soft shatter of stars.
The third bell is saffron and slow,
And I behold a long sunset over the sea
With wall on wall of castled cloud and glittering balustrades.
25 The fourth bell is colour of bronze,
I walk by a frozen lake in the dun light of dusk:
Muffled crackings run in the ice,
Trees creak, birds fly.
The fifth bell is cold clear azure,
30 Delicately tinged with green:
One golden star hangs melting in it,
And towards this, sleepily, I go.
The sixth bell is as if a pebble
Had been dropped into a deep sea far above me . . .
35 Rings of sound ebb slowly into the silence.

4

On the day when my uncle and I drove to the cemetery,
Rain rattled on the roof of the carriage;
And talking constrainedly of this and that
We refrained from looking at the child's coffin on the seat before us.
40 When we reached the cemetery
We found that the thin snow on the grass
Was already darkly transparent with rain;
And boards had been laid upon it
That we might walk without wetting our feet.

5

45 When I was a boy, and saw bright rows of icicles
In many lengths along a wall
I was disappointed to find
That I could not play music upon them:
I ran my hand lightly across them
50 And they fell, tinkling.
I tell you this, young man, so that your expectations of life
Will not be too great.

6

It is now two hours since I left you,
And the perfume of your hands is still on my hands.
55 And though since then
I have looked at the stars, walked in the cold blue streets,

And heard the dead leaves blowing over the ground
Under the trees,
I still remember the sound of your laughter.
₆₀ How will it be, lady, when there is none to remember you
Even as long as this?
Will the dust braid your hair?

7
The day opens with the brown light of snowfall
And past the window snowflakes fall and fall.
₆₅ I sit in my chair all day and work and work
Measuring words against each other.
I open the piano and play a tune
But find it does not say what I feel,
I grow tired of measuring words against each other,
₇₀ I grow tired of these four walls,
And I think of you, who write me that you have just had a daughter
And named her after your first sweetheart,
And you, who break your heart, far away,
In the confusion and savagery of a long war,
₇₅ And you who, worn by the bitterness of winter,
Will soon go south.
The snowflakes fall almost straight in the brown light
Past my window,
And a sparrow finds refuge on my window-ledge.
₈₀ This alone comes to me out of the world outside
As I measure word with word.

8
Many things perplex me and leave me troubled,
Many things are locked away in the white book of stars
Never to be opened by me.
₈₅ The starred leaves are silently turned,
And the mooned leaves;
And as they are turned, fall the shadows of life and death.
Perplexed and troubled,
I light a small light in a small room,
₉₀ The lighted walls come closer to me,
The familiar pictures are clear.
I sit in my favourite chair and turn in my mind
The tiny pages of my own life, whereon so little is written,
And hear at the eastern window the pressure of a long wind, coming
₉₅ From I know not where.

How many times have I sat here,
How many times will I sit here again,
Thinking these same things over and over in solitude
As a child says over and over
₁₀₀ The first word he has learned to say.

9

This girl gave her heart to me,
And this, and this.
This one looked at me as if she loved me,
And silently walked away.
105 This one I saw once and loved, and saw her never again.

Shall I count them for you upon my fingers?
Or like a priest solemnly sliding beads?
Or pretend they are roses, pale pink, yellow, and white,
And arrange them for you in a wide bowl
110 To be set in sunlight?
See how nicely it sounds as I count them for you—
'This girl gave her heart to me
And this, and this' . . . !
And nevertheless my heart breaks when I think of them,
115 When I think their names,
And how, like leaves, they have changed and blown
And will lie at last, forgotten,
Under the snow.

10

It is night-time, and cold, and snow is falling,
120 And no wind grieves the walls.
In the small world of light around the arc-lamp
A swarm of snowflakes falls and falls.
The street grows silent. The last stranger passes.
The sound of his feet, in the snow, is indistinct.

125 What forgotten sadness is it, on a night like this,
Takes possession of my heart?
Why do I think of a camellia tree in a southern garden,
With pink blossoms among dark leaves,
Standing, surprised, in the snow?
130 Why do I think of spring?

The snowflakes, helplessly veering,
Fall silently past my window;
They come from darkness and enter darkness.
What is it in my heart is surprised and bewildered
135 Like that camellia tree,
Beautiful still in its glittering anguish?
And spring so far away!

11

As I walked through the lamplit gardens,
On the thin white crust of snow,
140 So intensely was I thinking of my misfortune,
So clearly were my eyes fixed
On the face of this grief which has come to me,

That I did not notice the beautiful pale colouring
Of lamplight on the snow;
145 Nor the interlaced long blue shadows of trees;·

And yet these things were there,
And the white lamps and orange lamps, and lamps of lilac were there,
As I have seen them so often before;
As they will be so often again
150 Long after my grief is forgotten.

And still, though I know this, and say this, it cannot console me.

12
How many times have we been interrupted
Just as I was about to make up a story for you!
One time it was because we suddenly saw a firefly
155 Lighting his green lantern among the boughs of a fir-tree.
Marvellous! Marvellous! He is making for himself
A little tent of light in the darkness!
And one time it was because we saw a lilac lightning flash
Run wrinkling into the blue top of the mountain,—
160 We heard boulders of thunder rolling down upon us
And the plat-plat of drops on the window,
And we ran to watch the rain
Charging in wavering white clouds across the long grass of the field!
Or at other times it was because we saw a star
165 Slipping easily out of the sky and falling, far off,
Among pine-dark hills;
Or because we found a crimson eft
Darting in the cold grass!

These things interrupted us and left us wondering;
170 And the stories, whatever they might have been,
Were never told.
A fairy, binding a daisy down and laughing?
A golden-haired princess caught in a cobweb?
A love-story of long ago?
175 Some day, just as we are beginning again,
Just as we blow the first sweet note,
Death itself will interrupt us.

13
My heart is an old house, and in that forlorn old house,
In the very centre, dark and forgotten,
180 Is a locked room where an enchanted princess
Lies sleeping.
But sometimes, in that dark house,
As if almost from the stars, far away,
Sounds whisper in that secret room—
185 Faint voices, music, a dying trill of laughter?

And suddenly, from her long sleep,
The beautiful princess awakes and dances.

Who is she? I do not know.
Why does she dance? Do not ask me!—
190 Yet to-day, when I saw you,
When I saw your eyes troubled with the trouble of happiness,
And your mouth trembling into a smile,
And your fingers put shyly forward,—
Softly, in that room,
195 The little princess arose
And danced;
And as she danced the old house gravely trembled
With its vague and delicious secret.

14
Like an old tree uprooted by the wind
200 And flung down cruelly
With roots bared to the sun and stars
And limp leaves brought to earth—
Torn from its house—
So do I seem to myself
205 When you have left me.

15
The music of the morning is red and warm;
Snow lies against the walls;
And on the sloping roof in the yellow sunlight
Pigeons huddle against the wind.
210 The music of the evening is attenuated and thin—
The moon seen through a wave by a mermaid;
The crying of a violin.
Far down there, far down where the river turns to the west,
The delicate lights begin to twinkle
215 On the dusky arches of the bridge:
In the green sky a long cloud,
A smouldering wave of smoky crimson,
Breaks in the freezing wind: and above it, unabashed,
Remote, untouched, fierily palpitant,
220 Sings the first star.

PREFACE

IF "SENLIN: A BIOGRAPHY" may be said to provide the generic "I"
that underlies *The Divine Pilgrim*, the block unit of human reference,
and to illustrate, within prescribed limits, the apparent disintegration of the soul, or ego, with which modern psychology has con-
fronted us, "Changing Mind" carries the analysis a step farther. For
this might be called the specific "I," and at a specific moment in its

experience, in a specific predicament: the predicament, both private and social, of the writer or artist. Senlin is the purely racial exemplar —the basic stock reacting to basic situations. He is the inheritor of racial memories, and through these of even deeper instinctual responses, but beyond this he is not particularized, and was not meant to be. The wholly anonymous hero of "Changing Mind," on the other hand, and perhaps anonymous with reason, is not only particularized, he is also shown to be the willing participant, and perhaps to some extent even the instigator, in the process of seeing himself resolved into his constituent particles: and this with a purpose, that his increased awareness may be put at the service of mankind. Not only does he inherit the ordinary basic unconscious memory of Senlin—he also inherits the complete private situation of a highly complex and self-conscious contemporary individual whose neuroses have made it necessary or desirable that he should be an artist. He must make his experience articulate for the benefit of others, he must be, in the evolving consciousness of man, the servant-example, and in fact he has little choice in the matter. He is himself simply a part of that evolution.

1949

CHANGING MIND
from THE DIVINE PILGRIM
(1925)

1
The room filled with the sound of voices,
The voices weaving like vines or voices of viols,
And the voices mixed, filling the warm room
From wall to vibrant wall. It was then I saw
5   The talk itself, the fourfold torrent of talk
(Below the candles and above the fire)
Moving like golden water!

"Come under!" he said,
"Come down under the talk! Stoop your shoulders
10   And enter the darkness!"

Who could this be
Who spoke to me in secret, while those others
Wove with their spider-mouths the moving water?
It was not the small man, not the tall man,
15   And not the woman whose long hair of burnt gold
Fell on the talk and was woven into it;
Nor was it that other woman, who blew smoke
Over the golden hair and golden water.

"Come under!" he said;
20   And as he spoke I saw him! His white face

Came up laughing, with bright hair! He showed
(Turning upon his axis, a strong swimmer
Making himself a ball) how he could scoop
A hollow in bright air, turning within it;
His white arms, curving like a swimmer's, shaped
The dark sphere out of brightness. There he curled,
In that cold chrysalis, secret under the talk,
Carved in the light.

    "You! Narcissus!" I said!
And softly, under the four-voiced dialogue,
In the bright ether, in the golden river
Of cabbalistic sound, I plunged, I found
The silver rind of peace, the hollow round
Carved out of nothing; curled there like a god.

The blue-eyed woman, leaning above the water,
Shook her scarab ear-rings, while her voice
Entered the stream. "Nevertheless"—she said—
Leaning toward the golden foam her head—
"Nevertheless I am not dead;
Let him forget me at his peril!"—this she said,
Smiling, and showing the three rings on her finger,
The fourth of her left hand. Her arm was naked,
The low green bodice showed her bosom rising,
Rising more quickly, as with agitation.
"I can entice him still, my eye is quick
As a lizard's eye, my tongue is quick—"

     "—as quick
As an aspic's!"—this the tall man rang, and laughed.
The small man also laughed, and the bright stream
Rose deeper; and I felt myself submerged,
Submerged deliciously.

    The small man whistled:
After the four dull boulders of their laugh
Had sunk beside me, sending up four spouts
Of golden water. The long whistle
Ran like a nerve. It was blue, and reached
At the near end a gong, and at the far
A copper spring. This all four pressed at once,
And the long screaming nerve wound through the water,
While they above it leaned. Ah, did they see
How the blue nerve was grounded twice in me?
"Laugh if you like," she said, whose golden hair
Fell round me fine as water-sifted sunlight,
"Whistle derision from Rome to Jericho;
Sell him to Doctor Wundt the psycho-analyst
Whose sex-ray eyes will separate him out

Into a handful of blank syllables,—
Like a grammarian, whose beak can parse
A sentence till its gaudy words mean nothing;
70   Yet if I smile above him, ah, you'll see!
Each idiot syllable of what was once
The multitudinous meaning of that brain
Will beat devotion and speak its love again!"

(Alas, it is true I am dispersed thus,
75   Dissected out on the glass-topped table,
The tweezers picking up syllables and putting them down,
Particles so small they have no colour;
I am dispersed, and yet I know
That sovereign eye, if once it glare its love,
80   Will reassemble me.)
                The other woman,
Blowing her smoke above the outspread hair
And woven water and hair, and the dying nerve
Of sibilation, spoke at last, and while she spoke
85   I saw the four walls leaning inward above the stream,
And her with the rings upon her fingers, leaning,
And the two men smiling above me.
Venus too was there, and the evening star,_
And the inverted trees, and the terror-coloured sky.
90   Sky, trees, walls, gods, birds.
"Let him forget you at his peril, this you say?
O Alba, what a bloody jest is here!
If he remember you, the peril is yours.
You, then, are only you? this gold-ring-fingered,
95   Green-bodiced leman? No, no, be not deceived!
You are not only you, this one great golden
Goddess above the stream with sovereign eye!
You are not only the sea-cold marble, interfused
With sanguine warmth, yet pure as the sea-coral!
100   You are not only the one white god of forked
Flesh, bewildering ever, never sating!
How could this be?"

              She blew a round blue cloud
Of smoke across the golden moving water,
105   (Whereunder in my hollow I sat sleeping)
And smiled.

       "How could this be? You are but one
Of all our host; and us too he has seen.
Us he remembers when he remembers you:
110   The livid; the sore; the old; the worn; the wounded:
Hating the smell of us, you too he'll hate.
Ah, Alba, what a cruel jest is here!
For if you wake him, with that sovereign eye,

Teasing his flesh with the three-gold-ringed finger
115 Until, assembled, he again swims up:
Will it not be to me—to me also—he comes?
Me, the dead cormorant whom he so loathed
And buried by the sea?"

She leaned, and then
120 I saw her weeping. Intolerable pity
Broke in my heart when thus I saw her weeping.
Her in blue muslin, tall and meagre, her
The starved blue cormorant whom I betrayed.

Then Doctor Wundt, the tall man, walked beside
125 The sparkling stream. His face was like a star.
Between the leaves, inexorable, he shone,
While the brown thrush, sequestered, hushed the wood
With meditative song. Anon the youths
Came from the wood and laughed with Socrates:
130 They saw him drink the hemlock, heard him say
Alpha and Omega. Thence up the hill
To Golgotha they jeered, and with them took
The sponge, the spear, the flask of vinegar,
And that poor king, whose madness, on a Friday,
135 Burned to a beauty like the evening star.
Hegel, too, came shoreward in that evening,
Leaning above me, leaning above the stream,
Whose motion (so he sighed at length) was only
Manifestation of the dialectic.
140 And others, too; some singly, some in groups,
Talking a little, or silent. There at last
My father also came. The dead leaf's step
Was his, rapid and light; and his young face
Shone like the evening star, inexorable.

145 And he and Doctor Wundt together spoke,
Flinging one image on the moving water,
With one voice spoke, wherewith the bird's voice chimed;
But what it was they said I could not hear.
Only, I heard the bird-voice tinkling "peace"
150 Among the lapping leaves, and sound of weeping
Where the tall woman, the blue-muslined, leaned
Above the river; while the sovereign eye
Glared on the water to assemble me.
"Inheritor!"—this word my father said,
155 And Doctor Wundt said also. The word hung
Smokelike above the stream.

2

O Alba! Look! While thus Narcissus sleeps
Under the river, and beside him keeps

Conscious and yet unconscious my bright soul!
160 Look, how the dawn, the giant swimmer, comes
Over the sky, head downward, swimming slowly,
With powerful bright arms! Out of the east
The blue god looms, and with him come new worlds.
Those bubbles—look—that from his silver heel
165 Sparkle and burst, and those that from his mouth
Spiral, and those that bead his sides with light,
And those that globe his fingers—those are worlds,
That bursting seem to escape the godlike tether,
And yet do not escape. Is it from me they come—
170 From me to me? And is that sky myself?

It was the southeast wind, changing softly,
Who thus, eyes downward, swam upon my sky,
Bringing news of the southeast. The weather-vanes—
Golden cocks, ships, and a hundred arrows,—
175 All creaked at once, changed on a mile of steeples,
All changed at once, as thus the swimmer passed.
And all those bubbles
Whirling about him, voluting sleekly, bursting
With altered shape enlarged, these were the news
180 Of another country! These were the fields of corn!
These were the salt marshes, steaming in sunlight, where
The herons rise with trailed legs
And the wild horses stamp!
There, in long brightness, breaks the world-long sea!

185   The small man brooded
Darkly above me, darkly glowing,
Mephistopheles, holding in his wide hand
All these shapes. "It is the kite country,"
He laughed, "it is the land of kites; and there he walks."
190 . . . And as he glowed above me, Chinese lantern
Burning with grinning mouth beneath the leaves,
And the pierced eyes cruel as the eyes of the kite-flyers,
Those others laughed: the tall man first, and then
More musically, melodious derision,
195 She who had wept, the cormorant, and she
Who threatened, glaring, to assemble me.
Ha, ha, they laughed, descending scale of scorn.
Three towers leaned above me, beating bells,
So that the air was beaten and confused.
200 Through this (harsh sabbath) mocked the pursuing voice:

"Childe Roland, leaving behind him the dark tower,
Came in the evening to the land of kites.
Peril was past. The skull of the dead horse
His foot broke; and the desert, where wild dogs
205 Bay up the moon from tall grass, this he crossed

In the long light. And in the kite country—"
(Ha, ha, they laughed, merry descending scale)—
"He saw the diamond kites all rise at once
From the flat land. And on each kite was bound
210   A weeping woman, the arms outstretched, the feet
Nailed at the foot!"

                (Alas, how hard it is,
I helpless, bound thus, in my cave, asleep,
Bound in the stinging nerves of sound, these voices!)

215   "Under the sky of kites he steps, hearing
The sad singing and whimpering of the kites,
Seeing also the blood that drips from hands
Nailed to the Crosspiece, high in air. He climbs
Slowly in twilight to the weeping-cross . . .
220   Alas, good woman, you no sooner lust
Together concupiscent, your four arms
Enwreathed, your faces fused in one, your eyes
Sightless with foresight of the two-backed beast,
Than with derisive cries and cruel eyes
225   The kiteflyers come! Your outstretched hands they nail
Against the Crosspiece! Then down the hill they run
Drawing the kitecord with them, so that, weeping,
He hears you, weeping, blown aloft in air!"

Thus the small man, amid derisive laughter!
230   But it was not of the kites, nor the kite country,
The giant swimmer sang, who brought me news,
News of the southeast! O believe, believe!
Believe, grim four, believe me or I die!
It is from you this vision comes; while I
235   Dreamed that I swam, and with that swimmer came
Into the southeast of forgotten name.

           3
    The seven-man orchestra tuned up bubbling and squeaking.
Harry Frank, the conductor, stuffed a dirty handkerchief inside
his collar, turning goggle eyes to see if his friend Anne was in the
audience; and Tom, the drummer, with his prizefighter's mug,
was chatting with a couple of skirts in the front row. Lights!
Lights! O'Dwyer, his bloodshot eyes, looked round the cheru-
bimed corner of the proscenium arch to see what they were waiting for. What were they waiting for? "Hearts and Flowers."
245   Harry rapped his frayed bow on the lamplit tripod, turning his
smug Jewish profile from Tom to O'Dwyer, sleekly smiling. He
began briskly. The theatre was full. Three thousand faces. Faces
in rows like flowers in beds.
    And all this, mind you, was myself! myself still asleep under
250   the four-voiced dialogue! the fourfold river of talk! Here the

three thousand faces leaned down upon me, stamens and pistils!
and here I was the orchestra, a submarine orchestra, a telephone
exchange of blue nerves, and a bare stage on which something was
about to happen! Here I was Luvic, warbling, her white arms fat
at the shoulders, like hams powdered, her green-ringed fingers
making in a fold of her dress that pill-rolling motion which is a
symptom of paralysis agitans, bugling

> Falling life and fading tree,
> Lines of white in a sullen sea,
> Shadows rising on you and me—

her pale mouth opening and shutting, flexing and reflexing, in perfect time! Here I was Glozo, the card-eater, the ventriloquist, who
took goldfish out of his gold-toothed mouth, and Mrs. Glozo, his
plump-rumped assistant. Here I was Tozo, the Jap, and his family
of little Tozos, all exactly alike in pink fleshings, all shortlegged
and bowlegged, lying on their long backs and twirling purple barrels (gold-star-emblazoned) on their pat-slapping soft feet, tossing the purple barrels from one simian sole to another. Here I was
Nozo, the hobo, the awkward inflamed nose with a diamond sparkling on its horn. I was each of these in turn, and then also I was
Bozo, the muscular trapeze artist, and all the while I was Harry
cocking his left eye over his fiddle, and Tom rubbing sandpaper
together (wisha wisha) while Mrs. Bishop put her perfumed hand
in his pocket, and three thousand yellow faces perched in rows
like birds, and a humming marble foyer with gilt mirrors, and
O'Dwyer crowding into the same telephone booth with Mrs.
Harry Frank (naughty-naughty) and the electric sign in Bos-
worth Place—

All this I was, and also the amphitheatre itself,
All this, but also a small room, a forest,
Trees full of birds walking down to the water's edge,
Socrates in a basket hanging beside the full moon, eating a partridge,
The young men pushing, hubbub on Golgotha,
The mad king among them, terrified, smelling the sweat of the crowd,
Hegel arriving on a sea-scallop accompanied by Venus,—
All this I was, but also those four strangers
Leaning above me, leaning above the stream,
The tall man, the small man, and the blue-eyed woman,
And that other woman, whose beauty, on a kite,
Rose to a beauty like the evening star.
Golgotha, the skull, was the amphitheatre,
The skull was my skull, and within it played
The seven-man orchestra, while Luvic sang—

Lights! Lights! O'Dwyer hoarsely cried,
His bloodshot eyes peeped round the gilded smooth
Belly of a cherub, who supported

Chryselephantine pillar of fruits and lutes and leaves.
The lights changed, the walls
Came closer, the crowd was blue, obscure, the forest
Nodded, the blue smoke rolled among the leaves
And nests of birds. The orchestra sat playing

Typewriters, telephones and telegraphs
Under the calcium light
And on the stage red ropes had squared a ring.
Out of the forest flew the songs of birds,
While hid in leaves the saxophone made moan.
Bang! said the gong, and the red giant from his corner
Sprang to the ring, shaking the boards. The other
Rose terrified, submissive, his thin hands
Ungloved, his chin defenceless, and his heart
Visibly beating.

       "You! Narcissus!" I said!
And as I rose the giant's hard glove crashed
Black on the visible heart, and the sick man
Shot through the ropes and fell against the arch
Under the cherub at O'Dwyer's feet.

ONE TWO THREE FOUR FIVE
SIX SEVEN EIGHT NINE—
       the red hand
Counted, jerking. At the fatal nine
The sick man rose, crawled through the ropes, his face
White as a dead man's in the calcium light,
His dark eyes burning with fever, his weak hands
Uplifted, trembling.

       "You! Narcissus!" I said!
And saw again the hard black piston crash
Against the visible heart, and the sick man
Falling backward, on his back, in the dark corner,
Unconscious, motionless, his dark eyes
Wide open! Then the applause, roaring like rain!
The giant's bloody glove upheld! The gong clattering!
Bozo, Nozo, Glozo, the Tozos, cheering!
While from the forest blew a blast of sound,
Flutebirds and bubblebeaks, Harry and Tom,
The seven-man orchestra, the saxophone
Bubbling the *Himmelfahrt*, the Lo! the hero
Conquering comes!

       Lights! O'Dwyer rubbed
A bright alpaca sleeve across the cherub,
The forest darkened, the nodding lilies
Darkened also, the bare stage diminished,

Bozo, Nozo, Glozo, the Tozos, all were gone,
Only the half-dead man, who lay alone,
His white dead face propped up against the backdrop,
Staring, with dying eyes. To him I knelt,
While Doctor Wundt, above me, in a box,
Leaned down among the leaves
Pleasantly laughing, and that other man,
My father, chill from the grave, leaned down and smiled.
And it was then the blue-eyed woman triumphed
And glared with sovereign eye above the stream:
"What thinks he now? What peril seeks he now?
Digs now what magic?"

                "Digs in his heart a grave!"
Laughed Doctor Wundt. "It is the half-dead man,
Himself, who longs to die; for him he digs."

      (It is true I ran to the dead man
      And raised his head. Alas, what horror,
      When I saw the chest-wall rotted, the heart
      Hanging like a cluster of grapes,
      Beating weakly, uncovered and sick.
      Alas, too, what horror when he said:
      Daily I fight here,
      Daily I die for the world's delight
      By the giant blow on my visible heart!)

Then from the wood arose a sigh of sound
Where lapped in leaves the seven-man orchestra,
Flutebird and bubblebeak, Harry and Tom,
Blew blue nostalgia out of "Hearts and Flowers";
While Doctor Wundt, grown taller, and my father,
Flinging one haloed image on the stream,
Sang, with one voice, a mournful requiem.
"Inheritor!" This was the word they said,
But also sang, "Alas, Narcissus dead,
Narcissus daily dead, that we may live!"

           4
      My father which art in earth
      From whom I got my birth,
      What is it that I inherit?
      From the bones fallen apart
      And the deciphered heart,
      Body and spirit.
      My mother which art in tomb
      Who carriedst me in thy womb,
      What is it that I inherit?
      From the thought come to dust
      And the remembered lust,
      Body and spirit.

Father and mother, who gave
Life, love, and now the grave,
390 What is it that I can be?
Nothing but what lies here,
The hand still, the brain sere,
Naught lives in thee

Nor ever will live, save
395 It have within this grave
Roots in the mingled heart,
In the damp ashes wound
Where the past, underground,
Falls, falls apart.

LIMERICKS

1

The limerick's, admitted, a verse form:
a terse form: a curse form: a hearse form.
    It may not be lyric,
    and at best it's Satyric,
5 and a whale of a tail in perverse form.

7

It's time to make love: douse the glim.
The fireflies twinkle and dim.
    The stars lean together
    like birds of a feather
5 and the loin lies down with the limb.

11

Said a lovely Greek maiden named Clytie
I look mighty nice in my nightie:
    but beyond all compare
    I look cuter when bare,
5 and when I am bare I am bitey.

12

Farewell to the dear days of Genesis.
We do these things now all by synthesis.
    And who would not rather
    have a test-tube for father
5 than a *homo in loco parenthesis?*

27

Great archers and hitters of bull's-eyes,
you wingers of wren's eyes and gulls' eyes,
    Ulysses and Tell
    and Achilles as well,
5 where walk you now baring your skull's eyes?

E. E. Cummings (1894-1962)

Edward Estlin Cummings was born in Cambridge, Massachusetts, received his B.A. from Harvard in 1915 and his M.A. in 1916, and in 1917 joined the Norton Harjes Ambulance Corp in France. Through a military censor's error, he was imprisoned for three months—the experience on which *The Enormous Room* (1922) is based —and then joined the U.S. Army. After the war he settled in Paris for a time before returning to the United States, where he and his wife made their home in New York's Greenwich Village and in New Hampshire. He was a painter as well as a poet. He received the *Dial* Award in 1925 and the Bollingen Prize in 1957.

AT THE HEAD OF THIS STREET A GASPING ORGAN IS WAVING MOTH-

at the head of this street a gasping organ is waving moth-
eaten tunes. a fatish hand turns the crank; the box sprouts
fairies, out of it sour gnomes tumble clumsily, the little box
is spilling rancid elves upon neat sunlight into the flower-
5   stricken air which is filthy with agile swarming sonal creatures

—Children, stand with circular frightened faces glaring at
the shabby tiny smiling, man in whose hand the crank goes
desperately, round and round pointing to the queer monkey

10   (if you toss him a coin he will pick it cleverly from, the air
and stuff it seriously in, his minute pocket) Sometimes he
does not catch a piece of money and then his master will
yell at him over the music and jerk the little string and the
monkey will sit, up, and look at, you with his solemn blinky
15   eyeswhichneversmile and after he has caught a, penny or
three, pennies he will be thrown a peanut (which he will
open skilfully with his, mouth carefully holding, it, in his
little toylike hand) and then he will stiff-ly throw the shell
away with a small bored gesture that makes the children
20   laugh.

But i don't, the crank goes round desperate elves and hopeless gnomes and frantic fairies gush clumsily from the
battered box fatish and mysterious the flowerstricken sunlight is thickening dizzily is reeling gently the street and
25   the children and the monkeyandtheorgan and the man are
dancing slowly are tottering up and down in a trembly mist
of atrocious melody . . . . tiniest dead tunes crawl upon my
face my hair is lousy with mutilated singing microscopic

things in my ears scramble faintly tickling putrescent
30   atomies,
        and
          i feel the jerk of the little string! the tiny
smiling shabby man is yelling over the music i understand
him i shove my round red hat back on my head i sit up and
35   blink at you with my solemn eyeswhichneversmile

yes, By god.
for i am they are pointing at the queer monkey with a little
oldish doll-like face and hairy arms like an ogre and rub-
bercoloured hands and feet filled with quick fingers and a
40   remarkable tail which is allbyitself alive. (and he has a
little red coat with i have a real pocket in it and the round
funny hat with a big feather is tied under myhis chin.)
that climbs and cries and runs and floats like a toy on the
end of a string

The Cambridge Ladies Who Live in Furnished Souls

the Cambridge ladies who live in furnished souls
are unbeautiful and have comfortable minds
(also, with the church's protestant blessings
daughters, unscented shapeless spirited)
5   they believe in Christ and Longfellow, both dead,
are invariably interested in so many things—
at the present writing one still finds
delighted fingers knitting for the is it Poles?
perhaps. While permanent faces coyly bandy
10   scandal of Mrs. N and Professor D
. . . . the Cambridge ladies do not care, above
Cambridge if sometimes in its box of
sky lavender and cornerless, the
moon rattles like a fragment of angry candy

If You Can't Eat You Got To

If you can't eat you got to

smoke and we aint got
nothing to smoke:come on kid

let's go to sleep
5   if you can't smoke you got to

Sing and we aint got

nothing to sing;come on kid
let's go to sleep

if you can't sing you got to
10   die and we aint got

Nothing to die,come on kid

let's go to sleep
if you can't die you got to

dream and we aint got
15   nothing to dream(come on kid

Let's go to sleep)

I THANK YOU GOD FOR MOST THIS AMAZING

i thank You God for most this amazing
day:for the leaping greenly spirits of trees
and a blue true dream of sky;and for everything
which is natural which is infinite which is yes

5   (i who have died am alive again today,
and this is the sun's birthday;this is the birth
day of life and of love and wings:and of the gay
great happening illimitably earth)

how should tasting touching hearing seeing
10   breathing any—lifted from the no
of all nothing—human merely being
doubt unimaginable You?

(now the ears of my ears awake and
now the eyes of my eyes are opened)

THANKSGIVING
(1956)

a monstering horror swallows
this unworld me by you
as the god of our fathers' fathers bows
to a which that walks like a who

5   but the voice-with-a-smile of democracy
announces night & day
"all poor little peoples that want to be free
just trust in the u s a"

suddenly uprose hungary
10   and she gave a terrible cry

"no slave's unlife shall murder me
for i will freely die"

she cried so high thermopylae
heard her and marathon
15   and all prehuman history
and finally The UN

"be quiet little hungary
and do as you are bid
a good kind bear is angary
20   we fear for the quo pro quid"

uncle sam shrugs his pretty
pink shoulders you know how
and he twitches a liberal titty
and lisps "i'm busy right now"

25   so rah-rah-rah democracy
let's all be as thankful as hell
and bury the statue of liberty
(because it begins to smell)

ROSETREE, ROSETREE

rosetree,rosetree
—you're a song to see:whose
all(you're a sight to sing)
poems are opening,
5   as if an earth was
playing at birthdays

each(a wish no
bigger than)in roguish
am of fragrance
10   dances a honeydunce;
whirling's a frantic
struts a pedantic

proud or humble,
equally they're welcome
15   —as if the humble proud
youngest bud testified
"giving(and giving
only)is living"

worlds of prose mind
20   utterly beyond is
brief that how infinite

(deeply immediate
fleet and profound this)
beautiful kindness

25 sweet such(past can's
every can't)immensest
mysteries contradict
a deathful realm of fact
—by their precision
30 evolving vision

dreamtree,truthtree
tree of jubilee:with
aeons of(trivial
merely)existence,all
35 when may not measure
a now of your treasure

blithe each shameless
gaiety of blossom
—blissfully nonchalant
40 wise and each ignorant
gladness—unteaches
what despair preaches

myriad wonder
people of a person;
45 joyful your any new
(every more only you)
most emanation
creates creation

lovetree!least the
50 rose alive must three,must
four and(to quite become
nothing)five times,proclaim
fate isn't fatal
—a heart her each petal

Hart Crane (1899-1932)

Hart Crane was born in Garretsville, Ohio, and grew up in Cleveland.
In 1916 he went to New York. There, and in other places, he held
a variety of jobs to support himself while he wrote poetry. Receiving
financial help from Otto Kahn, the philanthropist, in 1925 Crane
worked for several years on *The Bridge*, which was published in 1930
and received the Levison Award from *Poetry* magazine. After a year

in Mexico on a Guggenheim Fellowship, he committed suicide by
jumping from the ship that was returning him to the United States.

THE HARBOR DAWN
from THE BRIDGE

Insistently through sleep—a tide of voices—   *400 years and more*
They meet you listening midway in your dream,   *. . . or is it from*
The long, tired sounds, fog-insulated noises: *the soundless shore*
Gongs in white surplices, beshrouded wails,   *of sleep that time*
5   Far strum of fog horns . . . signals dispersed in veils.

And then a truck will lumber past the wharves
As winch engines begin throbbing on some deck;
Or a drunken stevedore's howl and thud below
Comes echoing alley-upward through dim snow.

10   And if they take your sleep away sometimes
They give it back again. Soft sleeves of sound
Attend the darkling harbor, the pillowed bay;
Somewhere out there in blankness steam

Spills into steam, and wanders, washed away
15   —Flurried by keen fifings, eddied
Among distant chiming buoys—adrift. The sky,
Cool feathery fold, suspends, distills
This wavering slumber . . . . Slowly—
Immemorially the window, the half-covered chair,
20   Ask nothing but this sheath of pallid air.

And you beside me, blessèd now while sirens   *recalls you to your*
Sing to us, stealthily weave us into day—   *love, there in a*
Serenely now, before day claims our eyes   *waking dream to*
Your cool arms murmurously about me lay.   *merge your seed*

25   While myriad snowy hands are clustering at the panes—

         your hands within my hands are deeds;
         my tongue upon your throat—singing
         arms close; eyes wide, undoubtful
              dark
30   *drink the dawn—*
         a forest shudders in your hair!

The window goes blond slowly. Frostily clears.   *—with whom?*
From Cyclopean towers across Manhattan waters
—Two—three bright window-eyes aglitter, disk
35   The sun, released—aloft with cold gulls hither.

The fog leans one last moment on the sill.
Under the mistletoe of dreams, a star—
As though to join us at some distant hill—
Turns in the waking west and goes to sleep.

*Who is the woman
with us in the
dawn? . . . whose
is the flesh our feet
have moved upon?*

VIRGINIA
from THE BRIDGE

    O rain at seven,
    Pay-check at eleven—
    Keep smiling the boss away,
    Mary (what are you going to do?)
5   Gone seven—gone eleven,
    And I'm still waiting you—

O blue-eyed Mary with the claret scarf,
    Saturday Mary, mine!

    It's high carillon
10   From the popcorn bells!
    Pigeons by the million—
    And Spring in Prince Street
    Where green figs gleam
    By oyster shells!

15 O Mary, leaning from the high wheat tower,
    Let down your golden hair!

    High in the noon of May
    On cornices of daffodils
    The slender violets stray.
20   Crap-shooting gangs in Bleecker reign,
    Peonies with pony manes—
    Forget-me-nots at window panes:

Out of the way-up nickel-dime tower shine,
    Cathedral Mary,
25   shine!—

CHAPLINESQUE

We make our meek adjustments,
Contented with such random consolations
As the wind deposits
In slithered and too ample pockets.

5   For we can still love the world, who find
A famished kitten on the step, and know
Recesses for it from the fury of the street,
Or warm torn elbow coverts.

We will sidestep, and to the final smirk
10 Dally the doom of that inevitable thumb
That slowly chafes its puckered index toward us,
Facing the dull squint with what innocence
And what surprise!

And yet these fine collapses are not lies
15 More than the pirouettes of any pliant cane;
Our obsequies are, in a way, no enterprise.
We can evade you, and all else but the heart:
What blame to us if the heart live on.

The game enforces smirks; but we have seen
20 The moon in lonely alleys make
A grail of laughter of an empty ash can,
And through all sound of gaiety and quest
Have heard a kitten in the wilderness.

PASSAGE

Where the cedar leaf divides the sky
I heard the sea.
In sapphire arenas of the hills
I was promised an improved infancy.

5 Sulking, sanctioning the sun,
My memory I left in a ravine,—
Casual louse that tissues the buckwheat,
Aprons rocks, congregates pears
In moonlit bushels
10 And wakens alleys with a hidden cough.

Dangerously the summer burned
(I had joined the entrainments of the wind).
The shadows of boulders lengthened my back:
In the bronze gongs of my cheeks
15 The rain dried without odour.

"It is not long, it is not long;
See where the red and black
Vine-stanchioned valleys—": but the wind
Died speaking through the ages that you know
20 And hug, chimney-sooted heart of man!
So was I turned about and back, much as your smoke
Compiles a too well-known biography.

The evening was spear in the ravine
That throve through very oak. And had I walked
25 The dozen particular decimals of time?

Touching an opening laurel, I found
A thief beneath, my stolen book in hand.

"Why are you back here—smiling an iron coffin?"
"To argue with the laurel," I replied:
30 "Am justified in transience, fleeing
Under the constant wonder of your eyes—."

He closed the book. And from the Ptolemies
Sand troughed us in a glittering abyss.
A serpent swam a vertex to the sun
35 —On unpaced beaches leaned its tongue and drummed.
What fountains did I hear? what icy speeches?
Memory, committed to the page, had broke.

VOYAGES: VI

Where icy and bright dungeons lift
Of swimmers their lost morning eyes,
And ocean rivers, churning, shift
Green borders under stranger skies,

5 Steadily as a shell secretes
Its beating leagues of monotone,
Or as many waters trough the sun's
Red kelson past the cape's wet stone;

O rivers mingling toward the sky
10 And harbor of the phoenix' breast—
My eyes pressed black against the prow,
—Thy derelict and blinded guest

Waiting, afire, what name, unspoke,
I cannot claim: let thy waves rear
15 More savage than the death of kings,
Some splintered garland for the seer.

Beyond siroccos harvesting
The solstice thunders, crept away,
Like a cliff swinging or a sail
20 Flung into April's inmost day—

Creation's blithe and petaled word
To the lounged goddess when she rose
Conceding dialogue with eyes
That smile unsearchable repose—

25 Still fervid convenant, Belle Isle,
—Unfolded floating dais before

Which rainbows twine continual hair—
Belle Isle, white echo of the oar!

30 The imaged word, it is, that holds
Hushed willows anchored in its glow.
It is the unbetrayable reply
Whose accent no farewell can know.

IMPERATOR VICTUS

Big guns again
No speakee well
But plain.

Again, again—
5 And they shall tell
The Spanish Main

The Dollar from the Cross.

Big guns again.
But peace to thee,
10 Andean brain.

That defunct boss.

Big guns again,
Atahualpa,
Imperator Inca—

15 Slain.

IMPERATOR VICTUS. **13.** *Atahualpa:* last Inca of Peru, died 1533. In spite of a ransom payment of a roomful of gold and silver Atahualpa was put to death by the Spanish conqueror Francisco Pizzaro.

NINETEEN POETS
OF TODAY

Richard Eberhart (1904-   )

Born in Austin, Minnesota, Richard Eberhart was educated at Dartmouth (B.A., 1926), from which he also received an honorary Doctor of Letters degree in 1954. He also studied at St. John's College, Cambridge University (B.A., 1929, M.A., 1933). During World War II he served in the Navy, rising to the rank of lieutenant commander. After the war he entered the Butcher Polish Company of Boston, where he worked for six years; he is now honorary vice-president of the company and a member of the board of directors. Since 1956 he has been Professor of English and Poet in Residence at Dartmouth. He is married and the father of two children. His prizes and honors include the Harriet Monroe Memorial Prize, the Shelley Memorial Award, a grant from the National Institute of Arts and Letters, and the Bollingen Prize (co-winner) from Yale University Library in 1962. He was Consultant in Poetry at the Library of Congress from 1959 to 1961, was appointed by President Eisenhower to the Advisory Committee on the Arts for the National Cultural Center (renamed the John F. Kennedy Center for the Performing Arts) in Washington in 1959, and is a member of the National Institute of Arts and Letters. Here is his comment on the voice of the poet, written at Hanover, New Hampshire:

> The voice of poetry is a difficult concept. Recently Prof. Hans Frankel of Yale gave a seminar here for professors studying the poetry of Wang Wei. Our own Prof. Chan "sang" the Chinese characters in three different modes. One was Mandarin, one was Cantonese (his dialect) and one was a sort of demotic modern. We had the sounds on paper in English syllables and words. Nobody short of the author himself, dead 1000 years or more, could tell what was the voice of the poet. Prof. Frankel gave transliterations of 10 poems which came out to be anything but musical as set down in English. One of my students when shown the work in my undergraduate seminar held that it was not poetry at all. His convictions were strong against all arguments that the Chinese think differently or that a Chinese character represents several things, or images, or attitudes.

The voice of the poet must be an epitome of his being. It must be an essence of the self. It comes from the make of the man. Each poet has his own timbre, his own peculiarity because of the uniqueness of his physical and psychic make-up, I should think. The voice is as it were God-given, about which nothing can be done. It is something one has. It possesses a kind of constancy through the changes of decades. The meaning of a poem is in the words on paper. It is said that the Chinese always sing their poems, never read them silently. Yet they are first written. In reading a Shakespeare sonnet silently, for instance, there is no doubt of the tone, the vocal quality of the poem. The voice would seem to inhere in the make of the words.

As for the poet projecting a kind of voice by plan maybe some of them do. I do not, or at least not consciously. It is plain to me that I used a different tone in my verse plays than in my lyrics. I think of the voice of the poet as something subjective, given, inevitable, a constitutional heritage.

THIS FEVERS ME

This fevers me, this sun on green,
On grass glowing, this young spring.
The secret hallowing is come,
Regenerate sudden incarnation,
5 Mystery made visible
In growth, yet subtly veiled in all,
Unundertstandable in grass,
In flowers, and in the human heart,
This lyric mortal loveliness,
10 The earth breathing, and the sun.
The young lambs sport, none udderless.
Rabbits dash beneath the brush.
Crocuses have come; wind flowers
Tremble against quick April.
15 Violets put on the night's blue,
Primroses wear the pale dawn,
The gold daffodils have stolen
From the sun. New grass leaps up;
Gorse yellows, starred with day;
20 The willow is a graceful dancer
Poised; the poplar poises too.
The apple takes the seafoam's light,
And the evergreen tree is densely bright.
April, April, when will he
25 Be gaunt, be old, who is so young?
This fevers me, this sun on green,
On grass glowing, this young spring.

For a Lamb

I saw on the slant hill a putrid lamb,
Propped with daisies. The sleep looked deep,
The face nudged in the green pillow
But the guts were out for crows to eat.

5   Where's the lamb? whose tender plaint
Said all for the mute breezes.
Say he's in the wind somewhere,
Say, there's a lamb in the daisies.

The Soul Longs to Return Whence It Came

I drove up to the graveyard, which
Used to frighten me as a boy,
When I walked down the river past it,
And evening was coming on. I'd make sure
5   I came home from the woods early enough.
I drove in, I found to the place, I
Left the motor running. My eyes hurried,
To recognize the great oak tree
On the little slope, among the stones.
10   It was a high day, a crisp day,
The cleanest kind of Autumn day,
With brisk intoxicating air, a
Little wind that frisked, yet there was
Old age in the atmosphere, nostalgia,
15   The subtle heaviness of the Fall.
I stilled the motor. I walked a few paces;
It was good, the tree; the friendliness of it.
I touched it, I thought of the roots;
They would have pierced her seven years.
20   O all peoples! O mighty shadows!
My eyes opened along the avenue
Of tombstones, the common land of death.
Humiliation of all loves lost,
That might have had full meaning in any
25   Plot of ground, come, hear the silence,
See the quivering light. My mind worked
Almost imperceptibly, I
In the command, I the wilful ponderer.
I must have stood silent and thoughtful
30   There. A host of dry leaves
Danced on the ground in the wind.
They startled, they curved up from the ground,
There was a dry rustling, rattling.
The sun was motionless and brittle.
35   I felt the blood darken in my cheeks

And burn. Like running. My eyes
Telescoped on decay, I out of command.
Fear, tenderness, they seized me.
My eyes were hot, I dared not look
40   At the leaves. A pagan urge swept me.
Multitudes, O multitudes in one.
The urge of the earth, the titan
Wild and primitive lust, fused
On the ground of her grave.
45   I was a being of feeling alone.
I flung myself down on the earth
Full length on the great earth, full length,
I wept out the dark load of human love.
In pagan adoration I adored her.
50   I felt the actual earth of her.
Victor and victim of humility,
I closed in the wordless ecstasy
Of mystery: where there is no thought
But feeling lost in itself forever,
55   Profound, remote, immediate, and calm.
Frightened, I stood up, I looked about
Suspiciously, hurriedly (a rustling),
As if the sun, the air, the trees
Were human, might not understand.
60   I drew breath, it made a sound,
I stepped gingerly away. Then
The mind came like a fire, it
Tortured man, I thought of madness.
The mind will not accept the blood.
65   The sun and sky, the trees and grasses,
And the whispering leaves, took on
Their usual characters. I went away,
Slowly, tingling, elated, saying, saying
Mother, Great Being, O Source of Life
70   To whom in wisdom we return,
Accept this humble servant evermore.

THE HORSE CHESTNUT TREE

Boys in sporadic but tenacious droves
Come with sticks, as certainly as Autumn,
To assault the great horse chestnut tree.

There is a law governs their lawlessness.
5   Desire is in them for a shining amulet
And the best are those that are highest up.

They will not pick them easily from the ground.
With shrill arms they fling to the higher branches,
To hurry the work of nature for their pleasure.

10 I have seen them trooping down the street
Their pockets stuffed with chestnuts shucked, unshucked.
It is only evening keeps them from their wish.

Sometimes I run out in a kind of rage
To chase the boys away: I catch an arm,
15 Maybe, and laugh to think of being the lawgiver.

I was once such a young sprout myself
And fingered in my pocket the prize and trophy.
But still I moralize upon the day

And see that we, outlaws on God's property,
20 Fling out imagination beyond the skies,
Wishing a tangible good from the unknown.

And likewise death will drive us from the scene
With the great flowering world unbroken yet,
Which we held in idea, a little handful.

THE PLACE

I
Eventually one finds
There is no environment
Patent for the poetic.

Any place will do.
5 Alas! One thought of a gold
Hullabaloo, a place of glass

Refinement with subtleties
Crossing the transparency
As lively as mind's images.

10 One thought of a vast portico
With appropriate, energized
Gods and beings, rich purposes.

Alas! Any place will do.
There is no poetical place,
15 America continues its practices.

Final toughness of the word,
The word bawling imperfections,
Its paradox to be heard.

II
There used to be
20 The violent struggle
For place, the right

Place poetic in countries
Or cities or underground,
The right place

25 Was thought emergent
And to harbor you,
Hello! Poetry Place.

The subconscious was
Nearest, perhaps dearest,
30 Anyway sheerest

But always fleering off.
Ways you went! Allurement
In echoic happiness.

There was no place for poetry.
35 Entrenched, my flesh is
Poetry's environment.

THE RECORD

Reading the stars' epitaphy
I foredeemed empathy.
My hands were free,
Lined with sensuality.

5 Looking in the spring of the palm
I could perpetrate there without qualm;
All was calm,
Against breakneck violence, balm.

It was up in the stars' periphery
10 I read the soul's history
And victory,
The voyage of the soul's periptery.

I had enjoined the battle of being
In harshness of inner seeing,
15 Never fleeing
The antique duties of self-freeing.

Man, what was man, was
Man the ultimate cause
Of all laws,
20 The old game and the taws?

Laid up, elect, the ideational
Stars were sensational

And passional
Variations of the natural.

25 I would never descend to man
Without feeling ascend I can
And am
Ascentional by august plan.

Better to live in the higher light
30 Beyond animal fight,
Night—
Free from dualistic force and blight,

And in true sensuality
Discover the nativity
35 And history
Of the soul among its immortalities.

THE HEIGHT OF MAN

I am where the bluebell dies
But I, where Western storms are born,
Am ready for new mysteries,
I think of riding the bullock's horns

5 To sweaty dust; I climb Hermit's Peak
Ten thousand feet up beyond trees
Where in the last reaches high crosses
Mark the stages of the Penitentes.

Some say their savage mysteries
10 Were so guarded on the heights
That when a non-believer climbed to them
They slew him with a light slingshot.

Bluebells, bluebells, how frail and Spring-like,
Another world all fragile and intact,
15 O bluebells of the early memories and life,
A fair elixir before the killing facts.

HARK BACK

To have stepped lightly among European marbles
Dwelling in a pantheon of air;

THE HEIGHT OF MAN. **8.** *Penitentes:* religious sect of Southwest United States known
for practicing flagellation during Holy Week, until 1896 ending with a crucifixion;
condemned by the Roman Catholic Church in 1889.

To have altered the gods in a fact of being;

5 To have· envisaged the marriage
Of everything new with the old.

And sprung a free spirit in the world

Is to have caught my own spirit
On a bicycle in the morning

Riding out of Paris,
10 Heading South.

My flesh felt so good
I was my own god.

Stanley Kunitz (1905-   )

Born in Worcester, Massachusetts, Stanley Kunitz graduated summa
cum laude from Harvard in 1926, and received his M.A. in 1927.
He worked for many years as editor and biographer on such reference works as *Twentieth Century Authors,* edited the Wilson Library
Bulletin from 1928 to 1943, married in 1939 (one child), served in
the Air Transport Command from 1943 to 1945, and taught at Bennington College from 1946 to 1949, and at the New School from 1950
to 1957, with visiting professorships at the University of Washington,
Queens College, and Brandeis University from 1955 to 1958. From
1958 to 1962 he was director of the Poetry Workshop at the Poetry
Center in New York. Divorced in 1958, he married the painter-poet
Elise Asher. Since 1963 he has taught at Columbia. He lives in Greenwich Village. His honors include a Guggenheim Fellowship in 1945-
1946, the Amy Lowell Traveling Fellowship in 1953-1954, a Ford
Foundation grant in· 1958-1959, the Harriet Monroe Award from
the University of Chicago, and in· 1959 the Pulitzer Prize for his
Selected Poems. He is a member of the National Institute of Arts and
Letters. On the voice of the poet he writes:

> I never met a poet who was not convinced of his uniqueness, but
> some of us must be wrong, for clearly there are many more poets
> than there are voices. Every artist, Malraux has said, is born the
> prisoner of a style, by which I take it he means that the stamp of
> the age on our work is inescapable. More than we like to admit,
> the art of any given period is an unconscious agitation of the col-
> lective will, precipitating at calculable intervals a non-toxic sediment
> of reputations. *Anon.* still flourishes, through a multiplicity of sig-
> natures. In this decade, as always, the easiest poems to praise are
> those that incorporate the fashionable floating materials that will

make them seem for a while newer and better than they are. Does that matter so much? In time a handful who have listened to the prevailing tune will play it back, but different—modified by the accents of the great dead, set to their own living voice, beating in their own authentic measure.

I think of poetry partly as a game, partly as an ordeal, and I confess to ignorance of the boundaries. This is the danger of word-play: that it may lead to revelations. The path to "the true voice of feeling," as Keats called it, runs through a forest of lies. What do I really know except that I am living and dying at once? The taste of that knowledge on my tongue is the last secret I have to tell.

PROMISE ME

Only, when I am sudden loss
Of consequence for mind and stair,
Picking my dogged way from us
To whom, recessive in some where
5 Of recollection, with the cross
Fallen, the breast in disrepair:

Only, when loosening clothes, you lean
Out of your window sleepily,
And with luxurious, lidded mien
10 Sniff at the bitter dark—dear she,
Think somewhat gently of, between
Love ended and beginning, me.

SHE WEPT, SHE RAILED

She wept, she railed, she spurned the meat
Men toss into a muslin cage
To make their spineless doxy bleat
For pleasure and for patronage,
5 As if she had no choice but eat
The lewd bait of a squalid age.

That moment when the lights go out
The years shape to the sprawling thing,
A marmoset with bloodied clout,
10 A pampered flank that learns to sing,
Without the grace, she cried, to doubt
The postures of the underling.

I thought of Judith in her tent,
Of Helen by the crackling wall,
15 Of Cressida, her bone-lust spent,
Of Catherine on the holy wheel:

I heard their woman-dust lament
The golden wound that does not heal.

What a wild air her small joints beat!
20 I only poured the raging wine
Until our bodies filled with light,
Mine with hers and hers with mine,
And we went out into the night
Where all the constellations shine.

FOREIGN AFFAIRS

We are two countries girded for the war,
Whisking our scouts across the pricked frontier
To ravage in each other's fields, cut lines
Along the lacework of strategic nerves,
5 Loot stores; while here and there,
In ambushes that trace a valley's curves,
Stark witness to the dangerous charge we bear,
A house ignites, a train's derailed, a bridge
Blows up sky-high, and water floods the mines.
10 Who first attacked? Who turned the other cheek?
Aggression perpetrated is as soon
Denied, and insult rubbed into the injury
By cunning agents trained in these affairs,
With whom it's touch-and-go, don't-tread-on-me,
15 I-dare-you-to, keep-off, and kiss-my-hand.
Tempers could sharpen knives, and do; we live
In states provocative
Where frowning headlines scare the coffee cream
And doomsday is the eighth day of the week.

20 Our exit through the slammed and final door
Is twenty times rehearsed, but when we face
The imminence of cataclysmic rupture,
A lesser pride goes down upon its knees.
Two countries separated by desire!—
25 Whose diplomats speed back and forth by plane,
Portmanteaus stuffed with fresh apologies
Outdated by events before they land.
Negotiations wear them out: they're driven mad
Between the protocols of tears and rapture.

30 Locked in our fated and contiguous selves,
These worlds that too much agitate each other,
Interdependencies from hip to head,
Twin principalities both slave and free,
We coexist, proclaiming Peace together.
35 Tell me no lies! We are divided nations
With malcontents by thousands in our streets,

These thousands torn by inbred revolutions.
A triumph is demanded, not moral victories
Deduced from small advances, small retreats.
40 Are the gods of our fathers not still daemonic?
On the steps of the Capitol
The outraged lion of our years roars panic,
And we suffer the guilty cowardice of the will,
Gathering its bankrupt slogans up for flight
45 Like gold from ruined treasuries.
And yet, and yet, although the murmur rises,
We are what we are, and only life surprises.

The Dark and the Fair

A roaring company that festive night;
The beast of dialectic dragged his chains,
Prowling from chair to chair in the smoking light,
While the snow hissed against the windowpanes.

5 Our politics, our science, and our faith
Were whiskey on the tongue; I, being rent
By the fierce divisions of our time, cried death
And death again, and my own dying meant.

Out of her secret life, that griffin-land
10 Where ivory empires build their stage, she came,
Putting in mine her small impulsive hand,
Five-fingered gift, and the palm not tame.

The moment clanged: beauty and terror danced
To the wild vibration of a sister-bell,
15 Whose unremitting stroke discountenanced
The marvel that the mirrors blazed to tell.

A darker image took this fairer form
Who once, in the purgatory of my pride,
When innocence betrayed me in a room
20 Of mocking elders, swept handsome to my side,

Until we rose together, arm in arm,
And fled together back into the world.
What brought her now, in the semblance of the warm,
Out of cold spaces, damned by colder blood?

25 That furied woman did me grievous wrong,
But does it matter much, given our years?
We learn, as the thread plays out, that we belong
Less to what flatters us than to what scars;

So freshly turning, as the turn condones,
30   For her I killed the propitiatory bird,
Kissing her down. Peace to her bitter bones,
Who taught me the serpent's word, but yet the word.

FATHER AND SON

Now in the suburbs and the falling light
I followed him, and now down sandy road
Whiter than bone-dust, through the sweet
Curdle of fields, where the plums
5   Dropped with their load of ripeness, one by one.
Mile after mile I followed, with skimming feet,
After the secret master of my blood,
Him, steeped in the odor of ponds, whose indomitable love
Kept me in chains. Strode years; stretched into bird;
10   Raced through the sleeping country where I was young,
The silence unrolling before me as I came,
The night nailed like an orange to my brow.

How should I tell him my fable and the fears,
How bridge the chasm in a casual tone,
15   Saying, "The house, the stucco one you built,
We lost. Sister married and went from home,
And nothing comes back, it's strange, from where she goes.
I lived on a hill that had too many rooms:
Light we could make, but not enough of warmth,
20   And when the light failed, I climbed under the hill.
The papers are delivered every day;
I am alone and never shed a tear."

At the water's edge, where the smothering ferns lifted
Their arms, "Father!" I cried, "Return! You know
25   The way. I'll wipe the mudstains from your clothes;
No trace, I promise, will remain. Instruct
Your son, whirling between two wars,
In the Gemara of your gentleness,
For I would be a child to those who mourn
30   And brother to the foundlings of the field
And friend of innocence and all bright eyes.

O teach me how to work and keep me kind."
Among the turtles and the lilies he turned to me
The white ignorant hollow of his face.

DECIDUOUS BRANCH

Winter, that coils in the thickets now,
Will glide from the fields; the swinging rain

Be knotted with flowers; on every bough
A bird will meditate again.

5 Lord, in the night if I should die,
Who entertained your thrilling worm,
Corruption wastes more than the eye
Can pick from this imperfect form.

I lie awake, hearing the drip
10 Upon my sill; thinking, the sun
Has not been promised; we who strip
Summer to seed shall be undone.

Now, while the antler of the eaves
Liquefies, drop by drop, I brood
15 On a Christian thing: unless the leaves
Perish, the tree is not renewed.

If all our perishable stuff
Be nourished to its rot, we clean
Our trunk of death, and in our tough
20 And final growth are evergreen.

ORGANIC BLOOM

The brain constructs its systems to enclose
The steady paradox of thought and sense;
Momentously its tissued meaning grows
To solve and integrate experience.
5 But life escapes closed reason. We explain
Our chaos into cosmos, cell by cell,
Only to learn of some insidious pain
Beyond the limits of our charted hell,
A guilt not mentioned in our prayers, a sin
10 Conceived against the self. So, vast and vaster
The plasmic circles of gray discipline
Spread outward to include each new disaster.
Enormous floats the brain's organic bloom
Till, bursting like a fruit, it scatters doom.

THE WAR AGAINST THE TREES

The man who sold his lawn to standard oil
Joked with his neighbors come to watch the show
While the bulldozers, drunk with gasoline,
Tested the virtue of the soil
5 Under the branchy sky
By overthrowing first the privet-row.

Forsythia-forays and hydrangea-raids
Were but preliminaries to a war
Against the great-grandfathers of the town,
So freshly lopped and maimed.
They struck and struck again,
And with each elm a century went down.

All day the hireling engines charged the trees,
Subverting them by hacking underground
In grub-dominions, where dark summer's mole
Rampages through his halls,
Till a northern seizure shook
Those crowns, forcing the giants to their knees.

I saw the ghosts of children at their games
Racing beyond their childhood in the shade,
And while the green world turned its death-foxed page
And a red wagon wheeled,
I watched them disappear
Into the suburbs of their grievous age.

Ripped from the craters much too big for hearts
The club-roots bared their amputated coils,
Raw gorgons matted blind, whose pocks and scars
Cried Moon! on a corner lot
One witness-moment, caught
In the rear-view mirrors of the passing cars.

A CHOICE OF WEAPONS

Reviewing me without undue elation
A critic who has earned his reputation
By being always Johnny-on-the-spot
Where each contemporary starts to rot
Conceded me integrity and style
And stamina to walk a measured mile,
But wondered why a gang of personal devils
Need clank their jigging bones as public evils:

"The times are suited for the gay empiric,
The witty ironist, the casual lyric;
Apparently it's gristle-fare, not fat,
At certain tables: must we weep at that?
Though poets seem to rail at bourgeois ills
It is their lack of audience that kills.
Their metaphysics but reflects a folly:
'Read me or I'll be damned and melancholy.'
This poet suffers: that's his right, of course,
But we don't have to watch him beat his horse."

Sir, if appreciation be my lack,
20 You may appreciate me, front and back—
I won't deny that vaguely vulgar need:
But do not pity those whose motives bleed
Even while strolling in a formal garden.
Observe that tears are bullets when they harden;
25 The triggered poem's no water-pistol toy,
But shoots its cause, and is a source of joy.

Theodore Roethke (1908-1963)

Theodore Roethke was born in Saginaw, Michigan, received his B.A. from the University of Michigan in 1929 and his M.A. in 1936, and taught at Lafayette College, Pennsylvania State College, Bennington College, and—from 1947 until his death—the University of Washington. He married in 1953 and is survived by his wife; they had no children. His many honors include Guggenheim Fellowships in 1946 and 1950, the Pulitzer Prize in 1954 for *The Waking: Poems, 1933-1953*, the 1958 Bollingen Prize and the 1959 Edna St. Vincent Millay Prize for *Words for the Wind,* a two-year Ford Foundation Fellowship awarded in 1959, and, posthumously, the National Book Award in 1965 for *The Far Field.*

Open House

My secrets cry aloud.
I have no need for tongue.
My heart keeps open house,
My doors are widely swung.
5 An epic of the eyes
My love, with no disguise.

My truths are all foreknown,
This anguish self-revealed.
I'm naked to the bone,
10 With nakedness my shield.
Myself is what I wear:
I keep the spirit spare.

The anger will endure,
The deed will speak the truth
15 In language strict and pure.
I stop the lying mouth:
Rage warps my clearest cry
To witless agony.

No Bird

Now here is peace for one who knew
The secret heart of sound.
The ear so delicate and true
Is pressed to noiseless ground.

5 Slow swings the breeze above her head,
The grasses whitely stir;
But in this forest of the dead
No bird awakens her.

Transplanting

Watching hands transplanting,
Turning and tamping,
Lifting the young plants with two fingers,
Sifting in a palm-full of fresh loam,—
5 One swift movement,—
Then plumping in the bunched roots,
A single twist of the thumbs, a tamping and turning,
All in one,
Quick on the wooden bench,
10 A shaking down, while the stem stays straight,
Once, twice, and a faint third thump,—
Into the flat-box it goes,
Ready for the long days under the sloped glass:

The sun warming the fine loam,
15 The young horns winding and unwinding,
Creaking their thin spines,
The underleaves, the smallest buds
Breaking into nakedness,
The blossoms extending
20 Out into the sweet air,
The whole flower extending outward,
Stretching and reaching.

Elegy for Jane
MY STUDENT, THROWN BY A HORSE

I remember the neckcurls, limp and damp as tendrils;
And her quick look, a sidelong pickerel smile;
And how, once startled into talk, the light syllables leaped for her,
And she balanced in the delight of her thought,
5 A wren, happy, tail into the wind,
Her song trembling the twigs and small branches.
The shade sang with her;

The leaves, their whispers turned to kissing;
And the mold sang in the bleached valleys under the rose.

10 Oh, when she was sad, she cast herself down into such a pure depth,
Even a father could not find her:
Scraping her cheek against straw;
Stirring the clearest water.

My sparrow, you are not here,
15 Waiting like a fern, making a spiny shadow.
The sides of wet stones cannot console me,
Nor the moss, wound with the last light.

If only I could nudge you from this sleep,
My maimed darling, my skittery pigeon.
20 Over this damp grave I speak the words of my love:
I, with no rights in this matter,
Neither father nor lover.

REPLY TO A LADY EDITOR

If the Poem (beginning "I knew a woman, lovely
in her bones") in *The London Times Literary Supplement* has not appeared here, we offer you $75
for it. Could you wire us collect your answer?
                              Sincerely yours,
                              Alice S. Morris
            Literary Editor, *Harper's Bazaar*

Sweet Alice S. Morris, I *am* pleased, of course,
You take the *Times Supplement,* and read its verse,
And know that True Love is more than a Life-Force
—And so like my poem called *Poem.*

5 Dan Cupid, I tell you's a braw laddie-buck;
A visit from him is a piece of pure luck,
And should he arrive, why just lean yourself back
—And recite him my poem called *Poem.*

O print it, my dear, do publish it, yes,
10 That ladies their true natures never suppress,
When they come, dazedly, to the pretty pass
—Of acting my poem called *Poem.*

My darling, my dearest, most-honest-alive,
Just send me along that sweet seventy-five;
15 I'll continue to think on the nature of love,
—As I dance to my poem called *Poem.*

I Knew a Woman

I knew a woman, lovely in her bones,
When small birds sighed, she would sigh back at them;
Ah, when she moved, she moved more ways than one:
The shapes a bright container can contain!
5 Of her choice virtues only gods should speak,
Or English poets who grew up on Greek
(I'd have them sing in chorus, cheek to cheek).

How well her wishes went! She stroked my chin,
She taught me Turn, and Counter-turn, and Stand;
10 She taught me Touch, that undulant white skin;
I nibbled meekly from her proffered hand;
She was the sickle; I, poor I, the rake,
Coming behind her for her pretty sake
(But what prodigious mowing we did make).

15 Love likes a gander, and adores a goose:
Her full lips pursed, the errant note to seize;
She played it quick, she played it light and loose;
My eyes, they dazzled at her flowing knees;
Her several parts could keep a pure repose,
20 Or one hip quiver with a mobile nose
(She moved in circles, and those circles moved).

Let seed be grass, and grass turn into hay:
I'm martyr to a motion not my own;
What's freedom for? To know eternity.
25 I swear she cast a shadow white as stone.
But who would count eternity in days?
These old bones live to learn her wanton ways:
(I measure time by how a body sways).

The Voice

One feather is a bird,
I claim; one tree, a wood;
In her low voice I heard
More than a mortal should;
5 And so I stood apart,
Hidden in my own heart.

And yet I roamed out where
Those notes went, like the bird,
Whose thin song hung in air,
10 Diminished, yet still heard:
I lived with open sound,
Aloft, and on the ground.

That ghost was my own choice,
The shy cerulean bird;
It sang with her true voice,
And it was I who heard
A slight voice reply;
I heard; and only I.

Desire exults the ear:
Bird, girl, and ghostly tree,
The earth, the solid air—
Their slow song sang in me;
The long noon pulsed away,
Like any summer day.

JOURNEY TO THE INTERIOR

I

In the long journey out of the self,
There are many detours, washed-out interrupted raw places
Where the shale slides dangerously
And the back wheels hang almost over the edge
At the sudden veering, the moment of turning.
Better to hug close, wary of rubble and falling stones.
The arroyo cracking the road, the wind-bitten buttes, the canyons,
Creeks swollen in midsummer from the flash-flood roaring into the
    narrow valley.
Reeds beaten flat by wind and rain,
Gray from the long winter, burnt at the base in late summer.
—Or the path narrowing,
Winding upward toward the stream with its sharp stones,
The upland of alder and birchtrees,
Through the swamp alive with quicksand,
The way blocked at last by a fallen fir-tree,
The thickets darkening,
The ravines ugly.

II

I remember how it was to drive in gravel,
Watching for dangerous down-hill places, where the wheels whined
    beyond eighty—
When you hit the deep pit at the bottom of the swale,
The trick was to throw the car sideways and charge over the hill,
    full of the throttle.
Grinding up and over the narrow road, spitting and roaring.
A chance? Perhaps. But the road was part of me, and its ditches,
And the dust lay thick on my eyelids,—Who ever wore goggles?—
Always a sharp turn to the left past a barn close to the roadside,
To a scurry of small dogs and a shriek of children,
The highway ribboning out in a straight thrust to the North,

To the sand dunes and fish flies, hanging, thicker than moths,
Dying brightly under the street lights sunk in coarse concrete,
30   The towns with their high pitted road-crowns and deep gutters,
Their wooden stores of silvery pine and weather-beaten red court-
    houses,
An old bridge below with a buckled iron railing, broken by some
    idiot plunger;
Underneath, the sluggish water running between weeds, broken
    wheels, tires, stones.
And all flows past—
35   The cemetery with two scrubby trees in the middle of the prairie,
The dead snakes and muskrats, the turtles gasping in the rubble,
The spikey purple bushes in the winding dry creek bed—
The floating hawks, the jackrabbits, the grazing cattle—
I am not moving but they are,
40   And the sun comes out of a blue cloud over the Tetons,
While, farther away, the heat-lightning flashes.
I rise and fall in the slow sea of a grassy plain,
The wind veering the car slightly to the right,
Whipping the line of white laundry, bending the cottonwoods apart,
45   The scraggly wind-break of a dusty ranch-house.
I rise and fall, and time folds
Into a long moment;
And I hear the lichen speak,
And the ivy advance with its white lizard feet—
50   On the shimmering road,
On the dusty detour.

         III
I see the flower of all water, above and below me, the never receding,
Moving, unmoving in a parched land, white in the moonlight:
The soul at a still-stand,
55   At ease after rocking the flesh to sleep,
Petals and reflections of petals mixed on the surface of a glassy pool,
And the waves flattening out when the fishermen drag their nets
    over the stones.

In the moment of time when the small drop forms, but does not fall,
I have known the heart of the sun,—
60   In the dark and light of a dry place,
In a flicker of fire brisked by a dusty wind.
I have heard, in a drip of leaves,
A slight song,
After the midnight cries.
65   I rehearse myself for this:
The stand at the stretch in the face of death,
Delighting in surface change, the glitter of light on waves,
And I roam elsewhere, my body thinking,
Turning toward the other side of light,
70   In a tower of wind, a tree idling in air,

Beyond my own echo,
Neither forward nor backward,
Unperplexed, in a place leading nowhere.

As a blind man, lifting a curtain, knows it is morning,
75 I know this change:
On one side of silence there is no smile;
But when I breathe with the birds,
The spirit of wrath becomes the spirit of blessing,
And the dead begin from their dark to sing in my sleep.

LIGHT LISTENED

O what could be more nice
Than her ways with a man?
She kissed me more than twice
Once we were left alone.
5 Who'd look when he could feel?
She'd more sides than a seal.

The close air faintly stirred.
Light deepened to a bell,
The love-beat of a bird.
10 She kept her body still
And watched the weather flow.
We live by what we do.

All's known, all, all around:
The shape of things to be;
15 A green thing loves the green
And loves the living ground.
The deep shade gathers night;
She changed with changing light.

We met to leave again
20 The time we broke from time;
A cold air brought its rain,
The singing of a stem.
She sang a final song;
Light listened when she sang.

THE GERANIUM

When I put her out, once, by the garbage pail,
She looked so limp and bedraggled,
So foolish and trusting, like a sick poodle,
Or a wizened aster in late September,
5 I brought her back in again

For a new routine—
Vitamins, water, and whatever
Sustenance seemed sensible
At the time: she'd lived
10   So long on gin, bobbie pins, half-smoked cigars, dead beer,
Her shriveled petals falling
On the faded carpet, the stale
Steak grease stuck to her fuzzy leaves.
(Dried-out, she creaked like a tulip.)

15   The things she endured!—
The dumb dames shrieking half the night
Or the two of us, alone, both seedy,
Me breathing booze at her,
She leaning out of her pot toward the window.

20   Near the end, she seemed almost to hear me—
And that was scary—
So when that snuffling cretin of a maid
Threw her, pot and all, into the trash-can,
I said nothing.

25   But I sacked the presumptuous hag the next week,
I was that lonely.

ALL MORNING

Here in our aging district the wood pigeon lives with us,
His deep-throated cooing part of the early morning,
Far away, close-at-hand, his call floating over the on-coming traffic,
The lugubriously beautiful plaint uttered at regular intervals,
5   A protest from the past, a reminder.

They sit, three or four, high in the fir-trees back of the house,
Flapping away heavily when a car blasts too close,
And one drops down to the garden, the high rhododendron,
Only to fly over to his favorite perch, the cross-bar of a telephone
    pole;
10   Grave, hieratic, a piece of Assyrian sculpture,
A thing carved of stone or wood, with the dull iridescence of long-
    polished wood,
Looking at you without turning his small head,
With a round vireo's eye, quiet and contained,
Part of the landscape.

15   And the Steller jay, raucous, sooty headed, lives with us,
Conducting his long wars with the neighborhood cats,
All during mating season,
Making a racket to wake the dead,

To distract attention from the short-tailed ridiculous young ones
Hiding deep in the blackberry bushes—
What a scuttling and rapping along the drainpipes,
A fury of jays, diving and squawking,
When our spayed female cat yawns and stretches out in the sun-
    shine—
And the wrens scold, and the chickadees frisk and frolic,
Pitching lightly over the high hedgerows, dee-deeing,
And the ducks near Lake Washington waddle down the highway
    after a rain,
Stopping traffic, indignant as addled old ladies,
Pecking at crusts and peanuts, their green necks glittering;
And the hummingbird dips in and around the quince tree,
Veering close to my head,
Then whirring off sideways to the top of the hawthorn,
Its almost-invisible wings, buzzing, hitting the loose leaves intermit-
    tently—

A delirium of birds!
Peripheral dippers come to rest on the short grass,
Their heads jod-jodding like pigeons;
The gulls, the gulls far from their waves
Rising, wheeling away with harsh cries,
Coming down on a patch of lawn:

It is neither spring nor summer: it is Always,
With towhees, finches, chickadees, California quail, wood doves,
With wrens, sparrows, juncos, cedar waxwings, flickers,
With Baltimore orioles, Michigan bobolinks,
And those birds forever dead,
The passenger pigeon, the great auk, the Carolina paraquet,
All birds remembered, O never forgotten!
All in my yard, of a perpetual Sunday,
All morning! All morning!

THE MOMENT

We passed the ice of pain,
And came to a dark ravine,
And there we sang with the sea:
The wide, the bleak abyss
Shifted with our slow kiss.

Space struggled with time;
The gong of midnight struck
The naked absolute.
Sound, silence sang as one.

10   All flowed: without, within;
     Body met body, we
     Created what's to be.

     What else to say?
     We end in joy.

Elizabeth Bishop (1911-   )

Elizabeth Bishop was born in Worcester, Massachusetts, received an
A.B. from Vassar in 1934, was Consultant in Poetry at the Library
of Congress in 1949-1950, and now lives in Petropolis, Brazil. In
1945 she won the Houghton Mifflin poetry fellowship award, in 1947
a Guggenheim Fellowship, in 1952 the Shelley Memorial Award,
in 1956 the Pulitzer Prize for *A Cold Spring,* in 1957 an Amy Lowell
Fellowship, and in 1964 an award of $5000 from the Academy of
American Poets. Miss Bishop preferred not to comment on the voice
of the poet.

WADING AT WELLFLEET

In one of the Assyrian wars
a chariot first saw the light
that bore sharp blades around its wheels.

The chariot from Assyria
5   went rolling down mechanically
to take the warriors by the heels.

A thousand warriors in the sea
could not consider such a war
as that the sea itself contrives

10   but hasn't put in action yet.
This morning's glitterings reveal
the sea is "all a case of knives."

Lying so close, they catch the sun,
the spokes directed at the shin.
15   The chariot front is blue and great.

The war rests wholly with the waves:
they try revolving, but the wheels
give way, they will not bear the weight.

A MIRACLE FOR BREAKFAST

At six o'clock we were waiting for coffee,
waiting for coffee and the charitable crumb

that was going to be served from a certain balcony,
—like kings of old, or like a miracle.
It was still dark. One foot of the sun
steadied itself on a long ripple in the river.

The first ferry of the day had just crossed the river.
It was so cold we hoped that the coffee
would be very hot, seeing that the sun
was not going to warm us; and that the crumb
would be a loaf each, buttered, by a miracle.
At seven a man stepped out on the balcony.

He stood for a minute alone on the balcony
looking over our heads toward the river.
A servant handed him the makings of a miracle,
consisting of one lone cup of coffee
and one roll, which he proceeded to crumb,
his head, so to speak, in the clouds—along with the sun.

Was the man crazy? What under the sun
was he trying to do, up there on his balcony!
Each man received one rather hard crumb,
which some flicked scornfully into the river,
and, in a cup, one drop of the coffee.
Some of us stood around, waiting for the miracle.

I can tell what I saw next; it was not a miracle.
A beautiful villa stood in the sun
and from its doors came the smell of hot coffee.
In front, a baroque white plaster balcony
added by birds, who nest along the river,
—I saw it with one eye close to the crumb—

and galleries and marble chambers. My crumb
my mansion, made for me a miracle,
through ages, by insects, birds, and the river
working the stone. Every day, in the sun,
at breakfast time I sit on my balcony
with my feet up, and drink gallons of coffee.

We licked up the crumb and swallowed the coffee.
A window across the river caught the sun
as if the miracle were working, on the wrong balcony.

At the Fishhouses

Although it is a cold evening,
down by one of the fishhouses
an old man sits netting,

his net, in the gloaming almost invisible,
5 a dark purple-brown,
and his shuttle worn and polished.
The air smells so strong of codfish
it makes one's nose run and one's eyes water.
The five fishhouses have steeply peaked roofs
10 and narrow, cleated gangplanks slant up
to storerooms in the gables
for the wheelbarrows to be pushed up and down on.
All is silver: the heavy surface of the sea,
swelling slowly as if considering spilling over,
15 is opaque, but the silver of the benches,
the lobster pots, and masts, scattered
among the wild jagged rocks,
is of an apparent translucence
like the small old buildings with an emerald moss
20 growing on their shoreward walls.
The big fish tubs are completely lined
with layers of beautiful herring scales
and the wheelbarrows are similarly plastered
with creamy iridescent coats of mail,
25 with small iridescent flies crawling on them.
Up on the little slope behind the houses,
set in the sparse bright sprinkle of grass,
is an ancient wooden capstan,
cracked, with two long bleached handles
30 and some melancholy stains, like dried blood,
where the ironwork has rusted.

The old man accepts a Lucky Strike.
He was a friend of my grandfather.
We talk of the decline in the population
35 and of codfish and herring
while he waits for a herring boat to come in.
There are sequins on his vest and on his thumb.
He has scraped the scales, the principal beauty,
from unnumbered fish with that black old knife,
40 the blade of which is almost worn away.

Down at the water's edge, at the place
where they haul up the boats, up the long ramp
descending into the water, thin silver
tree trunks are laid horizontally
45 across the gray stones, down and down
at intervals of four or five feet.

Cold dark deep and absolutely clear,
element bearable to no mortal,
to fish and to seals . . . One seal particularly
50 I have seen here evening after evening.

He was curious about me. He was interested in music;
like me a believer in total immersion,
so I used to sing him Baptist hymns.
I also sang "A Mighty Fortress Is Our God."
He stood up in the water and regarded me
steadily, moving his head a little.
Then he would disappear, then suddenly emerge
almost in the same spot, with a sort of shrug
as if it were against his better judgment.
Cold dark deep and absolutely clear,
the clear gray icy water . . . Back, behind us,
the dignified tall firs begin.
Bluish, associating with their shadows,
a million Christmas trees stand
waiting for Christmas. The water seems suspended
above the rounded gray and blue-gray stones.
I have seen it over and over, the same sea, the same,
slightly, indifferently swinging above the stones,
icily free above the stones,
above the stones and then the world.
If you should dip your hand in,
your wrist would ache immediately,
your bones would begin to ache and your hand would burn
as if the water were a transmutation of fire
that feeds on stones and burns with a dark-gray flame.
If you tasted it, it would first taste bitter,
then briny, then surely burn your tongue.
It is like what we imagine knowledge to be:
dark, salt, clear, moving, utterly free,
drawn from the cold hard mouth
of the world, derived from the rocky breasts
forever, flowing and drawn, and since
our knowledge is historical, flowing, and flown.

INSOMNIA

The moon in the bureau mirror
looks out a million miles
(and perhaps with pride, at herself,
but she never, never smiles)
far and away beyond sleep, or
perhaps she's a daytime sleeper.

By the Universe deserted,
she'd tell it to go to hell,
and she'd find a body of water,
or a mirror, on which to dwell.
So wrap up care in a cobweb
and drop it down the well

into that world inverted
where left is always right,
where the shadows are really the body,
where we stay awake all night,
where the heavens are shallow as the sea
is now deep, and you love me.

15

VISITS TO ST. ELIZABETHS
1950

This is the house of Bedlam.

This is the man
that lies in the house of Bedlam.

This is the time
of the tragic man
that lies in the house of Bedlam.

5

This is a wristwatch
telling the time
of the talkative man
that lies in the house of Bedlam.

10

This is a sailor
wearing the watch
that tells the time
of the honored man
that lies in the house of Bedlam.

15

This is the roadstead all of board
reached by the sailor
wearing the watch
that tells the time
of the old, brave man
that lies in the house of Bedlam.

20

These are the years and the walls of the ward,
the winds and clouds of the sea of board
sailed by the sailor
wearing the watch
that tells the time
of the cranky man
that lies in the house of Bedlam.

25

This is a Jew in a newspaper hat
that dances weeping down the ward
over the creaking sea of board
beyond the sailor

30

winding his watch
that tells the time
35 of the cruel man
that lies in the house of Bedlam.

This is a world of books gone flat.
This is a Jew in a newspaper hat
that dances weeping down the ward
40 over the creaking sea of board
of the batty sailor
that winds his watch
that tells the time
of the busy man
45 that lies in the house of Bedlam.

This is a boy that pats the floor
to see if the world is there, is flat,
for the widowed Jew in the newspaper hat
that dances weeping down the ward
50 waltzing the length of a weaving board
by the silent sailor
that hears his watch
that ticks the time
of the tedious man
55 that lies in the house of Bedlam.

These are the years and the walls and the door
that shut on a boy that pats the floor
to feel if the world is there and flat.
This is a Jew in a newspaper hat
60 that dances joyfully down the ward
into the parting seas of board
past the staring sailor
that shakes his watch
that tells the time
65 of the poet, the man
that lies in the house of Bedlam.

This is the soldier home from the war.
These are the years and the walls and the door
that shut on a boy that pats the floor
70 to see if the world is round or flat.
This is a Jew in a newspaper hat
that dances carefully down the ward,
walking the plank of a coffin board
with the crazy sailor
75 that shows his watch
that tells the time
of the wretched man
that lies in the house of Bedlam.

The Armadillo
(for robert lowell)

This is the time of year
when almost every night
the frail, illegal fire balloons appear.
Climbing the mountain height,

5   rising toward a saint
still honored in these parts,
the paper chambers flush and fill with light
that comes and goes, like hearts.

Once up against the sky it's hard
10   to tell them from the stars—
planets, that is—the tinted ones:
Venus going down, or Mars,

or the pale green one. With a wind,
they flare and falter, wobble and toss;
15   but if it's still they steer between
the kite sticks of the Southern Cross,

receding, dwindling, solemnly
and steadily forsaking us,
or, in the downdraft from a peak
20   suddenly turning dangerous.

Last night another big one fell.
It splattered like an egg of fire
against the cliff behind the house.
The flame ran down. We saw the pair

25   of owls who nest there flying up
and up, their whirling black-and-white
stained bright pink underneath, until
they shrieked up out of sight.

The ancient owls' nest must have burned.
30   Hastily, all alone,
a glistening armadillo left the scene,
rose-flecked, head down, tail down,

and then a baby rabbit jumped out,
short-eared, to our surprise.
35   So soft!—a handful of intangible ash
with fixed, ignited eyes.

Too pretty, dreamlike mimicry!
O falling fire and piercing cry
and panic, and a weak mailed fist
40   *clenched ignorant against the sky!*

Karl Shapiro was born in Baltimore, attended the University of Virginia in 1932-1933 and Johns Hopkins from 1936 to 1939 (no degree), served in the army from 1941 to 1945, was Consultant in Poetry at the Library of Congress in 1946-1947, taught at Johns Hopkins from 1947 to 1950, edited *Poetry* magazine from 1950 to 1956, and since 1956 has been Professor of English at the University of Nebraska. He married in 1945 and has three children. His honors include Guggenheim Fellowships in 1945-1946 and 1953-1954, the Pulitzer Prize in 1945 for *V-Letter and Other Poems,* and the Shelley Memorial Award in 1945. He holds an honorary Doctor of Humane Letters degree from Wayne State University and is a member of the National Institute of Arts and Letters. To his extensive writing on poetry he adds this comment:

> Remember what Williams said, if he said it: a sonnet is a fascist form. Poets here and now who use "forms" are turning back the clock, winding the metronome, making the trains run on time— with black boots and whips. But mostpoets like it that way (mostpoets having the fascist or stalinist mentality). Or bringing it up to date, the poets are really using cybernetic forms and don't know it. The modern anthology is a feedback from the establishmentarian gut. Pardon these shapiroisms, too true to be taken seriously.

Elegy Written on a Frontporch

The sun burns on its sultry wick;
Stratus and cumulus unite.
I who am neither well nor sick
Sit in a wicker chair and write.

5   A hot wind presses at my lips.
I peel. Am totally undressed.
Pinkish, as though a part-eclipse,
Heat licks upon my naked breast.

Angles in quick succession rise.
10 Eyesight is stereopticon
As roof and roof geometrize
Perspective deviously drawn.

I face a heaven half-destroyed,
A skyscape alabaster, dead.
15 One living shadow on the void,
A Flying Fortress drones ahead.

Motion and fixity take shape;
The fallow rays intensify
Distinctness. Nothing can escape
20   The clean hard focus of the eye.

Noise into humming noise constricts;
The traffic mumbles deeper down.
Only a trolley contradicts,
Ticks by neurotically to town.

25   Stretched taut upon the light I scorch,
Writhe in my sweat and smoke and sun.
The evening paper hits the porch;
My honeymoon of peace is done.

Unmasticated pulp of life . . .
30   Decision finds me blind and deaf.
I do not finger for the strife
Of Delano and Mutt and Jeff,

Or bend upon my nudity's
Umbilicus, the fact of facts,
35   As one who drowns in light and sees
The newsreel of his private acts.

I do not hug my feet with glee
And smile into my cul-de-sac
Enamoured of the dignity
40   Of facing forward moving back.

But set my wired sight, reclaim
The rotted friendship and the fresh;
Tune in on him who changed his name
And her who stultified the flesh.

45   I see who came to marriage raw
With poverty and self-abuse;
Defendants to the general law,
Their ignorance was no excuse.

Instructors, graduates I see,
50   Scholars who sneered into their books,
The female doctors pouring tea,
Hundreds of victims of their looks.

The money-poise of some, the pride
Of those who whored on easy checks,
55   Sons of The Business, dressy, snide,
Disfigured in expensive wrecks.

Believers in the songhit, thin
With pounding to the hebroid jazz;
The studious drinkers feeding in
60 The cloaca of the middle-class.

I see too many who romanced
Defeat, unmasculine, debased;
The striptease puritans who danced
The long lewd ritual of waste.

65 All these I bury out of sight
Sans benefit of epitaph.
I turn my legs into the light,
Punch out a cigaret and laugh.

For one, the best against that rout,
70 Deserted, obdurate to see
Their weakly literate wear out
The old Horatian fallacy;

Spoke of the beauty-to-obey,
The life-expectancy of bone,
75 She turned her back upon the day
But will not lie at night alone.

HOLLYWOOD

Farthest from any war, unique in time
Like Athens or Baghdad, this city lies
Between dry purple mountains and the sea.
The air is clear and famous, every day
5 Bright as a postcard, bringing bungalows
    And sights. The broad nights advertise
For love and music and astonomy.

Heart of a continent, the hearts converge
On open boulevards where palms are nursed
10 With flare-pots like a grove, on villa roads
Where castles cultivated like a style
Breed fabulous metaphors in foreign stone,
    And on enormous movie lots
Where history repeats its vivid blunders.

15 Alice and Cinderella are most real.
Here may the tourist, quite sincere at last,
Rest from his dream of travels. All is new,
No ruins claim his awe, and permanence,
Despised like customs, fails at every turn.
20   Here where the eccentric thrives,
Laughter and love are leading industries.

Luck is another. Here the bodyguard,
The parasite, the scholar are well paid,
The quack erects his alabaster office,
25   The moron and the genius are enshrined,
And the mystic makes a fortune quietly;
    Here all superlatives come true
And beauty is marketed like a basic food.

O can we understand it? Is it ours,
30   A crude whim of a beginning people,
A private orgy in a secluded spot?
Or alien like the word *harem,* or true
Like hideous Pittsburgh or depraved Atlanta?
    Is adolescence just as vile
35   As this its architecture and its talk?

Or are they parvenus, like boys and girls?
Or ours and happy, cleverest of all?
Yes. Yes. Though glamorous to the ignorant
This is the simplest city, a new school.
40   What is more nearly ours? If soul can mean
    The civilization of the brain,
This is a soul, a possible proud Florence.

Homecoming

Lost in the vastness of the void Pacific
My thousand days of exile, pain,
Bid me farewell. Gone is the Southern Cross
To her own sky, fallen a continent
5   Under the wave, dissolved the bitterest isles
In their salt element,
And here upon the deck the mist encloses
My smile that would light up all darkness
And ask forgiveness of the things that thrust
10   Shame and all death on millions and on me.

We bring no raw materials from the East
But green-skinned men in blue-lit holds
And lunatics impounded between-decks;
The mighty ghoul-ship that we ride exhales
15   The sickly-sweet stench of humiliation,
And even the majority, untouched by steel
Or psychoneurosis, stare with eyes in rut,
Their hands a rabble to snatch the riches
Of glittering shops and girls.

20   Because I am angry at this kindness which
Is both habitual and contradictory

To the life of armies, now I stand alone
And hate the swarms of khaki men that crawl
Like lice upon the wrinkled hide of earth,
25 Infesting ships as well. Not otherwise
Could I lean outward piercing fog to find
Our sacred bridge of exile and return.
My tears are psychological, not poems
To the United States; my smile is prayer.

30 Gnawing the thin slops of anxiety,
Escorted by the ground swell and by gulls,
In silence and with mystery we enter
The territorial waters. Not till then
Does that convulsive terrible joy, more sudden
35 And brilliant than the explosion of a ship,
Shatter the tensions of the heaven and sea
To crush a hundred thousand skulls
And liberate in that high burst of love
The imprisoned souls of soldiers and of me.

QUINTANA LAY IN THE SHALLOW GRAVE OF CORAL
from THE BOURGEOIS POET

6

Quintana lay in the shallow grave of coral. The guns boomed
     stupidly fifty yards away. The plasma trickled into
     his arm. Naked and filthy, covered with mosquitoes, he
     looked at me as I read his white cloth tag. How do you
5   feel, Quintana? He looks away from my gaze. I lie:
     we'll get you out of here sometime today.

I never saw him again, dead or alive. Skin and bones, with
     eyes as soft as soot, neck long as a thigh, a cross on
     his breastbone not far from the dog tags. El Greco was
10   all I could think of. Quintana lying in his shallow fox-
     hole waiting to be evacuated. A dying man with a
     Spanish name equals El Greco. A truck driver from
     Dallas probably.

When the Japs were making the banzai charge, to add insult
15   to death, they came at us screaming the supreme insult:
     Babe Ruth, go to hell! The Americans, on the other
     hand, when the Japs flew over dropping sticks of ex-
     plosives, shouted into the air, as if they could hear:
     Tojo eat shit!

20   Soldiers fall in love with the enemy all too easily. It's the allies
     they hate. Every war is its own excuse. That's why
     they're all surrounded with ideals. That's why they're
     all crusades.

LOWER THE STANDARD: THAT'S MY MOTTO
from THE BOURGEOIS POET

9

Lower the standard: that's my motto. Somebody is always
putting the food out of reach. We're tired of falling off
ladders. Who says a child can't paint? A pro is somebody who does it for money. Lower the standards. Let's
all play poetry. Down with ideals, flags, convention
buttons, morals, the scrambled eggs on the admiral's
hat. I'm talking sense. Lower the standards. Sabotage
the stylistic approach. Let weeds grow in the subdivi-
sion. Putty up the incisions in the library façade, those
names that frighten grade-school teachers, those names
whose U's are cut like V's. Burn the *Syntopicon* and
The Harvard Classics. Lower the standard on classics,
battleships, Russian ballet, national anthems (but
they're low enough). Break through to the bottom. Be
natural as an American abroad who knows no language,
not even American. Keelhaul the poets in the vestry
chairs. Renovate the Abbey of cold-storage dreamers.
Get off the Culture Wagon. Learn how to walk the way
you want. Slump your shoulders, stick your belly out,
arms all over the table. How many generations will this
take? Don't think about it, just make a start. (You have
made a start.) Don't break anything you can step
around, *but don't pick it up.* The law of gravity is the
law of art. You first, poetry second, the good, the beautiful, the true come last. As the lad said: We must love
one another or die.

FROM THE TOP FLOOR OF THE TULSA HOTEL I GAZE
AT THE NIGHT BEAUTY OF THE CRACKING-PLANT
from THE BOURGEOIS POET

23

From the top floor of the Tulsa hotel I gaze at the night
beauty of the cracking-plant. Candlelit city of small gas
flames by the thousands, what a lovely anachronism
dancing below like an adolescent's dream of the 1880's,
the holy gas redeemed from Baudelaire's mustachioed
curses. Elsewhere are the white lights of the age, but
here, like a millionaire who frowns on electricity, the
opulence of flame. Descending on Rome from the air at
night, a similar beauty: the weak Italian bulbs like
faulty rheostats yellowly outline the baroque curves of
the Tiber, the semicircles of the monstrous Vatican,
endless broken parabolas.

The cracking-plant is equally palatial. Those oil men in the
silent elevator, like princes with their voices of natural

volume, their soft hats and their name-drops (like
balloons of words in the mouths of caricatures in
political cartoons), men of many mansions. The doors
of the room are mahogany. Through one which adjoins
and is locked I hear the guttural laughter of undress,
neither leisurely nor quick, indistinct wording, and all
is silent but a woman's moan. Now it rises like the grip
of pain; it is almost loud; it is certainly sincere, like the
pent-up grief of deep relief; now it is round, now
vibrant, now it is scaly as it grows. (Then it steps off
into nothingness.)

I stand awed in my stocking-feet and move respectfully
toward the window, as a man in an art gallery moves
toward a more distant masterpiece to avoid the musical
chatter of intruders. The cracking-plant sails on
through the delicate Oklahoma night, flying the thousand hot flags of Laputa.

WHY AM I HAPPY WRITING THIS TEXTBOOK?
from THE BOURGEOIS POET

77

Why am I happy writing this textbook? What sublime idiocy!
What a waste of time! A textbook on prosody at that.
Yet when I sit down to comb the business out, when I
address the easel of this task, I burn with an even
flame, I'm cooking with gas. There are some things
so dull they hypnotize like the pendulum of a clock;
so clockwork and quotidian they make the flesh de-
lirious like fresh water. X-ray the poem, give it a
thorough physical, a clean bill of health. We can see
everything but the flow of blood. What Latin and
Greek nomenclature! But this is order, order made to
order. This is system to plot and plan. This is definition, edges clean as razors. Simplification, boldface,
indented. I know there is no such thing as a textbook.
I know that all textbooks are sold the second the
course is over. I know that a book sold is a dead book.
And I dream, like others, of writing a textbook that
is not a textbook, a book that not even a student would
part with, a book that makes even prosody breathe.
So, when the sun shines with the nine o'clock brightness and the coffee swims in my throat and the smoke
floats over the page like the smoke of a ship's funnel,
then I romanticize. I make a muse of prosody, old hag.
She's just a registered nurse, I know, I know, but I
have her sashay, grind and bump, register Alcaics,
Sapphics, choriambs (my predilection). She's trained

all right. She's second nature herself. She knows her
job, I mine. We'll work it out: it may be poetry. Blue-
prints are blue. They have their dreams.

Randall Jarrell (1914-1965)

Randall Jarrell was born in Nashville, Tennessee, received an A.B.
from Vanderbilt in 1935 and an A.M. in 1938, taught at Kenyon
College from 1937 to 1939 and at the University of Texas from 1939
to 1942, served in the Army Air Force during World War II, and
subsequently taught at Sarah Lawrence College, Princeton, and the
Women's College of the University of North Carolina. From 1956
to 1958 he was Consultant in Poetry at the Library of Congress. He
married in 1952 and, until his sudden death when struck by a car
at the age of fifty-one, lived with his wife and two daughters in
Greensboro, North Carolina. He was a member of the National
Institute of Arts and Letters and a chancellor of the Academy of
American Poets. He won the National Book Award in 1961 for his
book of poems *The Woman at the Washington Zoo*. On the voice of the
poet he wrote:

> The poet *needs* to be deluded about his poems—for who can be
> sure that it is delusion? In his strongest hours the public hardly
> exists for the writer: he does what he ought to do, has to do, and
> if afterwards some Public wishes to come and crown him with laurel
> crowns, well, let it! if critics wish to tell people all that he isn't,
> well, let them—he knows what he is. But at night when he can't
> get to sleep it seems to him that it is what he is, his own particular
> personal quality, that he is being disliked for. It is this that the
> future will like him for, if it likes him for anything; but will it like
> him for anything?
>
> *He* can't know. He thinks of all those pieces of his he once thought
> good, and now thinks bad; how many of his current swans will turn
> out to be just such ducklings? All of them? If he were worse, would
> people like him better? If he were better, would people like him
> worse? If—
>
> What would an ideal public do? Mainly, essentially, it would just
> read the poet; read him with a certain willingness and interest;
> read him imaginatively and perceptively. It needs him, even if it
> doesn't know that; he needs it, even if he doesn't know that. It
> and he are like people in one army, one prison, one world: their
> interests are great and common, and deserve a kind of declaration
> of dependence. The public might treat him very much as it would
> like him to treat it. It has its faults, he has his; but both "are, after
> all," as a man said about women, "the best things that are offered
> in that line." The public ought not to demand the same old thing
> from the poet whenever he writes something very new, nor ought

to complain, *The same old thing!* whenever he writes something that isn't very new; and it ought to realize that it is not, unfortunately, in the writer's power to control what he writes: something else originates and controls it, whether you call that something else the unconscious or Minerva or the Muse. The poet writes what he writes just as the public likes what it likes; he can't help himself, it can't help itself, but each of them has to try: most of our morality, most of our culture are in the trying.

SECOND AIR FORCE

Far off, above the plain the summer dries,
The great loops of the hangars sway like hills.
Buses and weariness and loss, the nodding soldiers
Are wire, the bare frame building, and a pass
5   To what was hers; her head hides his square patch
And she thinks heavily: My son is grown.
She sees a world: sand roads, tar-paper barracks,
The bubbling asphalt of the runways, sage,
The dunes rising to the interminable ranges,
10   The dim flights moving over clouds like clouds.
The armorers in their patched faded green,
Sweat-stiffened, banded with brass cartridges,
Walk to the line; their Fortresses, all tail,
Stand wrong and flimsy on their skinny legs,
15   And the crews climb to them clumsily as bears.
The head withdraws into its hatch (a boy's),
The engines rise to their blind laboring roar,
And the green, made beasts run home to air.
Now in each aspect death is pure.
20   (At twilight they wink over men like stars
And hour by hour, through the night, some see
The great lights floating in — from Mars, from Mars.)
How emptily the watchers see them gone.

They go, there is silence; the woman and her son
25   Stand in the forest of the shadows, and the light
Washes them like water. In the long-sunken city
Of evening, the sunlight stills like sleep
The faint wonder of the drowned; in the evening,
In the last dreaming light, so fresh, so old,
30   The soldiers pass like beasts, unquestioning,
And the watcher for an instant understands
What there is then no need to understand;
But she wakes from her knowledge, and her stare,
A shadow now, moves emptily among
35   The shadows learning in their shadowy fields
The empty missions.
               Remembering,

She hears the bomber calling, *Little Friend!*
To the fighter hanging in the hostile sky,
40 And sees the ragged flame eat, rib by rib,
Along the metal of the wing into her heart:
The lives stream out, blossom, and float steadily
To the flames of the earth, the flames
That burn like stars above the lands of men.

45 She saves from the twilight that takes everything
A squadron shipping, in its last parade—
Its dogs run by it, barking at the band—
A gunner walking to his barracks, half-asleep,
Starting at something, stumbling (above, invisible,
50 The crews in the steady winter of the sky
Tremble in their wired fur); and feels for them
The love of life for life. The hopeful cells
Heavy with someone else's death, cold carriers
Of someone else's victory, grope past their lives
55 Into her own bewilderment: The years meant *this?*

But for them the bombers answer everything.

The Death of the Ball Turret Gunner

From my mother's sleep I fell into the State,
And I hunched in its belly till my wet fur froze.
Six miles from earth, loosed from its dream of life,
I woke to black flak and the nightmare fighters.
5 When I died they washed me out of the turret with a hose.

Deutsch Durch Freud

I believe my favorite country's German.

I wander in a calm folk-colored daze; the infant
Looks down upon me from his mother's arms
And says—oh, God knows what he says!
5 It's baby-talk? he's sick? or is it German?
That *Nachtigallenchor:* does it sing German?
Yoh, yoh: here mice, rats, tables, chairs,
Grossmütter, Kinder, der Herrgott im Himmel,
All, all but I—
10   all, all but I—
                    speak German.

DEUTSCH DURCH FREUD. *Deutsch Durch Freud:* cf. Mark Twain's essay "The Awful German Language." Appendix D in *A Tramp Abroad* (1879).

Have you too sometimes, by the fire, at evening,
Wished that you were—whatever you once were?
It is ignorance alone that is enchanting.
15 *Dearer to me than all the treasures of the earth*
Is something living, said old Rumpelstiltskin
And hopped home. Charcoal-burners heard him singing
And spoiled it all. . . . And all because—
If only he hadn't known his name!

20 In German I don't know my name.
                                   I am the log
The fairies left one morning in my place.
—In German I believe in them, in everything:
The world is everything that is the case.
25 How clever people are! I look on open-mouthed
As Kant reels down the road *im Morgenrot*
Humming *Mir ist so bang, so bang, mein Schatz*—
All the nixies set their watches by him
Two hours too fast. . . .
30   I think, *My calendar's*
Two centuries too fast, and give a sigh
Of trust. I reach out for the world and ask
The price; it answers, *One touch of your finger.*

In all *my* Germany there's no *Gesellschaft*
35 But one between *eine Katze* and *ein Maus.*
What's business? what's a teaspoon? what's a sidewalk?
Schweig stille, meine Seele! Such things are not for thee.
It is by Trust, and Love, and reading Rilke
Without *ein Wörterbuch,* that man learns German.
40 The Word rains in upon his blessed head
As glistening as from the hand of God
And means—what does it mean? Ah well, it's German.
Glaube, mein Herz! A Feeling in the Dark
Brings worlds, brings words that hard-eyed Industry
45 And all the schools' dark Learning never knew.

And yet it's hard sometimes, I won't deny it.
Take for example my own favorite daemon,
Dear good great Goethe: *ach,* what German!
Very idiomatic, very noble; very like a sibyl.
50 *My* favorite style is Leupold von Lerchenau's.
I've memorized his *da und da und da und da*
And whisper it when Life is dark and Death is dark.
There was someone who knew how to speak
To us poor *Kinder* here *im Fremde.*
55 And Heine! At the ninety-sixth *mir träumte*
I sigh as a poet, but dimple as *ein Schuler.*
And yet—if it's easy is it German?
And yet, that *wunderschöne Lindenbaum*
Im Mondenscheine! What if it is in Schilda?

It's moonlight, isn't it? *Mund, Mond, Herz,* and *Schmerz*
Sing round my head, in *Zeit* and *Ewigkeit,*
And my heart lightens at each *Sorge,* each *Angst:*
I know them well. And *Schicksal! Ach,* you Norns,
As I read I hear your—what's the word for scissors?
And *Katzen* have *Tatzen*—why can't I call someone *Kind?*
What a speech for Poetry (especially Folk-)!

And yet when, in my dreams, *eine schwartzbraune Hexe*
(Who mows on the Neckar, reaps upon the Rhine)
Riffles my yellow ringlets through her fingers,
She only asks me questions: *What is soap?*
I don't know. *A suitcase?* I don't know. *A visit?*
I laugh with joy, and try to say like Lehmann:
"*Quin-quin, es ist ein Besuch!*"
                    Ah, German!
Till the day I die I'll be in love with German
—If only I don't learn German. . . . I can hear my broken
Voice murmuring to *der Arzt: "Ich—sterber?"*
He answers sympathetically: "*Nein—sterbe.*"

If God gave me the choice—but I stole this from Lessing—
Of German and learning German, I'd say: Keep your German!

The thought of *knowing* German terrifies me.
—But surely, this way, no one could learn German?
And yet. . . .
                    It's difficult; is it impossible?
I'm hopeful that it is, but I can't say
For certain: I don't know enough German.

JEROME

Each day brings its toad, each night its dragon.
Der heilige Hieronymus—his lion is at the zoo—
Listens, listens. All the long, soft, summer day
Dreams affright his couch, the deep boils like a pot.
As the sun sets, the last patient rises,
Says to him, *Father;* trembles, turns away.

Often, to the lion, the saint said, *Son.*
To the man the saint says—but the man is gone.
Under a plaque of Gradiva, at gloaming,
The old man boils an egg. When he has eaten
He listens a while. The patients have not stopped.
At midnight, he lies down where his patients lay.

JEROME. **2.** *Der heilige Hieronymus:* i.e., Saint Jerome (c. 347-c. 420), one of the four great doctors of the western church. He spent two years in the desert searching for peace. **9.** *Gradiva:* Gradivus is a surname for Mars.

All night the old man whispers to the night.
It listens evenly. The great armored paws
Of its forelegs put together in reflection,
It thinks: *Where Ego was, there Id shall be.*
The world wrestles with it and is changed into it
And after a long time changes it. The dragon

Listens as the old man says, at dawn: *I see*
—There is an old man, naked, in a desert, by a cliff.
He has set out his books, his hat, his ink, his shears
Among scorpions, toads, the wild beasts of the desert.
I lie beside him—I am a lion.
He kneels listening. He holds in his left hand

The stone with which he beats his breast, and holds
In his right hand, the pen with which he puts
Into his book, the words of the angel:
The angel up into whose face he looks.
But the angel does not speak. He looks into the face
Of the night, and the night says—but the night is gone.

He has slept. . . . At morning, when man's flesh is young
And man's soul thankful for it knows not what,
The air is washed, and smells of boiling coffee,
And the sun lights it. The old man walks placidly
To the grocer's; walks on, under leaves, in light,
To a lynx, a leopard—he has come:

The man holds out a lump of liver to the lion,
And the lion licks the man's hand with his tongue.

A WELL-TO-DO INVALID

When you first introduced me to your nurse
I thought: "She's like your wife." I mean, I thought:
"She's like your nurse—" it was your wife.

She gave this old friend of her husband's
A pale ingratiating smile; we talked
And she agreed with me about everything.
I thought: "She's quite agreeable."
You gave a pleased laugh—you were feeling good.
She laughed and agreed with you.
                                    I said to her
—That is, I didn't say to her: "You liar!"
She held out
Her deck of smiles, I cut, and she dealt.

Almost as the years have sprung up, fallen back,
I've seen you in and out of bed; meanwhile,

Hovering solicitously alongside,
This governess, this mother
In her off-whites—pretty as a nurse
Is thinly and efficiently and optimistically
20 Pretty—has spoken with an enthusiasm
Like winter sunlight, of the comprehensiveness of insurance.
If you want it to, it can cover anything.

Like the governor on an engine, she has governed
Your rashness. And how many sins
25 She has forgiven in her big child! How many times
She has telephoned in an emergency
For the right specialist!

After I'd left your bed she'd take me to the door
And tell me about your heart and bowels.
30 When you were up and talking she would listen
A long time, oh so long! but go to bed
Before we did, with a limp, wan, almost brave
"Goodnight!" You are a natural
Disaster she has made her own. Meanly
35 Clinging to you, taking care—all praise
And understanding outside, and inside all insurance—
She has stood by you like a plaster Joan of Arc.
Prematurely tired, prematurely
Mature, she has endured
40 Much, indulgently
Repeating like a piece of white carbon paper
The opinions of that boisterous, sick thing, a man.
I can see through her—but then, who can't?
Her dishonesty is so transparent
45 It has about it a kind of honesty.
She has never once said what she thought, done what she wanted,
But (as if invented by some old economist
And put on an island, to trade with her mate)
Has acted in impersonal self-interest.

50 Never to do one thing for its own sake!

Year in, year out, with what sincerity
You said anything, demanded everything,
And she, the liar!
Was good to you—oh, insincerely good,
55 Good for all the worst reasons. Good.
And she was nice to me, and I was nice
To her: I *wanted* to be nice to her.
She was wrong, and I was right, and I was sick of it.
It wasn't right for her always to be wrong
60 And work so hard and get so little: I felt guilty
Because I wasn't on her side. I was on her side.

It was a terrible shock to me when she died.
I saw her cheeks red for the first time
Among the snowdrifts covering her coffin;
65 And you were up and talking, well with grief.
As I realized how easily you'd fill
This vacancy, I was sorry
For you and for that pale self-sufficient ghost
That had tended so long your self-sufficiency.

THE PLAYER PIANO

I ate pancakes one night in a Pancake House
Run by a lady my age. She was gay.
When I told her that I came from Pasadena
She laughed and said, "I lived in Pasadena
5 When Fatty Arbuckle drove the El Molino bus."

I felt that I had met someone from home.
No, not Pasadena, Fatty Arbuckle.
Who's that? Oh, something that we had in common
Like—like—the false armistice. Piano rolls.
10 She told me her house was the first Pancake House

East of the Mississippi, and I showed her
A picture of my grandson. Going home—
Home to the hotel—I began to hum,
"Smile the while I bid you sad adieu,
15 When the clouds roll by I'll come to you."

Let's brush our hair before we go to bed,
I say to the old friend who lives in my mirror.
I remember how I'd brush my mother's hair
Before she bobbed it. How long has it been
20 Since I hit my funnybone? had a scab on my knee?

Here are Mother and Father in a photograph,
Father's holding me. They both look so *young*.
I'm so much older than they are. Look at them,
Two babies with their baby. I don't blame you,
25 You weren't old enough to know any better;

If I could I'd go back, sit down by you both,
And sign our true armistice: you weren't to blame. . .
I shut my eyes and there's our living room,
The piano's playing something by Chopin,
30 And Mother and Father and their little girl

Listen. Look, the keys go down by themselves!
I go over, hold my hands out, play I play—
If only, somehow, I had learned to live!
The three of us sit watching, as my waltz
35   Plays itself out a half-inch from my fingers.

William Stafford (1914-   )

William Stafford was born and raised in Hutchinson, Kansas. He
received his B.A. from the University of Kansas in 1937 and his M.A.
from the same institution in 1946. An avowed pacifist, he served four
years in alternative service for religious objectors during World War
II and since World War II has been a member of the Fellowship of
Reconciliation, an international pacifist organization. He received
his Ph.D. from the State University of Iowa in 1953, and his first
collection of poems, *West of Your City* (1960), was published when he
was forty-six. In 1963 he won the National Book Award for his second
book of poems, *Traveling Through the Dark,* and in 1964 the Shelley
Memorial Award. Since 1948 he has taught at Lewis and Clark College in Portland, Oregon, where he specializes in teaching nineteenth-
century British literature. He lives in Oswego, Oregon, with his wife
and four children. He calls his comment on the voice of the poet *A
Poet's Voice: an Approach through Prose:*

> When you make a poem you merely speak or write the language
> of every day, capturing as many bonuses as possible and economiz-
> ing on losses; that is, you come awake to what always goes on in
> language, and you use it to the limit of your ability and your power
> of attention at the moment. You always fail, to some extent, since
> the opportunities are infinite—but think of the extent of your
> failure in ordinary conversation! Poetry bears the brunt, though;
> for in trying for the best it calls attention to its vivid failures.
>
> All of us know how to swim in language; most of the time we
> go slithering along, giving our hearers or readers a generally ade-
> quate communication, but for the most part being somewhat irre-
> sponsible about achievement. After all, prose is clear, pure, real-
> istic, accurate, and regular—isn't it? But meanwhile there exist
> always those sleeping resources in language—connotations, sound
> reinforcements, allusions, myth-residues, and so on. These ele-
> ments flicker on and off in anything we say or write, be it prose or
> poetry. Poets try to live up to those resources.
>
> Rather than giving poets the undeserved honor of telling us
> how distinctive and special poetry is, everyone should realize his
> own fair share of the joint risk and opportunity always present in
> language: through the social process of language all of us should
> help each other to become more aware of what being alive
> means.

West of Your City

West of your city into the fern
sympathy, sympathy rolls the train
all through the night on a lateral line
where the shape of game fish tapers down
5   from a reach where cougar paws touch water.

Corn that the starving Indians held
all through moons of cold for seed
and then they lost in stony ground
the gods told them to plant it in—
10   west of your city that corn still lies.

Cocked in that land tactile as leaves
wild things wait crouched in those valleys
west of your city outside your lives
in the ultimate wind, the whole land's wave.
15   Come west and see; touch these leaves.

A Ritual to Read to Each Other

If you don't know the kind of person I am
and I don't know the kind of person you are
a pattern that others made may prevail in the world
and following the wrong god home we may miss our star.

5   For there is many a small betrayal in the mind,
a shrug that lets the fragile sequence break
sending with shouts the horrible errors of childhood
storming out to play through the broken dyke.

And as elephants parade holding each elephant's tail,
10   but if one wanders the circus won't find the park,
I call it cruel and maybe the root of all cruelty
to know what occurs but not recognize the fact.

And so I appeal to a voice, to something shadowy,
a remote important region in all who talk:
15   though we could fool each other, we should consider—
lest the parade of our mutual life get lost in the dark.

For it is important that awake people be awake,
or a breaking line may discourage them back to sleep;
the signals we give—yes or no, or maybe—
20   should be clear: the darkness around us is deep.

THE TILLAMOOK BURN

These mountains have heard God;
they burned for weeks. He spoke
in a tongue of flame from sawmill trash
and you can read His word down to the rock.

5 In milky rivers the steelhead
butt upstream to spawn
and find a world with depth again,
starting from stillness and water across gray stone.

Inland along the canyons
10 all night weather smokes
past the deer and the widow-makers—
trees too dead to fall till again He speaks,

Mowing the criss-cross trees and the listening peaks.

IN RESPONSE TO A QUESTION

The earth says have a place, be what that place
requires; hear the sound the birds imply
and see as deep as ridges go behind
each other. (Some people call their scenery flat,
5 their only picture framed by what they know:
I think around them rise a riches and a loss
too equal for their chart—but absolutely tall.)

The earth says every summer have a ranch
that's minimum: one tree, one well, a landscape
10 that proclaims a universe—sermon
of the hills, hallelujah mountain,
highway guided by the way the world is tilted,
reduplication of mirage, flat evening:
a kind of ritual for the wavering.

15 The earth says where you live wear the kind
of color that your life is (gray shirt for me)
and by listening with the same bowed head that sings
draw all into one song, join
the sparrow on the lawn, and row that easy
20 way, the rage without met by the wings
within that guide you anywhere the wind blows.

Listening, I think that's what the earth says.

At Liberty School

Girl in the front row who had no mother
and went home every day to get supper,
the class became silent when you left early.

Elaborate histories were in our book
5   but of all the races you were the good:
the taxes of Rome were at your feet.

When the bell rang we did not write any more.
Traitor to everything else, we poured
to the fountain. I bent and thought of you.

10   Our town now is Atlantis, crystal-water-bound;
at the door of the schoolhouse fish are swimming round;
thinking in and out of the church tower go deep waves.

Girl in the front row who had no mother,
as I passed the alleys of our town toward supper
15   there were not spiteful nails in any board.

Requiem

Mother is gone. Bird songs wouldn't let her breathe.
The skating bug broke through the eternal veil.
A tree in the forest fell; the air remembered.
Two rocks clinked in the night to signal some meaning.

5   Traveler north, beyond where you can return,
hearing above you the last of the razor birds whizz
over the drift of dust that bore your name,
there's a kind of waiting you teach us—the art of not knowing.

Suicidal gestures of nobility driven to the wrist,
10   our molten bodies remembering some easier form,
we feel the bones assert the rites of yesterday
and the flow of angular events becoming destiny.

Summer and locusts own the elm part of town;
on the millpond moss is making its cream.
15   Our duty is just a certain high kind of waiting;
beyond our hearing is the hearing of the community.

The Only Card I Got on My Birthday Was from an Insurance Man

On upland farms into abandoned wells
on a line meridian high

state by state my birthday star comes on
and peers, my birthday night,
and in my eyes it stands while past its light
the world and I turn, just and far, till
every well scans over the year like spokes
of a wheel returning the long soft look of the sky.

Star in a well, dark message: when I die,
my glance drawn over galaxies,
all through one night let a candle nurse the dark
to mark this instant of what I was,
this once—not putting my hand out
blessing for business' sake any frail markers
of human years: we want real friends or none;
what's genuine will accompany every man.

Who travel these lonely wells can drink that star.

ADULTS ONLY

Animals own a fur world;
people own worlds that are variously, pleasingly, bare.
And the way these worlds *are* once arrived for us kids with a jolt,
that night when the wild woman danced
in the giant cage we found we were all in
at the state fair.

Better women exist, no doubt, than that one,
and occasions more edifying, too, I suppose.
But we have to witness for ourselves what comes for us,
nor be distracted by barkers of irrelevant ware;
and a pretty good world, I say, arrived that night
when that woman came farming right out of her clothes,
by God,

At the state fair.

THE TRIP

Our car was fierce enough;
no one could tell we were only ourselves;
so we drove, equals of the car,
and ate at a drive-in where Citizens were dining.
A waitress with eyes made up to be Eyes
brought food spiced by the neon light.

Watching, we saw the manager greet people—
hollow on the outside, some kind of solid veneer.

When we got back on the road we welcomed
10   it as a fierce thing welcomes the cold.
Some people you meet are so dull
that you always remember their names.

CHRISTIANITE

This new kind of metal will not suffer:
it either holds or bends.
Under stress it acts like a bar, or a hinge.

This metal possesses a lucky way,
5   always to respond by endurance, or
an eager collapse, and forget.

(The time between the loss and the end
costs all the wear: earlier,
you win; after, you start again.)

10   You think with it, make models,
save it for when you retire.
The impulsive cannot understand it.

Only something romantic or brittle
belongs in their hands.

MORNINGS

1. THE CEREMONY OF SLOW AWARENESS

Quiet,
rested, the brain begins to burn
and glow like a coal in the dark,
early—four in the morning, cold, with
5   frost on the lawn. The brain feels
in two directions of window, and as if
holding a taper follows the hall
that leads to the living room and silver
space; lets the town come close, the chains
10   of lights turned off, and purposeless feet
of chairs sprawled; lets it all rise and
subside, and the brain pulses larger
than the ordinary horizon, but deliberately
less than it wants to go. All benevolence,
15   the brain with its insistent little call
summons wraiths and mist layers near
from fields: the world arising and streaming
through the house, soundless, pitifully

elongated, inevitable, for review, like breathing,
20 quiet.

2. THE CEREMONY OF RECOGNIZING OTHERS

Waiting
in the town that flows for the brain, charmed,
weak as distance, no one can move or belong
till the brain finds them and says, "Live!"
25 There's one too far, the phantom beyond the brain
each day that can't hear the kindest call
(and kindness is volume in the brain's room)—
the stranger with the sudden face, of
erased body, who floats into my dream
30 again. Down the storm our lack of storm
implies I hear the lambs cry, every one
lost and myself lost by where I made our
home. I feel a wind inside my hand.
By a lack that life knows, life owns its greatness:
35 we are led one thing at a time through gain
to that pure gain—all that we lose. Stranger,
we are blind dancers in two different rooms;
we hear the music both heard long ago: wherever
you dance, that music finds you. When you turn,
40 I turn. Somewhere, whatever way you move
is ours; here, I keep our place,
repeat our turns, paced by my pulse,
waiting.

3. THE CEREMONY FOR HUMILITY

Lowly,
45 I listen as fur hears the air, and by will
I think one thing at a time while the world,
complete, turns—the farm where the wheat
votes, where they have already prayed the last day;
the glass of the ocean watching the storm;
50 all the extreme places; and I stand at the
prow of our house, an eye (for iris the attic window),
I gaze, and see so well my listening toes blur
on the rug and realize all the way to the island
of afternoon. My hands have given their gift,
55 then themselves. Can't the world see humility—my
trance, my face, the sober and steady spokes of my
bicycle? Many drive in piety and for the faith
an old car. Bishops in garages care, and presbyters
at the bank judge us—all that our shoes
60 and their crossed laces confess; angels behind
the counter inquire the name and send it up
the dizzying tube, and listen to the building

hum our estimation. Year by year the leaves
will come again, the suspicious grass, and the air
65   ever more tentative over the walls one color
at a time, fish of less than water, of evening;
shadows come and the bells get ready
before they sound, one part of a hum, like my self,
lowly.

4. THE CEREMONY OF ACKNOWLEDGING DAY

70   Light
comes inside the brain. It is early;
in the attic I hear the wind lie down.
"Stay!" I call, as we tell the dog. Sudden as
the telephone, day says "I am here!" And
75   in that clear light the brain comes home, lost
from all it wandered in, unable to be
sure for questioners, caught again by needs,
reduced to its trouble with my tongue.
The frank sycamore is at the window;
80   dark trails sink and go backward;
the sun comes over the world, aiming
the trees at the day, hill by hill.
Light.

John Ciardi (1916-   )

Born in Boston, John Ciardi graduated from Tufts (B.A., 1938) and
the University of Michigan (M.A., 1939), taught at the University
of Kansas City from 1940 to 1942, served in the Air Force from 1942
to 1945, and followed an academic career—University of Kansas
City, Harvard, and Rutgers—until 1961 when he resigned his position as Professor of English at Rutgers. Since 1955 he has been director of the Bread Loaf Writers Conference and since 1956 poetry
editor of *Saturday Review*. He married Myra Judith Hostetter in 1946
and now lives with his wife and three children in Metuchen, New
Jersey. A Fellow of the American Academy of Arts and Sciences and
a member of the National Institute of Arts and Letters, he holds
various awards given by *Poetry* magazine and received the Prix de
Rome in 1956. His comment on the voice of the poet turned into a
Manner of Speaking column called "Poetry and Personal Definition":

Poets are forever being given odd introspective assignments. Sir
Philip Sidney's command to his confused spirit was simply, "Look
in thy heart and write." Today the new exhortation seems to be
from the critic and it is more likely to read, "Look into your psyche
and explain yourself." It has become an article of the True Faith

that the introspection of poets will finally reveal a mystery called The Creative Source.

I have myself toiled in that abbey. In 1950 I published an anthology titled *Mid-Century American Poets,* a collection designed to introduce the work of fifteen poets of the 'forties, and as the editor-abbot I spent months in exhorting the poets to prayer and meditation that each might produce a prose "Statement of Intent" as a preface to his poems.

Now William Martz of Ripon College, a good man and a gentle abbot, is preparing an anthology to be called *The Distinctive Voice* and he is after me, in some sort of return of justice, to introspect (or to introspeculate) on the poetic voice. He says:

I am including in the head notes for each poet his comment (if he'll give it to me, which most have done or promised) on what he thinks, as of 1965, the voice of the poet is, or what he aims to be as a poetic voice. The question is admittedly vague. The accent is on personal definition.

As it happens I like vague personal questions and pray only that no man will ask precise ones about my character. Within that character, whatever it is, and with the accent on personal definition, I do have some strong feelings about the nature of the poetic voice, and I think my feelings run counter to what most teachers are telling the young, what most poets are practicing, and what most critics approve.

It was, I believe, André Malraux in, I believe, "Museum Without Walls" who observed that Van Gogh had carried personal style to the point at which he could paint (as he did) a simple chair with such individuality that he made of it as much a signature as an object represented. I am moved to generalize further that one mark of every artist we call "modern" may be found in his impulse to achieve not "style" but "a style." By "style" I mean the way the medium is used to forward what used to be called "the subject" and is now generally called "the aesthetic experience." By "a style" I mean the way the medium is used to forward the author's individuality. Nor need it be understood that one of these impulses can exist in a work of art without the other: I am after a matter of emphasis. "Style" is, at root, representational (whether of outward appearances or of inner-response-to) whereas "a style" is signatory.

So in poetry with "voice" and "a voice." Many contemporary poets, as it seems to me, are a bit drunken in their compulsion to emphasize the signatory way of writing, and even a number of good poets are self-limited by that compulsion. Robert Lowell, for example, is a good poet. Yet any given line of his is more likely to sound like Robert Lowell speaking than like a line reaching out to the nature of the thing spoken. Consider the following:

A brackish reach of shoal off Madaket—
Here the jack hammer jabs into the ocean
Bringing the landed promise and the faith

Once more where braced pig iron dragons grip
And crush the crab these Quaker sailors lost.

The lines are Lowell's but only as a pastiche from five different poems jammed together by a few syntactical violences intended to give the passage a spurious unity. A dirty trick, and for it I owe Lowell an apology and offer it honestly. I mean no malice. I mean only to show that such a pastiche has, in addition to the spurious unity I have imposed upon it, the true unity of "a voice," the lines being always signatory to themselves no matter what is being said.

Such a signatory voice is not necessarily bad and every good writer will inevitably identify himself by using some of his own habituated tonalities. Yet it is worth asking if contemporary taste has not gone too far in enshrining "a voice" at the expense of "voice." For when the impulse is first to achieve a unique way of speaking and then to find the world, the danger is that not enough world will be found.

For myself, and even at the risk of not believing everything I say, I still dream that "style" is potentially a better instrument than "a style." Since I am invited to personal definition, let me confess that I do not know enough about who I am to settle for "a style." Or perhaps I am merely formless and want them all—one for bird, one for bee, and one for Hell and the roaring sea. Let me dream that a willing reader might perhaps cull from the sum of my failures a few poems, each in its own voice, and with no two voices co-signatory, but with each (if only hopefully) formed to the subject-experience rather than to one habituated way of speaking.

I am dreaming, that is, of an act of language so entirely responsive to the poetic experience that my habituated way of speaking will be shattered and leave only the essential language called into being by the aesthetic experience itself. The dream is, finally, that the poem may seem to declare not "X spoke these words in his unique way" but rather "man spoke these words of himself."

Impossible? Probably so. Yet small steps may go toward unreachable distance. My dream will in any case identify my pleasure in some observations made by William Dickey in reviewing my "Person to Person" in *The Hudson Review,* Winter 1964-65.

The quality that I find most notable in Mr. Ciardi is that of observation: he sees things with an intensity and accuracy that no conventional language can wholly contain. The effect of a convention is to smooth out the differences between things; it expects, having established a form of language, that all objects will be equally amenable to its ministrations. But Mr. Ciardi's objects break these bounds; his sight is defined by the object itself, and he accepts and uses the object's own recalcitrance toward language that will soften it. "Hunchback bees in pirate pants," for example, is a phrase wholly determined by what its object looks like, rather than by a kind of language that is felt to be appropriate to the discussion of objects in general. Mr. Ciardi is often sententious or sentimental in his attitudes toward things he discusses, but these attitudes never prevent him from seeing what is before him. This ability to see is neither easy nor usual, and it represents one of the most important ways in which the floating world of poetic language can be given a persistent human relevance, a persistent reference back to the solidities of existence.

Since the passage, in isolation, sounds highly laudatory, and since I am after definition rather than self-advertisement, let me underline Mr. Dickey's notes on my faults (which the reader can see for himself) and let me point out (as the reader cannot see for himself) that Mr. Dickey was writing a round-up review and that he moved from my book to others he liked better. I was not the star of his show, but I shall settle happily if the ideas he identifies can be so taken. As Archibald MacLeish might have said, though he didn't, "A poem should not say but be."

Men Marry What They Need. I Marry You

Men marry what they need. I marry you,
morning by morning, day by day, night by night,
and every marriage makes this marriage new.

In the broken name of heaven, in the light
5   that shatters granite, by the spitting shore,
in air that leaps and wobbles like a kite,

I marry you from time and a great door
is shut and stays shut against wind, sea, stone,
sunburst, and heavenfall. And home once more

10   inside our walls of skin and struts of bone,
man-woman, woman-man, and each the other,
I marry you by all dark and all dawn

and learn to let time spend. Why should I bother
the flies about me? Let them buzz and do.
15   Men marry their queen, their daughter, or their mother

by names they prove, but that thin buzz whines through:
when reason falls to reasons, cause is true.
Men marry what they need. I marry you.

In Place of a Curse

At the next vacancy for God, if I am elected,
I shall forgive last the delicately wounded
who, having been slugged no harder than anyone else,
never got up again, neither to fight back,
5   nor to finger their jaws in painful admiration.

They who are wholly broken, and they in whom
mercy is understanding, I shall embrace at once

and lead to pillows in heaven. But they who are
the meek by trade, baiting the best of their betters
10   with extortions of a mock-helplessness

I shall take last to love, and never wholly.
Let them all into Heaven—I abolish Hell—
but let it be read over them as they enter:
"Beware the calculations of the meek, who gambled nothing,
15   gave nothing, and could never receive enough."

The Baboon and the State

A dog snout puzzles out the look of a man.
The wrong smell of a stranger tweaks the air.
"Fangs! Fangs! Why should we run? We are
Born of the chosen, first, and tallest tree!
5   Sons of the Sacred Banyan follow me!
Baboons are born to kill because they can."

Clemenceau said to the American
With the blue jaw and the fox-terrier hair,
"Above France, civilization." He made war
10   As if he strangled a mistress—tenderly,
But with a certain competence. A man
Must sacrifice for his own family.

Guido came trembling from the Vatican,
Roped up for God, God's moonspot in his hair.
15   "How shall I overthrow the Lateran?"
The Fat Pope said. "Speak up. God lives in me.
In His name teach me my cupidity."
And Guido spilled the malice in his ear.

Odysseus, that seven-minded man,
20   Piled up his kills to honor prophecy—
An indispensable, most Ithacan
Justification for a blood at war.
He spoke tongues and heard God-talk on the air,
But all his men were told was, "Follow me!"

25   Is man wrong for the State, or it for man?
High reasons and low causes make a war.
It is the Baboon kills, because he can

The Baboon and the State. 7. *Clemenceau:* Georges Clemenceau (1841-1929)
opposed Woodrow Wilson at the Peace Conference following World War I. 13. *Guido:*
Guido da Montefeltro (1223-1298), to whom Dante devotes Canto XXVII of *The Inferno.*
Guido entered the Franciscan Order in 1296, and thus wore the cord of his order and
a skullcap. He counseled Pope Boniface VIII in his feud with the Colonna family,
which broke into war in 1297. The castle of the Colonna, treacherously destroyed by
Boniface after an offer of amnesty, was in the Lateran district east of Rome.

But Presidents hear voices from the air.
So packs and parishes cry equally:
30   "God's first and last Law sounded from a tree."

The voices come to rest where they began.
Clemenceau nods to the American.
Guido comes praying from the Vatican.
An indispensable most Ithacan
35   Baboon snout puzzles out the look of a man.
The killers kill. They kill because they can.

To W. T. Scott
WITH THANKS FOR A POEM

I like that poem, Win. There's a green world in it.
Not just green acreage—any nature boy
can rhyme on that a dozen lines a minute:
put in a bluebird if you're out for joy,
5   put in a hayloft if you're out for plot,
put in a dead tree if you're out for thought.

I mean what's green in being what a man
touches to leave. Say, Mark Twain at the end;
the green of his last thought. Suppose it ran
10   to Huck or Jim drifting around a bend;
then stopped there with a sigh or with a smile,
or even wondering had it been worthwhile,

but still a life to think about that stood
green to itself. As God might lose a world
15   yet think back and be sad that it was good.
All green dies. But the sere manfingers curled
to their last pulse, touch in a memory.
Touch, and I think are justified. For me

that green is first. The green thought more than green
20   of Walden is Thoreau. The man unspared.
As queer as he was green. An in-between:
half-Cod, half-Buddha. But a system bared
to its own pulse. He had a mind with wings.
But best of all he had an eye for things.

25   God, how he could see green! He must have died
with time ablaze around him like spring fern
caught in a single ray of sun inside
a glacier-rumpled Stonehenge, while a churn
of swallows buttered him his last of light.
30   —All nothing till he held it in his sight.

That green. Say, Whitman like a stricken bear
thinking: "What is a sea?" Say, Henry James
thinking: "What country is it over there?"
on a long foggy walk beside the Thames.
35   Say, Melville thinking: "What have I left done
that will stay green to time for anyone?"

And *all* done. What a sea or country is.
What world can grow to, shaped round from the mind.
Such forests deeper than Yosemites
40   a man walks thinking in and leaves behind.
That last green, Win, after the first unrolled.
The eighth day of the world, by a man told.

BEDLAM REVISITED

Nobody told me anything much. I was born
free to my own confusions, though in hock
to Mother and Father Sweatshop's original stock
in Boston, Mass., four families to a john.
5   The spire of the Old North Church, like a tin horn
upside down on the roofs, was our kitchen clock,
and dropped the hours like rock onto a rock
over the Hull Street graveyard. "Gone. All gone,"

it thunked above the dead. The smells were sad.
10   And there were rats, of course, but nailed tin
could keep them down (or at least in)
to a noise between the hours. The graveyard had
left us a son in real estate and the lad
had grown to father our landlord, though Frank Glynn
15   was the wart-on-the-nose that came with a sneaky grin
to collect the rent. Till he died to Hell. Too bad.

Nobody told me anything much, and that
so wrong it cost me nothing—not even love—
to lose it. All but the Boss, the Cop and the Ghost of
20   the Irish Trinity. Those I sweated at
so hard I came up hating. But still grew fat
in a happy reek of garlic, bay, and clove.
I was crazy, of course, but always at one remove.
I tried on faces as if I were buying a hat.

25   Home was our Asylum. My father died
but my mother kept talking to him. My sisters screamed.
My aunt muttered. My uncle got drunk and dreamed
three numbers a night for a quarter with cock-eyed
Charlie Pipe-Dreams who moseyed along half-fried
30   every morning at seven. The old boy schemed

for twenty years that I knew of before he was reamed
by Family Morticians. But I'll say this—he tried.

Nobody told me anything much. Nobody had
anything much to tell me. I rolled my own
35   and scrounged for matches. How could I have known
everything about us was full-moon mad?
Or that I'd find few saner? It wasn't bad.
Someone always answered the telephone
when it had rung too long. You got only a tone
40   when they finally called you—far away and sad.
But it didn't matter. There would have been nothing to say.
Later they changed the number and we moved away.

A PLEA

I said to her tears: "I am fallible and hungry,
and refusal is no correction and anger no meal.
Feed me mercies from the first-bread of your heart.

I have invented no part of the error it is
5   to be human. The least law could jail me
and be upheld; the least theology, damn me

and be proved. But when, ever, have I come to you
to be judged? Set me straight to your last breath,
and mine, and feed me most what I need not deserve

10   —or starve yourself, and starve me, and be right."

ON BEING SURE AND OF WHAT

Salmon are very sure
of something. They endure
the eating sea, the falling
river and its hauling
5   edges of nets and spears,
and otters, too, and bears.
Then when at last they win
to the still waters in
the rock-pools of the sky
10   they spend their eggs and die.
What saint flings harder at
his martyrdom? Our cat
finishing the can
that we began
15   completes the commentary.
Here ends this bestiary.

A MISSOURI FABLE

A man named Finchley once
without thinking much about
it broke into the premises of
Mr. Billy Jo Trant of these
5   parts, by which felonious
entry he meant to separate
Mr. Billy Jo from various
properties, but stepping on
a noise without thinking
10 enough about it woke Mr.
Billy Jo who took in hand a
Colt .45 and, improvising the
order of his rebuttal, fired
three times in an entirely
15 accurate way and then said
"Hands up!" without thinking
that the man named Finchley
once was not listening as
carefully as he might have
20 had Mr. Billy Jo thought to
disagree with him in a
slightly different order.

Moral: commit yourself to
another man's premises and
25 you may, in logic, have to
accept his conclusion.

GULLS LAND AND CEASE TO BE

Spread back across the air, wings wide,
   legs out, the wind delicately
dumped in balance, the gulls ride
   down, down, hang, and exactly
5   touch, folding not quite at once
   into their gangling weight, but
taking one step, two, wings still askance,
   reluctantly, at last, shut,
      twitch one look around
10   and are aground.

TWO HOURS

I. EVENING

The low-fi scrapes the phrases from the strings
of something neither of us was listening to.

Whatever it is, the strings grate still, the drums
begin to cough a bronchial bass crack. You,
I, someone, thought a music, but it comes
wrong from the machine. Which brings

me to you-and-me as you start to undress
at last (which brings me to you) and how
frothily from foam-trim perkily your thighs
dimple and your arms reach and grow
till they are elements of the light and the wise
S's of your hips enter the great S
of your languor as, reaching behind,
you unstrap and unribbon and your breasts
go from the advertised to the invincible
first line of mantime, and a last rustle rests
you ungirdled at the bird-sung well
of gardens this twisted music cannot find,

of lights and airs and palpable here-and-now
to confound all Heaven's recorders and amplifiers.
How shall they hear us on any machine of theirs?
—your nakedness is more music than they have wires.
Yet, if it's true that angels watch in pairs,
they still may learn. Come here. We'll *show* them how.

II. MORNING

A morning of the life there is
in the house beginning again
its clutters in the sun

babbles and sways and tells
time from its sailing cribs. Enter
three pirate energies to murder sleep:

the bed rocks with their boarding:
a fusilade of blather
sweeps the white decks. We're taken!

—Goodmorning, sweet with chains.
We win all but the fight.
Do as they say—I'll meet you here tonight.

TENZONE

SOUL TO BODY
That affable, vital, inspired even, and well-paid
    persuader of sensibility with the witty asides
but, at core, lucent and unswayed—
    a gem of serenest ray—besides

TENZONE. *Tenzone:* Italian word for combat.

being the well-known poet, critic, editor, and middle-high
aesthete of the circuit is, alas, I.

Some weep for him: a waster of talent. Some
    snicker at the thought of talent in him. He leaves
in a Cadillac, has his home away from home
    where the dolls are, and likes it. What weaves
vine leaves in the hair weaves no laurel for the head.
The greedy pig, he might as well be dead—

to art at least—for wanting it all and more—
    cash, bourbon, his whim away from whom.
He's a belly, a wallet, a suit, a no-score
    of the soul. Sure, he looks like a boom
coming, but whatever he comes to, sits to, tries
to sit still to and say, is a bust. It's booby prize

time at the last dance whenever he
    lets a silence into himself. It grinds
against the jitter in him and dies. Poetry
    is what he gabs at, then dabbles in when he finds
hobby time for it between serious pitches
for cash, free-loading, and the more expensive bitches.

I give him up, say I. (And so say I.)
    There are no tears in him. If he does feel,
he's busier at Chateaubriand than at asking why.
    He lives the way he lives as if it were real.
A con man. A half truth. A swindler in the clear.
Look at him guzzle. He actually likes it here!

BODY TO SOUL

That grave, secretive, aspirant even, and bang-kneed
    eternalist of boneyards with the swallowed tongue
but, at dream source, flaming and fire-freed—
    a monk of dark-celled rays—along
with being heretic, ignorant, Jesuit, and who-
knows-what skeleton, is, alas, not wholly you.

I've watched you: a scratcher of scabs that are not
    there. An ectoplasmic jitter. Who was it spent
those twenty years and more in the polyglot
    of nightmares talking to Pa? If I went
over your head to God, it *was* over your head.
Whose butt grew stiff in the chair the nights you read

whose eyes blind and wrote whose nerves to a dither?
    And who got up in the cold to revise you by light?

You're a glowworm. A spook. A half-strung zither
    with a warped sounding box: you pluck all right
but if what whines out is music, an alley cat
in moon-heat on a trashcan is Kirsten Flagstadt.

Yes, I like it here. Make it twenty times worse
    and I'd still do it over again, even with you
like a monkey on my back. You dried-out wet-nurse,
    think you're the poet, do you? You're wind that blew
on ashes that wouldn't catch. You were gone
the instant I learned the poem is belly and bone.

I gave *you* up. Like a burp. For a better weather
    inside my guts. And, *yes,* I want it all—
grab, gaggle, and rut—as sure as death's no breather.
    Though you wouldn't know, being dead as yesterday's squall
where the sea's a diamond-spilling toss in the bright brace
    of today's air, to glitter me time and place.

Robert Lowell (1917-   )

Robert Lowell was born in Boston, attended Harvard from 1935 to
1937, graduated summa cum laude in 1940 from Kenyon College
(where he was a student of John Crowe Ransom), and was a con-
scientious objector in World War II, serving five months in prison.
His marriage to the novelist Jean Stafford ended in divorce in 1948,
and in 1949 he married Elizabeth Hardwick. They have one daughter. He was Consultant in Poetry at the Library of Congress in 1947,
and he has taught at various places, including Kenyon, Boston University, and Harvard. He lives with his wife and daughter in New
York City. His prizes and awards include the Pulitzer Prize in 1947
for *Lord Weary's Castle,* a Guggenheim Fellowship in 1947-1948, the
Guinness Poetry Award in 1959, the National Book Award in 1959
for *Life Studies,* and the Bollingen translation prize in 1962 for *Imitations.* Not disposed to comment on the voice of the poet, Mr. Lowell
nevertheless expresses a view which is something of an answer to the
question. If his comment seems abrupt, it should be taken into ac-
count that it is part of a correspondence rather than a prepared
statement:

I don't mean to seem parsimonious, but there is really nothing
worth reprinting that I can casually knock off about the poet's
voice. I wish I could, but these things too have to be inspired.

---

48. Kirsten Flagstadt: Norwegian soprano (1895-1963).

CHRISTMAS EVE IN THE TIME OF WAR
A CAPITALIST MEDITATES BY A CIVIL WAR MONUMENT
from LAND OF UNLIKENESS

"He neither shall be rocked
  In silver nor in gold
But in a wooden cradle
  That rocks upon the mould."

Tonight a blackout. Twenty years ago
I strung my stocking on the tree—if Hell's
Inactive sting stuck in the stocking's toe,
Money would draw it out. Stone generals
5 Perching upon a pillar of dead snow,
Two cannon and a cairn of cannon balls,
Livid in the unfinished marble, know
How Christmas drunkards left them in the cold,
While Christ the King is rocking on the mould.

10 A blizzard soaps our dirty linen, all
The crowsfoot feathers mossing Mars' brass hat
Whiten to angels' wings, but the War's snowfall
Has coffered the good-humored plutocrat
Who rattled down his brass like cannon balls
15 To keep the puppets dancing for the state.
Tonight the venery of capital
Hangs the bare Christ-child on a tree of gold,
Tomorrow Mars will break his bones. I am cold,

War's coddling will not warm me up again.
20 Brazenly gracious, Mars is open arms,
The sabers of his statues slash the moon:
Their pageantary understanding forms
Anonymous machinery from raw men,
It rides the whirlwind, it directs the drums.
25 I bawl for Santa Claus and Hamilton,
To break the price-controller's strangle-hold.
I ask for bread, my father gives me mould.

Tonight in Europe and America
All lights are out. Tonight the statesmen lurch
30 Into some shuttered houseboat, mosque or bar;
Blue lines of boys and girls are on the march:
The Child has come with water and with fire.
Stone Generals, do you tremble for your perch?
Tonight our ruler follows his own Star;
35 Pretorians shake the Magi's Star for gold.
How can I spare the Child a crust of mould,

His stocking is full of stones! Stone men at war,
Give me the garish summer of your bed—

Flaring poinsettia, sweet william, larkspur
40 And black-eyed susan with her frizzled head:
My child is dead upon the field of honor:
His blood has made the golden idol glimmer.
"I bring no peace, I bring the sword," Christ said,
"My nakedness was fingered and defiled."
45 But woe unto the rich that are with child.

CHRISTMAS EVE UNDER HOOKER'S STATUE
from LORD WEARY'S CASTLE

Tonight a blackout. Twenty years ago
I hung my stocking on the tree, and hell's
Serpent entwined the apple in the toe
To sting the child with knowledge. Hooker's heels
5 Kicking at nothing in the shifting snow,
A cannon and a cairn of cannon balls
Rusting before the blackened Statehouse, know
How the long horn of plenty broke like glass
In Hooker's gauntlets. Once I came from Mass;

10 Now storm-clouds shelter Christmas, once again
Mars meets his fruitless star with open arms,
His heavy saber flashes with the rime,
The war-god's bronzed and empty forehead forms
Anonymous machinery from raw men;
15 The cannon on the Common cannot stun
The blundering butcher as he rides on Time—
The barrel clinks with holly. I am cold:
I ask for bread, my father gives me mould;

His stocking is full of stones. Santa in red
20 Is crowned with wizened berries. Man of war,
Where is the summer's garden? In its bed
The ancient speckled serpent will appear,
And black-eyed susan with her frizzled head.
When Chancellorsville mowed down the volunteer,
25 "All wars are boyish," Herman Melville said;
But we are old, our fields are running wild:
Till Christ again turn wanderer and child.

CHRISTMAS IN BLACK ROCK

Christ God's red shadow hangs upon the wall
The dead leaf's echo on these hours
Whose burden spindles to no breath at all;
Hard at our heels the huntress moonlight towers
5 And the green needles bristle at the glass

Tiers of defense-plants where the treadmill night
Churns up Long Island Sound with piston-fist.
Tonight, my child, the lifeless leaves will mass,
Heaving and heaping, as the swivelled light
Burns on the bell-spar in the fruitless mist.

Christ Child, your lips are lean and evergreen
Tonight in Black Rock, and the moon
Sidles outside into the needle-screen
And strikes the hand that feeds you with a spoon
Tonight, as drunken Polish night-shifts walk
Over the causeway and their juke-box booms
Hosannah in excelsis Domino.
Tonight, my child, the foot-loose hallows stalk
Us down in the blind alleys of our rooms;
By the mined root the leaves will overflow.

December, old leech, has leafed through Autumn's store
Where Poland has unleashed its dogs
To bay the moon upon the Black Rock shore:
Under our windows, on the rotten logs
The moonbeam, bobbing like an apple, snags
The undertow. O Christ, the spiralling years
Slither with child and manger to a ball
Of ice; and what is man? We tear our rags
To hang the Furies by their itching ears,
And the green needles nail us to the wall.

THE QUAKER GRAVEYARD IN NANTUCKET
For WARREN WINSLOW, DEAD AT SEA

Let man have dominion over the fishes of the
sea and the fowls of the air and the beasts and
the whole earth, and every creeping creature
that moveth upon the earth.

I

A brackish reach of shoal off Madaket,—
The sea was still breaking violently and night
Had steamed into our North Atlantic Fleet,
When the drowned sailor clutched the drag-net. Light
Flashed from his matted head and marble feet,
He grappled at the net
With the coiled, hurdling muscles of his thighs:
The corpse was bloodless, a botch of reds and whites,
Its open, staring eyes
Were lustreless dead-lights
Or cabin-windows on a stranded hulk

THE QUAKER GRAVEYARD IN NANTUCKET. **1.** *Madaket:* Also Maddequet, or Mada-
quet, a point on the northwest corner of Nantucket Island. It appears on the map in
Starbuck's history of the Island, as well as in some of the publications of Henry S. Wyer.

Heavy with sand. We weight the body, close
Its eyes and heave it seaward whence it came,
Where the heel-headed dogfish barks its nose
15   On Ahab's void and forehead; and the name
Is blocked in yellow chalk.
Sailors, who pitch this portent at the sea
Where dreadnaughts shall confess
Its hell-bent deity,
20   When you are powerless
To sand-bag this Atlantic bulwark, faced
By the earth-shaker, green, unwearied, chaste
In his steel scales: ask for no Orphean lute
To pluck life back. The guns of the steeled fleet
25   Recoil and then repeat
The hoarse salute.

II

Whenever winds are moving and their breath
Heaves at the roped-in bulwarks of this pier,
The terns and sea-gulls tremble at your death
30   In these home waters. Sailor, can you hear
The Pequod's sea wings, beating landward, fall
Headlong and break on our Atlantic wall
Off 'Sconset, where the yawing S-boats splash
The bellbuoy, with ballooning spinnakers,
35   As the entangled, screeching mainsheet clears
The blocks: off Madaket, where lubbers lash
The heavy surf and throw their long lead squids
For blue-fish? Sea-gulls blink their heavy lids
Seaward. The winds' wings beat upon the stones,
40   Cousin, and scream for you and the claws rush
At the sea's throat and wring it in the slush
Of this old Quaker graveyard where the bones
Cry out in the long night for the hurt beast
Bobbing by Ahab's whaleboats in the East.

III

45   All you recovered from Poseidon died
With you, my cousin, and the harrowed brine
Is fruitless on the blue beard of the god,
Stretching beyond us to the castles in Spain,
Nantucket's westward haven. To Cape Cod
50   Guns, cradled on the tide,
Blast the eelgrass about a waterclock
Of bilge and backwash, roil the salt and sand
Lashing earth's scaffold, rock
Our warships in the hand

---

15. *Ahab's void:* Ahab was Captain of the Pequod (line 31) in Herman Melville's novel
Moby Dick (1851).

55 Of the great God, where time's contrition blues
Whatever it was these Quaker sailors lost
In the mad scramble of their lives. They died
When time was open-eyed,
Wooden and childish; only bones abide
60 There, in the nowhere, where their boats were tossed
Sky-high, where mariners had fabled news
Of IS, the whited monster. What it cost
Them is their secret. In the sperm-whale's slick
I see the Quakers drown and hear their cry:
65 "If God himself had not been on our side,
If God himself had not been on our side,
When the Atlantic rose against us, why,
Then it had swallowed us up quick."

IV

This is the end of the whaleroad and the whale
70 Who spewed Nantucket bones on the thrashed swell
And stirred the troubled waters to whirlpools
To send the Pequod packing off to hell:
This is the end of them, three-quarters fools,
Snatching at straws to sail
75 Seaward and seaward on the turntail whale,
Spouting out blood and water as it rolls,
Sick as a dog to these Atlantic shoals:
Clamavimus, O depths. Let the sea-gulls wail

For water, for the deep where the high tide
80 Mutters to its hurt self, mutters and ebbs.
Waves wallow in their wash, go out and out,
Leave only the death-rattle of the crabs,
The beach increasing, its enormous snout
Sucking the ocean's side.
85 This is the end of running on the waves;
We are poured out like water. Who will dance
The mast-lashed master of Leviathans
Up from this field of Quakers in their unstoned graves?

V

When the whale's viscera go and the roll
90 Of its corruption overruns this world
Beyond tree-swept Nantucket and Wood's Hole
And Martha's Vineyard, Sailor, will your sword
Whistle and fall and sink into the fat?
In the great ash-pit of Jehoshaphat
95 The bones cry for the blood of the white whale,
The fat flukes arch and whack about its ears,
The death-lance churns into the sanctuary, tears
The gun-blue swingle, heaving like a flail,
And hacks the coiling life out: it works and drags

100 And rips the sperm-whale's midriff into rags,
Gobbets of blubber spill to wind and weather,
Sailor, and gulls go round the stoven timbers
Where the morning stars sing out together
And thunder shakes the white surf and dismembers
105 The red flag hammered in the mast-head. Hide,
Our steel, Jonas Messias, in Thy side.

VI OUR LADY OF WALSINGHAM

There once the penitents took off their shoes
And then walked barefoot the remaining mile;
And the small trees, a stream and hedgerows file
110 Slowly along the munching English lane,
Like cows to the old shrine, until you lose
Track of your dragging pain.
The stream flows down under the druid tree,
Shiloah's whirlpools gurgle and make glad
115 The castle of God. Sailor, you were glad
And whistled Sion by that stream. But see:
Our Lady, too small for her canopy,
Sits near the altar. There's no comeliness
At all or charm in that expressionless
120 Face with its heavy eyelids. As before,
This face, for centuries a memory,
Non est species, neque decor,
Expressionless, expresses God: it goes
Past castled Sion. She knows what God knows,
125 Not Calvary's Cross nor crib at Bethlehem
Now, and the world shall come to Walsingham.

VII

The empty winds are creaking and the oak
Splatters and splatters on the cenotaph,
The boughs are trembling and a gaff
130 Bobs on the untimely stroke
Of the greased wash exploding on a shoal-bell
In the old mouth of the Atlantic. It's well;
Atlantic, you are fouled with the blue sailors,
Sea-monsters, upward angel, downward fish:
135 Unmarried and corroding, spare of flesh,
Mart once of supercilious, wing'd clippers;
Atlantic, where your bell-trap guts its spoil
You could cut the brackish winds with a knife

Walsingham: village in Norfolk, England, and site of Walsingham Abbey. **114.** *Shiloah's whirlpools:* Isaiah 8:5-7: "The Lord spake also unto me again, saying, Forasmuch as this people refuseth the waters of Shiloah that go softly, and rejoice in Rezin and Remaliah's son; Now therefore, behold, the Lord bringeth upon them the waters of the river, strong and many, *even* the king of Assyria, and all his glory: and he shall come up over all his channels, and go over all his banks." **122.** *Non est species, neque decor:* Lowell is accurate in his translation, "There's no comeliness At all or charm."

Here in Nantucket, and cast up the time
140 When the Lord God formed man from the sea's slime
And breathed into his face the breath of life,
And blue-lung'd combers lumbered to the kill.
The Lord survives the rainbow of his will.

WINTER IN DUNBARTON

Time smiling on this sundial of a world
Sweltered about the snowman and the worm,
Sacker of painted idols and the peers
Of Europe; but my cat is cold, is curled
5   Tight as a boulder: she no longer smears
Her catnip mouse from Christmas, for the germ—
Mindless and ice, a world against our world—
Has tamped her round of brains into her ears.

This winter all the snowmen turn to stone,
10   Or, sick of the long hurly-burly, rise
Like butterflies into Jehovah's eyes
And shift until their crystals must atone

In water. Belle, the cat that used to rat
About my father's books, is dead. All day
15   The wastes of snow about my house stare in
Through idle windows at the brainless cat;
The coke-barrel in the corner whimpers. May
The snow recede and red clay furrows set
In the grim grin of their erosion, in
20   The caterpillar tents and roadslides, fat

With muck and winter dropsy, where the tall
Snow-monster wipes the coke-fumes from his eyes
And scatters his corruption and it lies
Gaping until the fungus-eyeballs fall

25   Into this eldest of the seasons. Cold
Snaps the bronze toes and fingers of the Christ
My father fetched from Florence, and the dead
Chatters to nothing in the thankless ground
His father screwed from Charlie Stark and sold
30   To the selectmen. Cold has cramped his head
Against his heart: my father's stone is crowned
With snowflakes and the bronze-age shards of Christ.

THE DRUNKEN FISHERMAN

Wallowing in this bloody sty,
I cast for fish that pleased my eye

(Truly Jehovah's bow suspends
No pots of gold to weight its ends);
5   Only the blood-mouthed rainbow trout
Rose to my bait. They flopped about
My canvas creel until the moth
Corrupted its unstable cloth.

A calendar to tell the day;
10 A handkerchief to wave away
The gnats; a couch unstuffed with storm
Pouching a bottle in one arm;
A whiskey bottle full of worms;
And bedroom slacks: are these fit terms
15 To mete the worm whose molten rage
Boils in the belly of old age?

Once fishing was a rabbit's foot—
O wind blow cold, O wind blow hot,
Let suns stay in or suns step out:
20 Life danced a jig on the sperm-whale's spout—
The fisher's fluent and obscene
Catches kept his conscience clean.
Children, the raging memory drools
Over the glory of past pools.

25 Now the hot river, ebbing, hauls
Its bloody waters into holes;
A grain of sand inside my shoe
Mimics the moon that might undo
Man and Creation too; remorse,
30 Stinking, has puddled up its source;
Here tantrums thrash to a whale's rage.
This is the pot-hole of old age.

Is there no way to cast my hook
Out of this dynamited brook?
35 The Fisher's sons must cast about
When shallow waters peter out.
I will catch Christ with a greased worm,
And when the Prince of Darkness stalks
My bloodstream to its Stygian term . . .
40 On water the Man-Fisher walks.

MR. EDWARDS AND THE SPIDER

I saw the spiders marching through the air,
Swimming from tree to tree that mildewed day

MR. EDWARDS AND THE SPIDER. *Mr. Edwards:* Jonathan Edwards (1703-1758). American Calvinist writer and preacher. At twelve he wrote an essay on the spider, "On Insects," and used the spider in his later writings as a symbol of sin.

In latter August when the hay
Came creaking to the barn. But where
  The wind is westerly,
Where gnarled November makes the spiders fly
Into the apparitions of the sky,
They purpose nothing but their ease and die
Urgently beating east to sunrise and the sea;

What are we in the hands of the great God?
It was in vain you set up thorn and briar
  In battle array against the fire
  And treason crackling in your blood;
    For the wild thorns grow tame
And will do nothing to oppose the flame;
Your lacerations tell the losing game
You play against a sickness past your cure.
How will the hands be strong? How will the heart endure?

A very little thing, a little worm,
Or hourglass-blazoned spider, it is said,
  Can kill a tiger. Will the dead
  Hold up his mirror and affirm
    To the four winds the smell
And flash of his authority? It's well
If God who holds you to the pit of hell,
Much as one holds a spider, will destroy,
Baffle and dissipate your soul. As a small boy

On Windsor Marsh, I saw the spider die
When thrown into the bowels of fierce fire:
  There's no long struggle, no desire
  To get up on its feet and fly—
    It stretches out its feet
And dies. This is the sinner's last retreat;
Yes, and no strength exerted on the heat
Then sinews the abolished will, when sick
And full of burning, it will whistle on a brick.

But who can plumb the sinking of that soul?
Josiah Hawley, picture yourself cast
  Into a brick-kiln where the blast
  Fans your quick vitals to a coal—
    If measured by a glass,
How long would it seem burning! Let there pass
A minute, ten, ten trillion; but the blaze
Is infinite, eternal: this is death,
To die and know it. This is the Black Widow, death.

THE DEAD IN EUROPE

After the planes unloaded, we fell down
Buried together, unmarried men and women;
Not crown of thorns, not iron, not Lombard crown,
Not grilled and spindle spires pointing to heaven
5   Could save us. Raise us, Mother, we fell down
Here hugger-mugger in the jellied fire:
Our sacred earth in our day was our curse.

Our Mother, shall we rise on Mary's day
In Maryland, wherever corpses married
10   Under the rubble, bundled together? Pray
For us whom the blockbusters marred and buried;
When Satan scatters us on Rising-day,
O Mother, snatch our bodies from the fire:
Our sacred earth in our day was our curse.

15   Mother, my bones are trembling and I hear
The earth's reverberations and the trumpet
Bleating into my shambles. Shall I bear,
(O Mary!) unmarried man and powder-puppet,
Witness to the Devil? Mary, hear,
20   O Mary, marry earth, sea, air and fire;
Our sacred earth in our day is our curse.

WORDS FOR HART CRANE

"When the Pulitzers showered on some dope
or screw who flushed our dry mouths out with soap,
few people would consider why I took
to stalking sailors, and scattered Uncle Sam's
5   phoney gold-plated laurels to the birds.
Because I knew my Whitman like a book,
stranger in America, tell my country: I,
Catullus redivivus, once the rage
of the Village and Paris, used to play my role
10   of homosexual, wolfing the stray lambs
who hungered by the Place de la Concorde.
My profit was a pocket with a hole.
Who asks for me, the Shelley of my age,
must lay his heart out for my bed and board."

FOR SALE

Poor sheepish plaything,
organized with prodigal animosity,
lived in just a year—

my Father's cottage at Beverly Farms
5   was on the market the month he died.
Empty, open, intimate,
its town-house furniture
had an on tiptoe air
of waiting for the mover
10   on the heels of the undertaker.
Ready, afraid
of living alone till eighty,
Mother mooned in a window,
as if she had stayed on a train
15   one stop past her destination.

MEMORIES OF WEST STREET AND LEPKE

Only teaching on Tuesdays, book-worming
in pajamas fresh from the washer each morning,
I hog a whole house on Boston's
"hardly passionate Marlborough Street,"
5   where even the man
scavenging filth in the back alley trash cans,
has two children, a beach wagon, a helpmate,
and is a "young Republican."
I have a nine months' daughter,
10   young enough to be my granddaughter.
Like the sun she rises in her flame-flamingo infants' wear.

These are the tranquillized *Fifties*
and I am forty. Ought I to regret my seedtime?
I was a fire-breathing Catholic C.O.,
15   and made my manic statement,
telling off the state and president, and then
sat waiting sentence in the bull pen
beside a Negro boy with curlicues
of marijuana in his hair.

20   Given a year,
I walked on the roof of the West Street Jail, a short
enclosure like my school soccer court,
and saw the Hudson River once a day
through sooty clothesline entanglements
25   and bleaching khaki tenements.
Strolling, I yammered metaphysics with Abramowitz,
a jaundice-yellow ("it's really tan")
and fly-weight pacifist,
so vegetarian,
30   he wore rope shoes and preferred fallen fruit.
He tried to convert Bioff and Brown,
the Hollywood pimps, to his diet.

Hairy, muscular, suburban,
wearing chocolate double-breasted suits,
35   they blew their tops and beat him black and blue.

I was so out of things, I'd never heard
of the Jehovah's Witnesses.
"Are you a C.O.?" I asked a fellow jailbird.
"No," he answered, "I'm a J.W."
40   He taught me the "hospital tuck,"
and pointed out the T shirted back
of *Murder Incorporated's* Czar Lepke,
there piling towels on a rack,
or dawdling off to his little segregated cell full
45   of things forbidden the common man:
a portable radio, a dresser, two toy American
flags tied together with a ribbon of Easter palm.
Flabby, bald, lobotomized,
he drifted in a sheepish calm,
50   where no agonizing reappraisal
jarred his concentration on the electric chair-
hanging like an oasis in his air
of lost connections. . . .

MAN AND WIFE

Tamed by *Miltown,* we lie on Mother's bed;
the rising sun in war paint dyes us red;
in broad daylight her gilded bed-posts shine,
abandoned, almost Dionysian.
5   At last the trees are green on Marlborough Street,
blossoms on our magnolia ignite
the morning with their murderous five days' white.
All night I've held your hand,
as if you had
10   a fourth time faced the kingdom of the mad—
its hackneyed speech, its homicidal eye—
and dragged me home alive. . . . Oh my *Petite,*
clearest of all God's creatures, still all air and nerve:
you were in your twenties, and I,
15   once hand on glass
and heart in mouth,
outdrank the Rahvs in the heat
of Greenwich Village, fainting at your feet—
too boiled and shy
20   and poker-faced to make a pass,
while the shrill verve
of your invective scorched the traditional South.

Now twelve years later, you turn your back.
Sleepless, you hold

25 your pillow to your hollows like a child;
    your old-fashioned tirade—
    loving, rapid, merciless—
    breaks like the Atlantic Ocean on my head.

from Introduction to IMITATIONS

"I have been reckless with literal meaning, and labored hard to get
the tone. Most of this has been *a* tone, for *the* tone is something that
will always more or less escape transference to another language and
cultural moment. I have tried to write alive English and to do what
my authors might have done if they were writing their poems now
and in America."

THE INFINITE
LEOPARDI: *L'infinito*
from IMITATIONS

    That hill pushed off by itself was always dear
    to me and the hedges near
    it that cut away so much of the final horizon.
    When I would sit there lost in deliberation,
5   I reasoned most on the interminable spaces
    beyond all hills, on their antediluvian resignation
    and silence that passes
    beyond man's possibility.
    Here for a little while my heart is quiet inside me;
10 and when the wind lifts roughing through the trees,
    I set about comparing my silence to those voices,
    and I think about the eternal, the dead seasons,
    things here at hand and alive,
    and all their reasons and choices.
15 It's sweet to destroy my mind
    and go down
    and wreck in this sea where I drown.

TO THE READER
(FOR STANLEY KUNITZ)
BAUDELAIRE: *Au lecteur*
from IMITATIONS

    Infatuation, sadism, lust, avarice
    possess our souls and drain the body's force;
    we spoonfeed our adorable remorse,
    like whores or beggars nourishing their lice.

5   Our sins are mulish, our confessions lies;
    we play to the grandstand with our promises,

we pray for tears to wash our filthiness,
importantly pissing hogwash through our styes.

10 The devil, watching by our sickbeds, hissed
old smut and folk-songs to our soul, until
the soft and precious metal of our will
boiled off in vapor for this scientist.

Each day his flattery makes us eat a toad,
and each step forward is a step to hell,
15 unmoved, though previous corpses and their smell
asphyxiate our progress on this road.

Like the poor lush who cannot satisfy,
we try to force our sex with counterfeits,
die drooling on the deliquescent tits,
20 mouthing the rotten orange we suck dry.

Gangs of demons are boozing in our brain—
ranked, swarming, like a million warrior-ants,
they drown and choke the cistern of our wants;
each time we breathe, we tear our lungs with pain.

25 If poison, arson, sex, narcotics, knives
have not yet ruined us and stitched their quick,
loud patterns on the canvas of our lives,
it is because our souls are still too sick.

Among the vermin, jackals, panthers, lice,
30 gorillas and tarantulas that suck
and snatch and scratch and defecate and fuck
in the disorderly circus of our vice,

there's one more ugly and abortive birth.
It makes no gestures, never beats its breast,
35 yet it would murder for a moment's rest,
and willingly annihilate the earth.

It's BOREDOM. Tears have glued its eyes together.
You know it well, my Reader. This obscene
beast chain-smokes yawning for the guillotine—
40 you—hypocrite Reader—my double—my brother!

SELF-PORTRAIT
RILKE: *Selbstbildnis aus dem Jahre 1906*
from IMITATIONS

The bone-build of the eyebrows has a mule's
or Pole's noble and narrow steadfastness.

A scared blue child is peering through the eyes,
and there's a kind of weakness, not a fool's,
5   yet womanish—the gaze of one who serves.
The mouth is just a mouth . . . untidy curves,
quite unpersuasive, yet it says its *yes,*
when forced to act. The forehead cannot frown,
and likes the shade of dumbly looking down.

10   A still life, *nature morte*—hardly a whole!
It has done nothing worked through or alive,
in spite of pain, in spite of comforting . . .
Out of this distant and disordered thing
something in earnest labors to unroll.

Richard Wilbur (1921-   )

Richard Wilbur was born in New York City, graduated from Amherst
College in 1942, served in the U.S. Army from 1943 to 1945, received
an A.M. from Harvard in 1947, taught at Harvard from 1950 to
1954 and at Wellesley from 1955 to 1957, and since 1957 has taught
at Wesleyan, where he is now Professor of English and an editor of
a series of volumes of new poetry published by Wesleyan University
Press. His translation of Moliere's *Misanthrope* was performed off-
Broadway at Theater East in 1956-1957, and his translation of *Tar-
tuffe* played from mid-January until May 1965 at the Lincoln Center
Repertory Theater in New York. Married and the father of four
children, he lives in Portland, Connecticut. His numerous prizes and
honors include the Pulitzer Prize and the National Book Award in
1957 for *Things of This World,* a Guggenheim Fellowship in 1952-1953,
the Prix de Rome in 1954, and a Ford Fellowship in 1960-1961. He
is also a member of the American Academy of Arts and Sciences and
of the National Institute of Arts and Letters. His statement on the
voice of the poet seems to read like a short poem:

> The "poet's voice" is the natural voice of the man who is writing
> the poem, but it is that voice moved to attempt its maximum range.
> It is that natural voice trying to invent a version of itself in which
> all of the man's selves, worlds, and tongues may speak at once, and
> clearly, and without apparent strain.

CIGALES

You know those windless summer evenings, swollen to stasis
by too-substantial melodies, rich as a
running-down record, ground round
to full quiet. Even the leaves
5   have thick tongues.

And if the first crickets quicken then,
other inhabitants, at window or door
or rising from table, feel in the lungs
a slim false-freshness, by this
10 trick of the ear.

Chanters of miracles took for a simple sign
the Latin cigale, because of his long waiting
and sweet change in daylight, and his singing
all his life, pinched on the ash leaf,
15 heedless of ants.

Others made morals; all were puzzled and joyed
by this gratuitous song. Such a plain thing
morals could not surround, nor listening:
not "chirr" nor "cri-cri." There is no straight
20 way of approaching it.

This thin uncomprehended song it is
springs healing questions into binding air.
Fabre, by firing all the municipal cannon
under a piping tree, found out
25 cigales cannot hear.

MIND

Mind in its purest play is like some bat
That beats about in caverns all alone,
Contriving by a kind of senseless wit
Not to conclude against a wall of stone.

5 It has no need to falter or explore;
Darkly it knows what obstacles are there,
And so may weave and flitter, dip and soar
In perfect courses through the blackest air.

And has this simile a like perfection?
10 The mind is like a bat. Precisely. Save
That in the very happiest intellection
A graceful error may correct the cave.

FRANCIS JAMMES: A PRAYER TO GO TO PARADISE WITH THE DONKEYS

When I must come to you, O my God, I pray
It be some dusty-roaded holiday,
And even as in my travels here below,
I beg to choose by what road I shall go
5 To Paradise, where the clear stars shine by day.

I'll take my walking-stick and go my way,
And to my friends the donkeys I shall say,
"I am Francis Jammes, and I'm going to Paradise,
For there is no hell in the land of the loving God."
10   And I'll say to them: "Come, sweet friends of the blue skies,
Poor creatures who with a flap of the ears or a nod
Of the head shake off the buffets, the bees, the flies . . ."

Let me come with these donkeys, Lord, into your land,
These beasts who bow their heads so gently, and stand
15   With their small feet joined together in a fashion
Utterly gentle, asking your compassion.
I shall arrive, followed by their thousands of ears,
Followed by those with baskets at their flanks,
By those who lug the carts of mountebanks
20   Or loads of feather-dusters and kitchen-wares,
By those with humps of battered water-cans,
By bottle-shaped she-asses who halt and stumble,
By those tricked out in little pantaloons
To cover their wet, blue galls where flies assemble
25   In whirling swarms, making a drunken hum.
Dear God, let it be with these donkeys that I come,
And let it be that angels lead us in peace
To leafy streams where cherries tremble in air,
Sleek as the laughing flesh of girls; and there
30   In that haven of souls let it be that, leaning above
Your divine waters, I shall resemble these donkeys,
Whose humble and sweet poverty will appear
Clear in the clearness of your eternal love.

ADVICE TO A PROPHET

When you come, as you soon must, to the streets of our city,
Mad-eyed from stating the obvious,
Not proclaiming our fall but begging us
In God's name to have self-pity,

5   Spare us all word of the weapons, their force and range,
The long numbers that rocket the mind;
Our slow, unreckoning hearts will be left behind,
Unable to fear what is too strange.

Now shall you scare us with talk of the death of the race.
10   How should we dream of this place without us?—
The sun mere fire, the leaves untroubled about us,
A stone look on the stone's face?

Speak of the world's own change. Though we cannot conceive
Of an undreamt thing, we know to our cost

15   How the dreamt cloud crumbles, the vines are blackened by frost,
How the view alters. We could believe,

If you told us so, that the white-tailed deer will slip
Into perfect shade, grown perfectly shy,
The lark avoid the reaches of our eye,
20   The jack-pine lose its knuckled grip

On the cold ledge, and every torrent burn
As Xanthus once, its gliding trout
Stunned in a twinkling. What should we be without
The dolphin's arc, the dove's return,

25   These things in which we have seen ourselves and spoken?
Ask us, prophet, how we shall call
Our natures forth when that live tongue is all
Dispelled, that glass obscured or broken

In which we have said the rose of our love and the clean
30   Horse of our courage, in which beheld
The singing locust of the soul unshelled,
And all we mean or wish to mean.

Ask us, ask us whether with the worldless rose
Our hearts shall fail us; come demanding
35   Whether there shall be lofty or long standing
When the bronze annals of the oak-tree close.

PANGLOSS'S SONG:
A COMIC-OPERA LYRIC

I

Dear boy, you will not hear me speak
    With sorrow or with rancor
Of what has paled my rosy cheek
    And blasted it with canker;
5   'Twas Love, great Love, that did the deed
    Through Nature's gentle laws,
And how should ill effects proceed
    From so divine a cause?

Sweet honey comes from bees that sting,
10   As you are well aware;
To one adept in reasoning,
Whatever pains disease may bring
Are but the tangy seasoning
    To Love's delicious fare.

II

15   Columbus and his men, they say,
    Conveyed the virus hither

Whereby my features rot away
    And vital powers wither;
Yet had they not traversed the seas
20   And come infected back,
Why, think of all the luxuries
    That modern life would lack!

All bitter things conduce to sweet,
    As this example shows;
25 Without the little spirochete
We'd have no chocolate to eat,
Nor would tobacco's fragrance greet
    The European nose.

III
Each nation guards its native land
30   With cannon and with sentry,
Inspectors look for contraband
    At every port of entry,
Yet nothing can prevent the spread
    Of Love's divine disease:
35 It rounds the world from bed to bed
    As pretty as you please.

Men worship Venus everywhere,
    As plainly may be seen;
The decorations which I bear
40 Are nobler than the Croix de Guerre,
And gained in service of our fair
    And universal Queen.

James Dickey (1923-   )

James Dickey was born in Atlanta, Georgia, was Phi Beta Kappa at Vanderbilt, served in the Air Force in World War II and in the Korean war, and has taught at Rice Institute and the University of Florida. In 1963-1964 he was poet in residence at Reed College and in 1964-1965 at San Fernando Valley State College. In 1966 he was appointed Consultant in Poetry to the Library of Congress. Married and the father of two sons, he has been a Guggenheim Fellow, and has won various prizes for his poetry, including several given by *Poetry* magazine. On the poet's voice he writes:

> One is never sure whether it is heard or overheard, whether it is saying something immortal or delusionary. It comes, mixed in with other things: clichés, other poets' good and mediocre lines, tags from newspapers and grammar school history books. It is not always unmistakable when it is heard, but there is usually, even in the first word, something arresting about it, something that has a

sound of unusualness, of a quickening of interest in an untoward part of the world. At this accent, one sits still, afraid even to move the lips, for the thread of the voice can be instantly broken, and nothing can call it back from the silence into which it has gone. At these times, hearing the voice—one's own deepest, strangest, most necessary and best voice, the voice with which one most tellingly exclaims against the void—is like wearing the earphones of an old crystal radio set, when the fragile hair of the wire is touching the pure crystal, by instants, where it lives. The sound is mainly that of static, the roaring of the void, but now and again a voice speaks clearly through it, and says something remarkable, something never before heard—or overheard—in human time. This language, this fragment which seems to belong to a larger whole that the void swallows when the crystal instantaneously converts, as it will do, from being a touchstone to common matter, is yet connected in such intimate and profound ways with what the poet really does feel about things, about his own experience and about a dreamed-of mode of speaking of it, that it appears to belong to a self other than the one which tries to articulate these experiences in poems using the ordinary means of mortal poets. It belongs, really, to a better thing, a better order of things within himself than he has yet been able to achieve.

It is the poet's sovereign challenge to make the poem rise to the level, insofar as its enveloping context and tone are concerned, of a few words overheard by chance. The poet's voice at the only time it ever really matters is the one he never suspected he had. It is his own voice when it surprises him most: when it pronounces on the events of his life as though it knew something he didn't.

THE LIFEGUARD

In a stable of boats I lie still,
From all sleeping children hidden.
The leap of a fish from its shadow
Makes the whole lake instantly tremble.
5   With my foot on the water, I feel
The moon outside

Take on the utmost of its power.
I rise and go out through the boats.
I set my broad sole upon silver,
10   On the skin of the sky, on the moonlight,
Stepping outward from earth onto water
In quest of the miracle

This village of children believed
That I could perform as I dived
15   For one who had sunk from my sight.
I saw his cropped haircut go under.

I leapt, and my steep body flashed
Once, in the sun.

20   Dark drew all the light from my eyes.
Like a man who explores his death
By the pull of his slow-moving shoulders,
I hung head down in the cold,
Wide-eyed, contained, and alone
Among the weeds,

25   And my fingertips turned into stone
From clutching immovable blackness.
Time after time I leapt upward
Exploding in breath, and fell back
From the change in the children's faces
30   At my defeat.

Beneath them I swam to the boathouse
With only my life in my arms
To wait for the lake to shine back
At the risen moon with such power
35   That my steps on the light of the ripples
Might be sustained.

Beneath me is nothing but brightness
Like the ghost of a snowfield in summer.
As I move toward the center of the lake,
40   Which is also the center of the moon,
I am thinking of how I may be
The savior of one

Who has already died in my care.
The dark trees fade from around me.
45   The moon's dust hovers together.
I call softly out, and the child's
Voice answers through blinding water.
Patiently, slowly,

He rises, dilating to break
50   The surface of stone with his forehead.
He is one I do not remember
Having ever seen in his life.
The ground I stand on is trembling
Upon his smile.

55   I wash the black mud from my hands.
On a light given off by the grave
I kneel in the quick of the moon
At the heart of a distant forest
And hold in my arms a child
60   Of water, water, water.

In the Mountain Tent

I am hearing the shape of the rain
Take the shape of the tent and believe it,
Laying down all around where I lie
A profound, unspeakable law.
5   I obey, and am free-falling slowly

Through the thought-out leaves of the wood
Into the minds of animals.
I am there in the shining of water
Like dark, like light, out of Heaven.

10   I am there like the dead, or the beast
Itself, which thinks of a poem—
Green, plausible, living, and holy—
And cannot speak, but hears,
Called forth from the waiting of things,

15   A vast, proper, reinforced crying
With the sifted, harmonious pause,
The sustained intake of all breath
Before the first word of the Bible.

At midnight water dawns
20   Upon the held skulls of the foxes
And weasels and tousled hares
On the eastern side of the mountain.
Their light is the image I make

As I wait as if recently killed,
25   Receptive, fragile, half-smiling,
My brow watermarked with the mark
On the wing of a moth

And the tent taking shape on my body
Like ill-fitting, Heavenly clothes.
30   From holes in the ground comes my voice
In the God-silenced tongue of the beasts.
"I shall rise from the dead," I am saying.

Cherrylog Road

Off Highway 106
At Cherrylog Road I entered
The '34 Ford without wheels,
Smothered in kudzu,

CHERRYLOG ROAD. **4.** *kudzu:* a twining, rapidly growing, hardy perennial with large
leaves and purple flowers.

5   With a seat pulled out to run
    Corn whiskey down from the hills,

    And then from the other side
    Crept into an Essex
    With a rumble seat of red leather
10   And then out again, aboard
    A blue Chevrolet, releasing
    The rust from its other color,

    Reared up on three building blocks.
    None had the same body heat;
15   I changed with them inward, toward
    The weedy heart of the junkyard,
    For I knew that Doris Holbrook
    Would escape from her father at noon

    And would come from the farm
20   To seek parts owned by the sun
    Among the abandoned chassis,
    Sitting in each in turn
    As I did, leaning forward
    As in a wild stock-car race

25   In the parking lot of the dead.
    Time after time, I climbed in
    And out the other side, like
    An envoy or movie star
    Met at the station by crickets.
30   A radiator cap raised its head,

    Become a real toad or a kingsnake
    As I neared the hub of the yard,
    Passing through many states,
    Many lives, to reach
35   Some grandmother's long Pierce-Arrow
    Sending platters of blindness forth

    From its nickel hubcaps
    And spilling its tender upholstery
    On sleepy roaches,
40   The glass panel in between
    Lady and colored driver
    Not all the way broken out,

    The back-seat phone
    Still on its hook.
45   I got in as though to exclaim,

8, 35. *Essex, Pierce-Arrow:* low-priced and large luxury cars, respectively, known mainly in the first quarter of the twentieth century.

"Let us go to the orphan asylum,
John; I have some old toys
For children who say their prayers."

50   I popped with sweat as I thought
I heard Doris Holbrook scrape
Like a mouse in the southern-state sun
That was eating the paint in blisters
From a hundred car tops and hoods.
She was tapping like code,

55   Loosening the screws,
Carrying off headlights,
Sparkplugs, bumpers,
Cracked mirrors and gear-knobs,
Getting ready, already,
60   To go back with something to show

Other than her lips' new trembling
I would hold to me soon, soon,
Where I sat in the ripped back seat
Talking over the interphone,
65   Praying for Doris Holbrook
To come from her father's farm

And to get back there
With no trace of me on her face
To be seen by her red-haired father
70   Who would change, in the squalling barn,
Her back's pale skin with a strop,
Then lay for me

In a bootlegger's roasting car
With a string-triggered 12-gauge shotgun
75   To blast the breath from the air.
Not cut by the jagged windshields,
Through the acres of wrecks she came
With a wrench in her hand,

Through dust where the blacksnake dies
80   Of boredom, and the beetle knows
The compost has no more life.
Someone outside would have seen
The oldest car's door inexplicably
Close from within:

85   I held her and held her and held her,
Convoyed at terrific speed
By the stalled, dreaming traffic around us,
So the blacksnake, stiff

With inaction, curved back
90   Into life, and hunted the mouse

With deadly overexcitement,
The beetles reclaimed their field
As we clung, glued together,
With the hooks of the seat springs
95   Working through to catch us red-handed
Amidst the gray, breathless batting

That burst from the seat at our backs.
We left by separate doors
Into the changed, other bodies
100   Of cars, she down Cherrylog Road
And I to my motorcycle
Parked like the soul of the junkyard

Restored, a bicycle fleshed
With power, and tore off
105   Up Highway 106, continually
Drunk on the wind in my mouth,
Wringing the handlebar for speed,
Wild to be wreckage forever.

THE SHARK'S PARLOR
from BUCKDANCER'S CHOICE

Memory: I can take my head and strike it on a wall   on Cumberland Island
Where the night tide came crawling under the stairs   came up
   the first
Two or three steps   and the cottage stood on poles all night
With the sea sprawled under it   as we dreamed of the great fin
   circling
5   Under the bedroom floor. In daylight there was my first brassy taste
   of beer
And Payton Ford and I came back from the Glynn County slaughter-
   house
With a bucket of entrails and blood. We tied one end of a hawser
To a spindling porch-pillar and rowed straight out of the house
Three hundred yards into the vast front yard of windless blue water
10   The rope outslithering its coil   the two-gallon jug stoppered and
   sealed
With wax   and a ten-foot chain leader   a drop-forged shark
   hook nestling.
We cast our blood on the waters   the land blood easily passing
For sea blood   and we sat in it for a moment with the stain spread-
   ing
Out from the boat   sat in a new radiance   in the pond of blood
   in the sea

15 Waiting for fins   waiting to spill our guts also in the glowing water.
  We dumped the bucket, and baited the hook with a run-over collie
      pup. The jug
  Bobbed, trying to shake off the sun as a dog would shake off the sea.
  We rowed to the house   feeling the same water lift the boat a new
      way,
  All the time seeing where we lived rise and dip with the oars.
20 We tied up and sat down in rocking chairs, one eye or the other
      responding
  To the blue-eye wink of the jug. Payton got us a beer and we sat

  All morning sat there with blood on our minds   the red mark out
  In the harbor slowly failing us   then   the house groaned   the
      rope
  Sprang out of the water   splinters flew   we leapt from our chairs
25 And grabbed the rope   hauled   did nothing   the house
      coming subtly
  Apart   all   around   us   underfoot   boards beginning to
      sparkle like sand
  With the glinting of the bright hidden parts of ten-year-old nails
  Pulling out   the tarred poles we slept propped-up on   leaning
      to sea
  As in land wind   crabs scuttling from under the floor   as we
      took turns about
30 Two more porch pillars   and looked out and saw   something
      a fish-flash
  An almighty fin in trouble   a moiling of secret forces   a false
      start
  Of water   a round wave growing: in the whole of Cumberland
  Sound the one ripple.
  Payton took off without a word   I could not hold him either

  But clung to the rope anyway: it was the whole house bending
35 Its nails that held whatever it was   coming in a little and like a fool
  I took up the slack on my wrist. The rope drew gently   jerked   I
      lifted
  Clean off the porch and hit the water   the same water it was in
  I felt in blue blazing terror at the bottom of the stairs and scrambled
  Back up looking desperately into the human house as deeply as I
      could
40 Stopping my gaze before it went out the wire screen of the back door
  Stopped it on the thistled rattan   the rugs I lay on and read
  On my mother's sewing basket with next winter's socks spilling from it
  The flimsy vacation furniture   a bucktoothed picture of myself.
  Payton came back with three men from a filling station   and
      glanced at me
45 Dripping water   inexplicable   then we all grabbed hold like
      a tug-of-war.

  We were gaining a little   from us a cry went up   from every-
      where

People came running. Behind us the house filled with men and boys.
On the third step from the sea I took my place   looking down the rope
Going into the ocean, humming and shaking off drops. A houseful
Of people put their backs into it   going up the steps from me
Into the living room   through the kitchen   down the back stairs
Up and over a hill of sand   across a dust road   and onto a raised field
Of dunes   we were gaining   the rope in my hands began to be wet
With deeper water   all other haulers retreated through the house
But Payton and I on the stairs   drawing hand over hand on our blood
Drawing into existence by the nose   a huge body   becoming
A hammerhead   rolling in beery shallows   and I began to let up
But the rope still strained behind me   the town had gone
Pulling-mad in our house: far away in a field of sand they struggled
They had turned their backs on the sea   bent double   some on their knees
The rope over their shoulders like a bag of gold   they strove for the ideal
Esso station across the scorched meadow   with the distant fish coming up
The front stairs   the sagging boards   still coming in   up taking
Another step   toward the empty house   where the rope stood straining
By itself through the rooms   in the middle of the air. "Pass the word,"
Payton said, and I screamed it: "Let up, good God, let up!"   to no one there.
The shark flopped on the porch, grating with salt-sand   driving back in
The nails he had pulled out   coughing chunks of his formless blood.
The screen door banged and tore off   he scrambled on his tail slid
Curved   did a thing from another world   and was out of his element and in
Our vacation paradise   cutting all four legs from under the dinner table
With one deep-water move   he unwove the rugs in a moment throwing pints
Of blood over everything we owned   knocked the buck teeth out of my picture
His odd head full of crushed jelly-glass splinters and radio tubes thrashing
Among the pages of fan magazines   all the movie stars drenched in sea-blood.
Each time we thought he was dead   he struggled back and smashed

One more thing   in all coming back to die   three or four more
    times after death.
At last we got him out   log-rolling him   greasing his sandpaper
    skin
With lard to slide him   pulling on his chained lips as the tide came
80 Tumbled him down the steps as the first night wave went under the
    floor.
He drifted off   head back   belly white as the moon. What could
    I do but buy
That house   for the one black mark still there   against death
    a forehead-
toucher in the room he circles beneath   and has been invited to
    wreck?
Blood hard as iron on the wall   black with time   still bloodlike
85 Can be touched whenever the brow is drunk enough: all changes:
    Memory:
Something like three-dimensional dancing in the limbs   with age
Feeling more in two worlds than one   in all worlds the growing
    encounters.

REINCARNATION 2

the white thing was so white, its wings
so wide, and in those for ever exiled waters
                    MELVILLE

As apparitional as sails that cross
Some page of figures to be filed away
                    HART CRANE

One can do   one begins to   one can only

Circle   eyes wide with fearing the spirit

Of weight   as though to be born   to awaken to what one is
Were to be carried   passed out
5   With enormous cushions of air under the arms
Straight up   the head growing stranger
And released between wings near an iceberg

It is too much to ask   to ask
For   under the white mild sun
10 On that huge frozen point to move

As one is so easily doing

Boring into it with one's new
Born excessive eye   after a long
Half-sleeping self-doubting voyage   until

15 The unbased mountain falters
   Turns over like a whale   one screams for the first time

   With a wordless voice   swings over
   The berg's last treasured bubble
   Straightens   wings trembling   RIDING!
20 Rises into a new South

   Sensitive current   checks each wing
   It is living there
                  and starts out.

   There is then this night
25 Crawling slowly in under one wing
   This night of all nights
   Aloft   a night five thousand feet up
   Where he soars among the as-yet-unnamed
   The billion unmentionable stars
30 Each in its right relation
   To his course   he shivers   changes his heading
   Slightly   feels the heavenly bodies
   Shake   alter   line up in the right conjunction
   For mating   for the plunge
35 Toward the egg   he soars   borne toward his offspring

   By the Dragon balanced exactly
   Against the Lion   the sense of the galaxies
   Right from moment to moment
   Drawing slowly for him a Great
40 Circle   all the stars in the sky
   Embued with the miracle of
   The single human Christmas one
   Conjoining to stand now over
   A rocky island ten thousand
45 Miles of water away.
                       With a cold new heart
   With celestial feathered crutches
   A "new start" like a Freudian dream
   Of a new start   he hurtles as if motionless
50 All the air in the upper world
   Splitting apart on his lips.

   Sleep   *wingless*—NO!
   The stars appear, rimmed with red
   Space under his breastbone maintains
55 Itself   he sighs like a man
   Between his cambered wings
   Letting down now   curving around
   Into the wind   slowly toward
   Any wave   that—

60 That one.   He folds his wings and moves
    With the mid-Pacific
    Carried for miles in no particular direction
    On a single wave   a wandering hill
    Surging softly along in a powerful
65 Long-lost phosphorous seethe   folded in those wings
    Those ultimate wings   home is like   home is
    A folding of wings   Mother
    Something whispers   one eye opens   a star shifts
    Does not fall   from the eye of the Swan   he dreams

70 He sees the Southern Cross
    Painfully over the horizon   drawing itself
    Together   inching
    Higher each night of the World   thorn
    Points   tilted   he watches   not to be taken in
75 By the False Cross   as in   in
    Another life   not taken

    Knowing the true south rises
    In a better make of cross   smaller   compact
    And where its lights must appear.
80 Just after midnight he rises
    And goes for it   joy with him
    Springing out of the water
    Disguised as wind   he checks each feather
    As the stars burn out   waiting
85 Taking his course on faith until
    The east begins
    To pulse with unstoppable light.
    Now darkness and dawn melt exactly
    Together on one indifferent rill
90 Which sinks and is
    Another   he lives

    In renewed light, utterly alone!

    In five days there is one ship
    Dragging its small chewed off-white
95 Of ship-water   one candle in a too-human cabin
    One vessel moving embedded
    In its blue unendurable country

    Water warms   thereafter it is not
    That the sea begins to tinge
100 Like a vast, laid smoke
    But that he closes his eyes and feels himself
    Turning whiter and whiter   upheld

    At his whitest it is

Midnight   the equator   the center of the world
105   He sneaks across   afire
With himself   the stars change all their figures
Reach toward him   closer
And now begin to flow
Into his cracked-open mouth   down his throat
110   A string of lights   emblems   patterns of fire   all
Directions   myths   Hydras
Centaurs   Wolves   Virgins
Eating them all   eating
The void   possessing
115   Music   order   repose
Hovering   moving on his armbones   crawling
On warm air   covering the whole ocean   the sea deadens
He dulls   new constellations pale off
Him   unmapped roads open out of his breast
120   Beyond the sick feeling
Of those whose arms drag at treasures   it is like

Roosting   like holding one's arms out
In a clean nightshirt   a good dream   it is all
Instinct   he thinks   I have been born
125   This way.
            Goes on
His small head holding
It all   the continents firmly fixed
By his gaze   five new ships turned
130   Rusty by his rich shadow.
His seamless shoulders of dawn-gold
Open   he opens
Them wider   an inch wider and he would

Trees   voices   white garments   meadows

135   Fail   under him again are
Mullet believing their freedom
Is to go anywhere they like in their collected shape
The form of an unthrown net
With no net anywhere near them.
140   Of these he eats.
            Taking off again
He rocks forward three more days
Twenty-four hours a day
Balancing without thinking—
145   In doubt, he opens his bill
And vastness adjusts him
He trims his shoulders and planes   up

Up   stalls

In midocean   falls off
150 Comes down in a long, unbeheld
Curve that draws him into

                              evening
Incredible pasture.

The Cross is up.   Looking in through its four panes
155 He sees something   a clean desk-top
Papers shuffled   hears
Something   a bird-word
A too-human word   a word
That should have been somewhere spoken
160 That now can be frankly said
With long stiff lips into
The center of the Southern Cross
A word enabling one to fly
Out the window of office buildings
165 Lifts up on wings of its own
To say itself over and over   sails on
Under the unowned stars   sails as if walking
Out the window
That is what I said
170 That is what I should   that is

Dawn.   Panic   one moment of thinking
Himself in the hell of thumbs   once more   a man
Disguised in these wings   alone   No   again
He thinks   I am here   I have been born
175 This way   raised up from   raised up in
Myself   my soul
Undivided at last   thrown slowly forward
Toward an unmanned island.

Day overcomes   night comes over
180 Day with day already

Coming behind it   the sun halved in the east
The moon pressing feathers together.
Who thinks his bones are light
Enough, should try it   it is for everyone
185 He thinks   the world is for everything born—
I always had
These wings   buried deep in my back:
There is a wing-growing motion
Half-alive in every creature.

190 Comes down   skims for fifty miles
All afternoon lies skimming
His white shadow burning his breast

The flying-fish darting before him
In and out of the ash-film glaze

195 Or "because it is there"   into almighty cloud

In rain crying hoarsely
No place to go except
Forward into water in the eyes
Tons of water falling on the back
200 For hours   no sight   no insight
Beating up   trying
To rise above it   not knowing which way
Is up   no stars   crying
Home   fire   windows   for God
205 Sake   beating down   up   up-down
No help   streaming   another
Death   vertigo   falling
Upward   mother   God   country
Then seizing one grain of water in his mouth
210 Glides forward   heavy with cloud
Enveloped   gigantic   blazing with St. Elmo's
Fire   alone at the heart
Of rain   pure bird   heaving up   going

Up from that

215   and from that

Finally breaking

Out   where the sun is violently shining

On the useless enormous ploughland
Of cloud   then up
220 From just above it   up
Reducing the clouds more and more
To the color of their own defeat
The beauty of history   forgotten bird-

kingdoms packed in batting
225 The soft country   the endless fields
Raining away beneath him   to be dead
In one life is to enter
Another   to break out   to rise above   the clouds
Fail   pull back their rain

230 Dissolve. All the basic blue beneath
Comes back, tattering through. He cries out
As at sight of home   a last human face
In a mirror dazzles   he reaches

Glides off on one wing   stretching himself wider
235 Floats into night   dark follows
At his pace

                        the stars' threads all connect
On him   and, each in its place, the islands
Rise   small form of beaches

240 Treeless   tons of guano   eggshells
Of generations

                        down

                        circling

Mistrusting

245 The land   coming in
Wings ultra-sensitive
To solids   the ground not reflecting his breast
Feet tentatively out
Creaking   close   closer
250 Earth blurring   tilt back and brace
Against the wind   closest   touch

Sprawl.   In ridiculous wings, he flounders.
He waddles   he goes to sleep
In a stillness of body not otherwhere to be found
255 Upheld for one night
With his wings closed   the stiff land failing to rock him.

Here mating   the new life
Shall not be lost   wings tangle
Over the beaches   over the pale
260 Sketches of coral reefs   treading the air
The father moving almost
At once out the vast blue door
He feels it swing open
The island fall off him   the sun

265 Rise in the shape of an egg   enormous
Over the islands
                        passing out
Over the cliffs   scudding
Fifteen feet from the poor skinned sod
270 Dazing with purity the eyes of turtles
Lizards   then feeling the world at once
Sheerly restore the sea   the island not
Glanced back at   where the egg
Fills with almighty feathers

275   The dead rise, wrapped in their wings
        The last thread of white
        Is drawn from the foot of the cliffs
        As the great sea takes itself back
        From around the island

280   And he sails out   heads north
        His eyes already on icebergs
        Ten thousand miles off   already feeling
        The shiver of the equator as it crosses
        His body at its absolute
285   Midnight whiteness
                         and death also
        Stands waiting   years away
        In midair   beats
        Balanced on a starpoints
290   Latitude and longitude correct
        Oriented by instinct   by stars
        By the sun in one eye the moon
        In the other   bird-death

        Hovers for years on its wings
295   With a time-sense that cannot fail
        Waits to change
        Him again   circles   abides   no feather
        Falling   conceived by stars and the void
        Is born perpetually
300   In midair   where it shall be
        Where it is.

Alan Dugan (1923-   )

Alan Dugan was born in Brooklyn, graduated from Mexico City College, and married a daughter of painter Ben Shahn. He now lives in New York City and works for a medical supply house. His first book, *Poems,* won the Yale Series of Younger Poets Award in 1961 and in 1962 the National Book Award and the Pulitzer Prize. He also received the Rome Fellowship of the American Academy of Arts and Letters for 1962-1963. He writes on his voice as a poet, July 14, 1965:

> I don't know what my voice is or was, but I know that my voice is changing; I'm sick of wit and eloquence in neat form and am trying to say what is hardest to say; that is, words wrung out of intense experience and not constructed. Also I'm still trying to write political polemics in which what I say is personally dangerous. I let the lines fall in terms of breath, terminal emphasis, and, sometimes, completeness of statement. Minimum juggling. This is not a plan

but an observation. I don't know what I'm doing until I do it. Even then I'm not so sure. Also, on July 12, I got four rimed quatrains straight out, after not having rimed in months, so this whole statement is suspect.

On July 16, he added:

Reconsidering my statement on the poet's voice in my letter of July 14 to you, I decide I was a little too ambiguous. I said I wrote 4 quatrains on July 12, but did not include them, so here they are, as assonant irregulars, abba:

What's the balm
for dying life;
dope, drink, or, Christ,
is there one?

I puke and choke
with it and find
no Peace of Mind
in flesh, and no hope.

It flows away
in mucous-juice.
Nothing I can do
can make it stay,

so I give out!,
and water the garden: It
is all shit
for flowers anyhow.

How's that for a hard-made affirmation? I hate cheap affirmations about how nice the universe is to human beings.

The verses, though off-rimed, demonstrate demonstrate? some of my technical preferences, like terminal emphasis and so forth and so what. In an effort not to be clever, I remain, Yours truly, Alan Dugan.

TRIBUTE TO KAFKA FOR SOMEONE TAKEN

The party is going strong.
The doorbell rings. It's
for someone named me.
I'm coming. I take
a last drink, a last
puff on a cigarette,
a last kiss at a girl,
and step into the hall,
              bang,

shutting out the laughter. "Is
your name you?" "Yes."
"Well come along then."
"See here. See here. See here."

ON A SEVEN-DAY DIARY

Oh I got up and went to work
and worked and came back home
and ate and talked and went to sleep.
Then I got up and went to work
and worked and came back home
from work and ate and slept.
Then I got up and went to work
and worked and came back home
and ate and watched a show and slept.
Then I got up and went to work
and worked and came back home
and ate steak and went to sleep.
Then I got up and went to work
and worked and came back home
and ate and fucked and went to sleep.
Then it was Saturday, Saturday, Saturday!
Love must be the reason for the week!
We went shopping! I saw clouds!
The children explained everything!
I could talk about the main thing!
What did I drink on Saturday night
that lost the first, best half of Sunday?
The last half wasn't worth this "word."
Then I got up and went to work
and worked and came back home
from work and ate and went to sleep,
refreshed but tired by the week-end.

FABRICATION OF ANCESTORS
FOR OLD BILLY DUGAN, SHOT IN THE ASS IN THE CIVIL WAR,
MY FATHER SAID.

The old wound in my ass
has opened up again, but I
am past the prodigies
of youth's campaigns, and weep
where I used to laugh
in war's red humors, half
in love with silly-assed pains
and half not feeling them.
I have to sit up with

10 an indoor unsittable itch
    before I go down late
    and weeping to the storm-
    cellar on a dirty night
    and go to bed with the worms.
15 So pull the dirt up over me
    and make a family joke
    for Old Billy Blue Balls,
    the oldest private in the world
    with two ass-holes and no
20 place more to go to for a laugh
    except the last one. Say:
    The North won the Civil War
    without much help from me
    although I wear a proof
25 of the war's obscenity.

VARIATION ON A THEME BY STEVENS

    In fall and whiskey weather when
    the eye clears with the air and blood
    comes up to surface one last time
    before the winter and its sleeps,
5   the weeds go down to straws,
    the north wind strips most birds
    out of the atmosphere and they
    go southward with the sunlight,
    the retired people, and rich airs.
10 All appetites revive and love
    is possible again in clarity
    without the sweats of heat: it makes
    warmth. The wall-eyed arctic birds
    arrive to summer in the fall,
15 warmed by these chills; geese
    practice their noisy "V"s,
    half a horizon wide, and white owls
    hide from their crows in the pines.
    Therefore it is not tragic to stay
20 and not tragic or comic to go,
    but it is absolutely typical to say
    goodbye while saying hello.

Louis Simpson (1923-   )

Louis Simpson was born in Jamaica, British West Indies, attended Monro College there, and studied at Columbia University (B.S., 1948; A.M., 1950; Ph.D., 1959). He married in 1949, divorced in

1954. He married again in 1955, has one child by his first marriage and two by his second. He taught at Columbia from 1956 to 1959 and since then has taught at the University of California at Berkeley. In 1957 he received the Prix de Rome, in 1962 a Guggenheim Fellowship, and in 1964 the Pulitzer Prize for *At the End of the Open Road.* On the voice of the poet he writes:

> The development of modern poetry is in the direction: Symbolism —Imagism—Surrealism.
>
> The old-fashioned verse of epithets and opinions—writing of the will rather than the imagination—which is still practiced by poets who think of themselves as avant-garde—is dead. And objective verse, which is only photography, is boring. Those who still write in these ways are at the mercy of their surroundings; they are depressed, and create nothing.
>
> Only in Surrealism, creating images and therefore realities, is there any joy. But Surrealist poets have often failed to see that mere images, however new, are not enough. Their images are drawn from a deeper level, the subconscious. But they are merely projected on a screen, where they remain motionless. The deepest image, if it does not move, is only an object. And it's no use multiplying images . . . nothing happens.
>
> The next step—it is already occurring—is to reveal the movements of the subconscious. The Surrealist poet—rejecting on the one hand the clichés of the rational mind, and on the other, a mere projection of irrational images—will reveal the drama and narrative of the subconscious. The images move, with the logic of dreams. I believe there is no limit to what may be achieved in this new kind of verse.

To the Western World

A siren sang, and Europe turned away
From the high castle and the shepherd's crook.
Three caravels went sailing to Cathay
On the strange ocean, and the captains shook
5   Their banners out across the Mexique Bay.

And in our early days we did the same.
Remembering our fathers in their wreck
We crossed the sea from Palos where they came
And saw, enormous to the little deck,
10   A shore in silence waiting for a name.

The treasures of Cathay were never found.
In this America, this wilderness
Where the axe echoes with a lonely sound,
The generations labor to possess
15   And grave by grave we civilize the ground.

On the Lawn at the Villa

On the lawn at the villa—
That's the way to start, eh, reader?
We know where we stand—somewhere expensive—
You and I *imperturbes*, as Walt would say,
5   Before the diversions of wealth, you and I *engagés*.

On the lawn at the villa
Sat a manufacturer of explosives,
His wife from Paris,
And a young man named Bruno,

10   And myself, being American,
Willing to talk to these malefactors,
The manufacturer of explosives, and so on,
But somehow superior. By that I mean democratic.
It's complicated, being an American,
15   Having the money and the bad conscience, both at the same time.
Perhaps, after all, this is not the right subject for a poem.

We were all sitting there paralyzed
In the hot Tuscan afternoon,
And the bodies of the machine-gun crew were draped over the
    balcony.
20   So we sat there all afternoon.

Walt Whitman at Bear Mountain

"... life which does not give the preference to
any other life, of any previous period, which
therefore prefers its own existence ..."
                ORTEGA Y GASSET

Neither on horseback nor seated,
But like himself, squarely on two feet,
The poet of death and lilacs
Loafs by the footpath. Even the bronze looks alive
5   Where it is folded like cloth. And he seems friendly.

"Where is the Mississippi panorama
And the girl who played the piano?
Where are you, Walt?
The Open Road goes to the used-car lot.

10   "Where is the nation you promised?
These houses built of wood sustain
Colossal snows,
And the light above the street is sick to death.

"As for the people—see how they neglect you!
Only a poet pauses to read the inscription."
"I am here," he answered.
"It seems you have found me out.
Yet, did I not warn you that it was Myself
I advertised? Were my words not sufficiently plain?

"I gave no prescriptions,
And those who have taken my moods for prophecies
Mistake the matter."
Then, vastly amused—"Why do you reproach me?
I freely confess I am wholly disreputable.
Yet I am happy, because you have found me out."

A crocodile in wrinkled metal loafing . . .

Then all the realtors,
Pickpockets, salesmen, and the actors performing
Official scenarios,
Turned a deaf ear, for they had contracted
American dreams.

But the man who keeps a store on a lonely road,
And the housewife who knows she's dumb,
And the earth, are relieved.

All that grave weight of America
Cancelled! Like Greece and Rome.
The future in ruins!
The castles, the prisons, the cathedrals
Unbuilding, and roses
Blossoming from the stones that are not there. . . .

The clouds are lifting from the high Sierras,
The Bay mists clearing.
And the angel in the gate, the flowering plum,
Dances like Italy, imagining red.

THINGS

A man stood in the laurel tree
Adjusting his hands and feet to the boughs.
He said, "Today I was breaking stones
On a mountain road in Asia,

When suddenly I had a vision
Of mankind, like grass and flowers,
The same over all the earth.

We forgave each other; we gave ourselves
Wholly over to words.
10   And straightway I was released
And sprang through an open gate."

I said, "Into a meadow?"

He said, "I am impervious to irony.
I thank you for the word. . . .
15   I am standing in a sunlit meadow.
Know that everything your senses reject
Springs up in the spiritual world."

I said, "Our scientists have another opinion.
They say, you are merely phenomena."

20   He said, "Over here they will be angels
Singing, Holy holy be His Name!
And also, it works in reverse.
Things which to us in the pure state are mysterious,
Are your simplest articles of household use—
25   A chair, a dish, and meaner even than these,
The very latest inventions.
Machines are the animals of the Americans—
Tell me about machines."

I said, "I have suspected
30   The Mixmaster knows more than I do,
The air conditioner is the better poet.
My right front tire is as bald as Odysseus—
How much it must have suffered!

Then, as things have a third substance
35   Which is obscure to both our senses,
Let there be a perpetual coming and going
Between your house and mine."

CRISTINA

I have sat in this room
All day. There is a room
Where a man stares at the wall
All day, and nothing moves.
5   Indolence . . . it is pure indolence . . .
My life is passing
Slowly under the scrutiny
Of goggle eyes and lights that are vaguely
Uncovering monsters.

10 And now the moon is rising
Over the trees and dark rooftops.
Light ripples around the shoreline.
Love, is it you?
Cristina . . . I had forgotten
15 This rustling of bright stars.
I had forgotten
The night, and the smell of hibiscus
That clings to the skin of a girl.

Yet when April returns,
20 When the little fish-leaves of March-April
Swim in the wind,
Cristina whispers,
"Wake now, and feel the pangs
Of sensual love."
25 She lies in the darkness breathing,
She floats on the waves regarding
The luminous world.

Tonight it is not the loved one
Alone that enters,
30 But an arm of the moon,
A chain that enters slowly.
I am mildly exhilarated.
Lifting my heavy arms and feet
I move on the ocean floor.
35 I stamp on the ooze of the ocean floor
While light floats on the surface.

AMERICAN DREAMS

In dreams my life came toward me,
My loves that were slender as gazelles.
But America also dreams.
Dream, you are flying over Russia.
5 Dream, you are falling in Asia.

As I look down the street
On a typical sunny day in California
It is my house that is burning
And my dear ones that lie in the gutter
10 As the American army enters.

Every day I wake far away
From my life, in a foreign country.
These people are speaking a strange language.
It is strange to me,
15 And strange, I think, even to themselves.

Philip Booth (1925-   )

Philip Booth was born in Hanover, New Hampshire, served as a pilot in the United States Air Force in 1944-1945, married in 1946, received his B.A. from Dartmouth in 1948, and received his M.A. from Columbia in 1949. He has taught at Bowdoin, Dartmouth, and Wellesley and is now Associate Professor of English and Poet in Residence at Syracuse University. His first book of poems, *Letter from a Distant Land,* won the Lamont Prize of the Academy of American Poets in 1956. He was a Guggenheim Fellow in 1958 and again in 1965, the second award enabling him to move with his wife and three daughters to Castine, Maine, to work on his third book of poems. On the voice of the poet he writes:

> I don't think about "voice" as such; I talk aloud to myself when I write, but I mostly listen for rhythms and how they get shaped and paced by internal patterns of sound. I suppose I have a New England voice, in some larger sense: direct, slightly flat, perhaps dry. My sense of a subject and my attitude as I'm writing makes, I hope, for various voices in various poems; but within that flexibility I want tones constant to my way of seeing and saying: a kind of understatement that's not (however wry) without some sense of humor.
>
> I'm tired of irony; it's been taught to death. What I want to hear in a poem is not a teacher's voice talking (my own included); I'm after something closer to conversational metaphors, to how stories shape themselves into self-resolution through casual re-telling. I revise and revise, line by line, but not until I've first found the rhythms and tones that feel native to the poem that the poem is trying to become. I write from the beginning, as well as I word-by-word can, trying to discover how the experience of the poem may, in the end, resolve.
>
> The world's not apt to be resolved by a poem, but a poem can make the world's landscape more humanly bearable, maybe more bearably human. Whether that impulse is what charges "a poet's voice," this year or any year, I don't presume to guess. I'm certain, though, that we don't need another *Waste Land* to tell us where we live. Our problem is less to define the world's complexity than it is to discover, within that complexity, some marginal way of sustaining how we relate to it. A poem does nothing for me if it doesn't stretch to do that. The voice of any good poem, whatever wilderness it cries from, cries less than it says "Hello, out there!" I forget the name of the one-act play that Saroyan built from that line, but the line is one act of a poem. A good poem greets with world; it welcomes the sharing a listening reader completes. The world's always out there, often mute but seldom inglorious: a poem or a person waiting for words.
>
> But maybe my hope for a poem's too ideal. I know that I also write to make sense of my own experience. There are days when I'm short of courage when I selfishly write to hear my own voice: when I need to speak back some old "hello" to myself.

First Lesson

Lie back, daughter, let your head
be tipped back in the cup of my hand.
Gently, and I will hold you. Spread
your arms wide, lie out on the stream
5   and look high at the gulls. A dead-
man's float is face down. You will dive
and swim soon enough where this tidewater
ebbs to the sea. Daughter, believe
me, when you tire on the long thrash
10   to your island, lie up, and survive.
As you float now, where I held you
and let go, remember when fear
cramps your heart what I told you:
lie gently and wide to the light-year
15   stars, lie back, and the sea will hold you.

Convoy

One blueberry morning in Maine,
turned home with a full quart pail
in the bilge, I saw a dog seal
on a ledge across from Castine.

5   In the flooding tide, like a rock
awash on that shoal ridge,
the seal lay stretched on warm ledge,
sunning until my struck oarlock

warned him awake. Aloof
10   yet inquisitive, he at first arched
his trick back and then as I watched
him upwind, flipped, and slid off.

I ate a berry, sure
he'd surface to see what fool
15   creature I was. No seal.
Then by my leeward oar

his wet dog head slid up.
I saw a salt drop drip
off his whiskers and *plop,*
20   he was gone. He was fed up

with man, I thought. I was wrong:
he came up to try the port side,
silver-brown, eyes still wide.
An expanding silver ring

25 of millpond framed him, but beneath
    that mirror I could not see.
    I looked at him. He
    regarded me. Then with deep breath

    he dove as if under my skiff
30 and I heard a new breath drift
    downwind. Only a ring was left
    when I looked; my neck was stiff

    with watching, I'd turned too slow,
    and as my mind encompassed
35 such double luck, I focused
    on my error. His alter ego

    or twin had submerged to explore.
    Only one seal or his true love
    surfaced in corners of
40 my sight, for a full half-hour.

    I never saw both; the sport
    was submarine: when a starboard
    nose broke water, then, with a hard
    seal slap, a tail submerged to port.

45 That was my convoy home: a seal
    splash (not caught crab or riptide)
    rippling one or the other side.
    At least one seal was real.

    And I, least wise in Maine,
50 with double delight and half dread
    flooding two good eyes and one head,
    rowed home on my single plane.

    FIRST DRAFT
    FOR J.W.

    Wanting a poem, Jim,
    waking blank, I try
    to count old oak leaves
    rusted in the rain;
5   I want to stay the wind,
    and make my rainy saying
    move you as your mind,
    at equinox, moves me;
    to let you see the leaves,
10 and how their drift,
    outward more than down,

leaves time, for once,
to play at playing God
and trying one right word;
but I hear you, far inland,
speak back to my island:
Time is always left,
there's no last word for love;
there's only this first world,
the poem all poems are part of.

MAINE

When old cars get retired, they go to Maine.
Thick as cows in backlots off the blacktop,
East of Bucksport, down the washboard
from Penobscot to Castine,
they graze behind frame barns: a Ford
turned tractor, Hudsons chopped to half-ton
trucks, and Chevy panels, jacked up,
tireless, geared to saw a cord of wood.

Old engines never die. Not in Maine,
where men grind valves the way their wives grind axes.
Ring-jobs burned-out down the Turnpike
still make revolutions, turned marine.
If Hardscrabble Hill makes her knock,
Maine rigs the water-jacket salt: a man
can fish forever on converted sixes,
and for his mooring, sink a V-8 block.

When fishing's poor, a man traps what he can.
Even when a one-horse hearse from Bangor fades
away, the body still survives:
painted lobster, baited—off Route 1—
with home preserves and Indian knives,
she'll net a parlor-full of Fords and haul in
transient Cadillacs like crabs. Maine trades
in staying power, not shiftless drives.

HE

He was fifteen. And she, Wisconsin:
rolling, vernal, a fern to the sun
who answered her green questionmark.

There were fields beyond them: clover
and buttercup, paintbrush, lupin,
daisy and daisy, over and over,

under bobolink, goldfinch, and lark.
He laughed out like a jack-in-the-pulpit,
woken up from the difficult dark.

CIDER

Downhill through this upland meadow
   aster and chicory, sumac,
     poplar and apple,
distill into Fall: its cider light
5   opens the deepening woods, de-
   canting, through leaves, this
   stillness a hundred feet tall.

Secret in their seasonal shadow,
   chipmunk-quip, the tick
10   of felled acorns, thick bees,
speak only their season's self-praise.
There is no password or resident
   God; only this upland light,
   fallen through miles of trees.

W. D. Snodgrass (1926-   )

W. D. Snodgrass was born in Wilkinsburg, Pennsylvania, attended
Geneva College in Pennsylvania, spent three years in the Navy (1944-
1947), graduated from the State University of Iowa (B.A., 1949;
M.A., 1951; M.F.A., 1953), and has taught at Cornell University,
the University of Rochester, and, since 1959, Wayne State University. Married in 1946 and the father of a daughter, he was divorced
in 1953 and remarried in 1954. He has two children by his second
marriage. In 1960 he won the Pulitzer Prize for *Heart's Needle,* and
in 1964 he held a Ford grant in the theatre. Asked to comment on
the voice of the poet, he replied:

> Elsewhere, I stated that I ask a poem for depth of sincerity. But
> I must underline the word *depth.* The psyche is a texture of opposi-
> tions. And very often, any real discovery must come from the less
> conscious areas—obviously, we already know what's in the con-
> scious areas.
>
>   Thus, the poet's voice must embody not the expedient certain-
> ties of his daily life and belief, but rather in its style, in its way of
> treating details and images (how discrete are they, how firm, how
> extensive?), above all in its sounds, its subrational structure of aural
> textures and rhythms. It is here he must hope to find those mean-
> ings which may remain beyond the consciousness of his own period,
> but which may be deep enough to endure into the consciousness
> of another.

RETURNED TO FRISCO, 1946

We shouldered like pigs along the rail to try
And catch that first gray outline of the shore
Of our first life. A plane hung in the sky
From which a girl's voice sang: ". . . you're home once more."

5   For that one moment, we were dulled and shaken
By fear. What could still catch us by surprise?
We had known all along we would be taken
By hawkers, known what authoritative lies

Would plan us as our old lives had been planned.
10   We had stood years and, then, scrambled like rabbits
Up hostile beaches; why should we fear this land
Intent on luxuries and its old habits?

A seagull shrieked for garbage. The Bay Bridge,
Busy with noontime traffic, rose ahead.
15   We would have liberty, the privilege
Of lingering over steak and white, soft bread

Served by women, free to get drunk or fight,
Free, if we chose, to blow in our back pay
On smart girls or trinkets, free to prowl all night
20   Down streets giddy with lights, to sleep all day,

Pay our own way and make our own selections;
Free to choose just what they meant we should;
To turn back finally to our old affections,
The ties that lasted and which must be good.

25   Off the port side, through haze, we could discern
Alcatraz, lavender with flowers. Barred,
The Golden Gate, fading away astern,
Stood like the closed gate of your own backyard.

THE MARSH

Swampstrife and spatterdock
   lull in the heavy waters;
some thirty little frogs
   spring with each step you walk;
5   a fish's belly glitters
   tangled near rotting logs.

Over by the gray rocks
   muskrats dip and circle.
Out of his rim of ooze

10   a silt-black pond snail walks
inverted on the surface
    toward what food he may choose.

You look up; while you walk
    the sun bobs and is snarled
15 in the enclosing weir
    of trees, in their dead stalks.
Stick in the mud, old heart,
    what are you doing here?

Winter Bouquet

Her hands established, last time she left my room,
this dark arrangement for a winter bouquet:
collected bittersweet, brittle stemmed Scotch broom,
perennial straw-flowers, grasses gone to seed,
5 lastly, the dry vaginal pods of milkweed.
These relics stay here for her when she's away.

Bulging like a coin purse fallen on the ground
of damp woods, overgrained with moss, mould and frost,
their husks are horned like the Venus'-combs I found
10 on Garipan. Those war years, many a wife
wandered the fields after such pods to fill life
preservers so another man might not be lost.

Now she's home. Today I lifted them, like charms
in the March sunshine to part the pods and blow
15 white bursts of quilly weedseed for the wide arms
and eyes of the children squealing where they drift
across the neighbors' cropped lawns like an airlift
of satyrs or a conservative, warm snow.

Heart's Needle

7

Here in the scuffled dust
    is our ground of play.
I lift you on your swing and must
    shove you away,
5 see you return again,
    drive you off again, then

stand quiet till you come.
    You, though you climb
higher, farther from me, longer,
10   will fall back to me stronger.

Bad penny, pendulum,
    you keep my constant time

to bob in blue July
    where fat goldfinches fly
15 over the glittering, fecund
    reach of our growing lands.
Once more now, this second,
    I hold you in my hands.

THE LOVERS GO FLY A KITE

What's up, today, with our lovers?
    Only bright tatters—a kite
That plunges and bobs where it hovers
    At no improbable height.

5 It's shuddery like a hooked fish
    Or stallion. They reel in string
And sprint, compassing their wish:
    To keep in touch with the thing.

They tear up their shirts for a tail
10   In hopes that might steady
It down. Wobbling, frail,
    They think it may not be ready

And balance their hawk aloft—
    Poor moth of twigs and tissue
15 That would spill if one chill wind coughed,
    Dive down to tear, or to kiss you,

Yet still tugs the line they keep
    Like some exquisite sting ray
Hauled from a poisonous deep
20   To explore the bright coasts of day.

Or say it's their weather ear
    Keeping the heart's patrol of
A treacherous, washed-out year,
    Searching for one sprig of olive.

25 What air they breathe is wrung
    With twenty subtleties;
Sharp bones of failure, hung
    In all the parkway trees;

It's enough to make you laugh—
30   In these uncommitted regions
On an invisible staff
    To run up an allegiance!

Allen Ginsberg (1926-   )

Allen Ginsberg was born in Newark, New Jersey, went to high school in Paterson, studied at Columbia University from 1943 to 1945, was dismissed, was readmitted, and received his B.A. in 1949. *Howl* (1956) made him the best known of the "beat" poets. In 1966 he received a Guggenheim Fellowship in poetry. Here is his comment on the voice of the poet, dated July 11, 1965:

In 1948 I had a vision and heard William Blake's voice reciting "The Sunflower": deep, earthen, tender, suffused with the feeling of the ancient of days. After that experience I imagined a "Voice of Rock" as the sound of prophesy.

Subsequent composition, following the prosodiac precepts of W. C. Williams based on breath-measure and the fresh swift naturalness of thought-voice in Kerouac's poetry and prose, circa 1955, brought me to my native New Jersey voice issuing from throat and breast and mind.

Subsequent experience in Benares with mantra chanting (short magic formulae sung or repeated aloud as invocation to inner divinity) and in Kyoto with Zen belly-breathing delivered my accustomed voice (and center of self) from upper chest and throat to solar plexus and lower abdomen. The timbre, range and feeling-quality of the physical voice was thus physiologically deepened, till it actually approximated what I'd youthfully imagined to be the voice of rock.

Feeling, and rhythm, which is concomitant bodily potential of feeling, take place in the *whole* body, not just the larynx. The voice cometh from the whole body, when the voice is full, when feeling is full. (Poesy may be seen as a rhythmic articulation of feeling.)

Practice chanting and reciting aloud before other souls has confirmed my pleasure in this unexpected occurrence of Voice.

Ideological consequences follow naturally—revolution and Eternity and Death.

HOWL
FOR CARL SOLOMON

1

I saw the best minds of my generation destroyed by madness, starving hysterical naked,

dragging themselves through the negro streets at dawn looking for an angry fix,

angelheaded hipsters burning for the ancient heavenly connection to the starry dynamo in the machinery of night,

who poverty and tatters and hollow-eyed and high sat up smoking in the supernatural darkness of cold-water flats floating across the tops of cities contemplating jazz,

who bared their brains to Heaven under the El and saw Moham-
medan angels staggering on tenement roofs illuminated,
who passed through universities with radiant cool eyes hallucinating
Arkansas and Blake-light tragedy among the scholars of war,
who were expelled from the academies for crazy & publishing obscene
odes on the windows of the skull,
who cowered in unshaven rooms in underwear, burning their money
in wastebaskets and listening to the Terror through the wall,
who got busted in their pubic beards returning through Laredo with
a belt of marijuana for New York,
10 who ate fire in paint hotels or drank turpentine in Paradise Alley,
death, or purgatoried their torsos night after night
with dreams, with drugs, with waking nightmares, alcohol and cock
and endless balls,
incomparable blind streets of shuddering cloud and lightning in the
mind leaping toward poles of Canada & Paterson, illuminating all
the motionless world of Time between,
Peyote solidities of halls, backyard green tree cemetery dawns, wine
drunkenness over the rooftops, storefront boroughs of teahead
joyride neon blinking traffic light, sun and moon and tree vibra-
tions in the roaring winter dusks of Brooklyn, ashcan rantings and
kind king light of mind,
who chained themselves to subways for the endless ride from Battery
to holy Bronx on benzedrine until the noise of wheels and children
brought them down shuddering mouth-wracked and battered bleak
of brain all drained of brilliance in the drear light of Zoo,
15 who sank all night in submarine light of Bickford's floated out and
sat through the stale beer afternoon in desolate Fugazzi's, listening
to the crack of doom on the hydrogen jukebox,
who talked continuously seventy hours from park to pad to bar to
Bellevue to museum to the Brooklyn Bridge,
a lost battalion of platonic conversationalists jumping down the stoops
off fire escapes off windowsills off Empire State out of the moon,
yacketayakking screaming vomiting whispering facts and memories
and anecdotes and eyeball kicks and shocks of hospitals and jails
and wars,
whole intellects disgorged in total recall for seven days and nights
with brilliant eyes, meat for the Synagogue cast on the pavement,
20 who vanished into nowhere Zen New Jersey leaving a trail of ambiguous picture postcards of Atlantic City Hall,
suffering Eastern sweats and Tangerian bone-grindings and mi-
graines of China under junk-withdrawal in Newark's bleak furnished room,
who wandered around and around at midnight in the railroad yard
wondering where to go, and went, leaving no broken hearts,
who lit cigarettes in boxcars boxcars boxcars racketing through snow
toward lonesome farms in grandfather night,
who studied Plotinus Poe St. John of the Cross telepathy and bop
kaballa because the cosmos instinctively vibrated at their feet in
Kansas,

25   who loned it through the streets of Idaho seeking visionary indian
angels who were visionary indian angels,
who thought they were only mad when Baltimore gleamed in supernatural ecstasy,
who jumped in limousines with the Chinaman of Oklahoma on the
impulse of winter midnight streetlight smalltown rain,
who lounged hungry and lonesome through Houston seeking jazz
or sex or soup, and followed the brilliant Spaniard to converse
about America and Eternity, a hopeless task, and so took ship to
Africa,
who disappeared into the volcanoes of Mexico leaving behind nothing
but the shadow of dungarees and the lava and ash of poetry scattered in fireplace Chicago,

30   who reappeared on the West Coast investigating the F.B.I. in beards
and shorts with big pacifist eyes sexy in their dark skin passing out
incomprehensible leaflets,
who burned cigarette holes in their arms protesting the narcotic
tobacco haze of Capitalism,
who distributed Supercommunist pamphlets in Union Square weeping and undressing while the sirens of Los Alamos wailed them
down, and wailed down Wall, and the Staten Island ferry also
wailed,
who broke down crying in white gymnasiums naked and trembling
before the machinery of other skeletons,
who bit detectives in the neck and shrieked with delight in police-
cars for committing no crime but their own wild cooking pederasty
and intoxication,

35   who howled on their knees in the subway and were dragged off the
roof waving genitals and manuscripts,
who let themselves be fucked in the ass.by saintly motorcyclists,
and screamed with joy,
who blew and were blown by those.human seraphim, the sailors,
caresses of Atlantic and Caribbean love,
who balled in the mornings in the evenings in rosegardens and the
grass of public parks and cemeteries scattering their semen freely
to whomever come who may,
who hiccupped endlessly trying to giggle but wound up with a sob
behind a partition in a Turkish Bath when the blonde & naked
angel came to pierce them with a sword,

40   who lost their loveboys to the three old shrews of fate the one eyed
shrew of the heterosexual dollar the one eyed shrew that winks
out of the womb and the one eyed shrew that does nothing but sit
on her ass and snip the intellectual golden threads of the crafts-
man's loom,
who copulated ecstatic and insatiate with a bottle of beer a sweetheart
a package of cigarettes a candle and fell off the bed, and continued
along the floor and down the hall and ended fainting on the wall
with a vision of ultimate cunt and come eluding the last gyzym of
consciousness,
who sweetened the snatches of a million girls trembling in the sunset,

and were red eyed in the morning but prepared to sweeten the snatch of the sunrise, flashing buttocks under barns and naked in the lake,

who went out whoring through Colorado in myriad stolen night-cars, N.C., secret hero of these poems, cocksman and Adonis of Denver —joy to the memory of his innumerable lays of girls in empty lots & diner backyards, moviehouses, rickety rows on mountaintops in caves or with gaunt waitresses in familiar roadside lonely petticoat upliftings & especially secret gas-station solipisisms of johns, & hometown alleys too,

who faded out in vast sordid movies, were shifted in dreams, woke on a sudden Manhattan, and picked themselves up out of basements hungover with heartless Tokay and horrors of Third Avenue iron dreams & stumbled to unemployment offices,

45   who walked all night with their shoes full of blood on the snowbank docks waiting for a door in the East River to open to a room full of steamheat and opium,

who created great suicidal dramas on the apartment cliff-banks of the Hudson under the wartime blue floodlight of the moon & their heads shall be crowned with laurel in oblivion,

who ate the lamb stew of the imagination or digested the crab at the muddy bottom of the rivers of Bowery,

who wept at the romance of the streets with their pushcarts full of onions and bad music,

who sat in boxes breathing in the darkness under the bridge, and rose up to build harpsichords in their lofts,

50   who coughed on the sixth floor of Harlem crowned with flame under the tubercular sky surrounded by orange crates of theology,

who scribbled all night rocking and rolling over lofty incantations which in the yellow morning were stanzas of gibberish,

who cooked rotten animals lung heart feet tail borsht & tortillas dreaming of the pure vegetable kingdom,

who plunged themselves under meat trucks looking for an egg,

who threw their watches off the roof to cast their ballot for Eternity outside of Time, & alarm clocks fell on their heads every day for the next decade,

55   who cut their wrists three times successively unsuccessfully, gave up and were forced to open antique stores where they thought they were growing old and cried,

who were burned alive in their innocent flannel suits on Madison Avenue amid blasts of leaden verse & the tanked-up clatter of the iron regiments of fashion & the nitroglycerine shrieks of the fairies of advertising & the mustard gas of sinister intelligent editors, or were run down by the drunken taxicabs of Absolute Reality,

who jumped off the Brooklyn Bridge this actually happened and walked away unknown and forgotten into the ghostly daze of Chinatown soup alleyways & firetrucks, not even one free beer,

who sang out of their windows in despair, fell out of the subway window, jumped in the filthy Passaic, leaped on negroes, cried all over

the street, danced on broken wineglasses barefoot smashed phono-
graph records of nostalgic European 1930's German jazz finished
the whiskey and threw up groaning into the bloody toilet, moans
in their ears and the blast of colossal steamwhistles,

who barreled down the highways of the past journeying to each
other's hotrod-Golgotha jail-solitude watch or Birmingham jazz
incarnation,

60   who drove crosscountry seventytwo hours to find out if I had a vision
or you had a vision or he had a vision to find out Eternity,

who journeyed to Denver, who died in Denver, who came back to
Denver & waited in vain, who watched over Denver & brooded &
loned in Denver and finally went away to find out the Time, & now
Denver is lonesome for her heroes,

who fell on their knees in hopeless cathedrals praying for each other's
salvation and light and breasts, until the soul illuminated its hair
for a second,

who crashed through their minds in jail waiting for impossible crim-
inals with golden heads and the charm of reality in their hearts
who sang sweet blues to Alcatraz,

who retired to Mexico to cultivate a habit, or Rocky Mount to tender
Buddha or Tangiers to boys or Southern Pacific to the black loco-
motive or Harvard to Narcissus to Woodlawn to the daisychain
or grave,

65   who demanded sanity trials accusing the radio of hypnotism & were
left with their insanity & their hands & a hung jury,

who threw potato salad at CCNY lecturers on Dadaism and subsequently presented themselves on the granite steps of the madhouse
with shaven heads and harlequin speech of suicide, demanding
instantaneous lobotomy,

and who were given instead the concrete void of insulin metrasol
electricity hydrotherapy psychotherapy occupational therapy pingpong & amnesia,

who in humorless protest overturned only one symbolic pingpong
table, resting briefly in catatonia,

returning years later truly bald except for a wig of blood, and tears
and fingers, to the visible madman doom of the wards of the mad-
towns of the East,

70   Pilgrim State's Rockland's and Greystone's foetid halls, bickering
with the echoes of the soul, rocking and rolling in the midnight
solitude-bench dolmen-realms of love, dream of life a nightmare,
bodies turned to stone as heavy as the moon,

with mother finally ******, and the last fantastic book flung out of
the tenement window, and the last door closed at 4 AM and the
last telephone slammed at the wall in reply and the last furnished
room emptied down to the last piece of mental furniture, a yellow
paper rose twisted on a wire hanger in the closet, and even that
imaginary, nothing but a hopeful little bit of hallucination—

ah, Carl, while you are not safe I am not safe, and now you're really
in the total animal soup of time—

and who therefore ran through the icy streets obsessed with a sudden flash of the alchemy of the use of the ellipse the catalog the meter & the vibrating plane,

who dreamt and made incarnate gaps in Time & Space through images juxtaposed, and trapped the archangel of the soul between 2 visual images and joined the elemental verbs and set the noun and dash of consciousness together jumping with sensation of Pater Omnipotens Aeterna Deus

75 to recreate the syntax and measure of poor human prose and stand before you speechless and intelligent and shaking with shame, rejected yet confessing out the soul to conform to the rhythm of thought in his naked and endless head,

the madman bum and angel beat in Time, unknown, yet putting down here what might be left to say in time come after death,

and rose reincarnate in the ghostly clothes of jazz in the goldhorn shadow of the band and blew the suffering of America's naked mind for love into an eli eli lamma lamma sabacthani saxophone cry that shivered the cities down to the last radio

with the absolute heart of the poem of life butchered out of their own bodies good to eat a thousand years.

2

What sphinx of cement and aluminum bashed open their skulls and ate up their brains and imagination?

80 Moloch! Solitude! Filth! Ugliness! Ashcans and unobtainable dollars! Children screaming under the stairways! Boys sobbing in armies! Old men weeping in the parks!

Moloch! Moloch! Nightmare of Moloch! Moloch the loveless! Mental Moloch! Moloch the heavy judger of men!

Moloch the incomprehensible prison! Moloch the crossbone soulless jailhouse and Congress of sorrows! Moloch whose buildings are judgement! Moloch the vast stone of war! Moloch the stunned governments!

Moloch whose mind is pure machinery! Moloch whose blood is running money! Moloch whose fingers are ten armies! Moloch whose breast is a cannibal dynamo! Moloch whose ear is a smoking tomb!

Moloch whose eyes are a thousand blind windows! Moloch whose skyscrapers stand in the long streets like endless Jehovahs! Moloch whose factories dream and croak in the fog! Moloch whose smokestacks and antennae crown the cities!

85 Moloch whose love is endless oil and stone! Moloch whose soul is electricity and banks! Moloch whose poverty is the specter of genius! Moloch whose fate is a cloud of sexless hydrogen! Moloch whose name is the Mind!

Moloch in whom I sit lonely! Moloch in whom I dream Angels! Crazy in Moloch! Cocksucker in Moloch! Lacklove and manless in Moloch!

Moloch who entered my soul early! Moloch in whom I am a consciousness without a body! Moloch who frightened me out of my natural

---

HOWL. **77.** *eli eli lamma lamma sabacthani:* "My God, my God, why why hast thou forsaken me," the words of Christ on the cross. See Matthew 27:46. Ginsberg adds a *lamma.*

ecstasy! Moloch whom I abandon! Wake up in Moloch! Light streaming out of the sky!

Moloch! Moloch! Robot apartments! invisible suburbs! skeleton treasuries! blind capitals! demonic industries! spectral nations! invincible madhouses! granite cocks! monstrous bombs!

They broke their backs lifting Moloch to Heaven! Pavements, trees, radios, tons! lifting the city to Heaven which exists and is everywhere about us!

90 Visions! omens! hallucinations! miracles! ecstasies! gone down the American river!

Dreams! adorations! illuminations! religions! the whole boatload of sensitive bullshit!

Breakthroughs! over the river! flips and crucifixions! gone down the flood! Highs! Epiphanies! Despairs! Ten years' animal screams and suicides! Minds! New loves! Mad generation! down on the rocks of Time!

Real holy laughter in the river! They saw it all! the wild eyes! the holy yells! They bade farewell! They jumped off the roof! to solitude! waving! carrying flowers! Down to the river! into the street!

3

Carl Solomon! I'm with you in Rockland
    where you're madder than I am
95 I'm with you in Rockland
    where you must feel very strange
I'm with you in Rockland
    where you imitate the shade of my mother
I'm with you in Rockland
    where you've murdered your twelve secretaries
I'm with you in Rockland
    where you laugh at this invisible humor
I'm with you in Rockland
    where we are great writers on the same dreadful typewriter
100 I'm with you in Rockland
    where your condition has become serious and is reported on
    the radio
I'm with you in Rockland
    where the faculties of the skull no longer admit the worms
    of the senses
I'm with you in Rockland
    where you drink the tea of the breasts of the spinsters of Utica
I'm with you in Rockland
    where you pun on the bodies of your nurses the harpies of
    the Bronx
I'm with you in Rockland
    where you scream in a straightjacket that you're losing the
    game of the actual pingpong of the abyss
105 I'm with you in Rockland
    where you bang on the catatonic piano the soul is innocent

and immortal it should never die ungodly in an armed madhouse
I'm with you in Rockland
where fifty more shocks will never return your soul to its body
again from its pilgrimage to a cross in the void
I'm with you in Rockland
where you accuse your doctors of insanity and plot the Hebrew
socialist revolution against the fascist national Golgotha
I'm with you in Rockland
where you will split the heavens of Long Island and resurrect
your living human Jesus from the superhuman tomb
I'm with you in Rockland
where there are twentyfive-thousand mad comrades all together singing the final stanzas of the Internationale
110 I'm with you in Rockland
where we hug and kiss the United States under our bedsheets
the United States that coughs all night and won't let us sleep
I'm with you in Rockland
where we wake up electrified out of the coma by our own souls'
airplanes roaring over the roof they've come to drop angelic
bombs the hospital illuminates itself imaginary walls collapse
O skinny legions run outside O starry-spangled shock of mercy
the eternal war is here O victory forget your underwear we're
free
I'm with you in Rockland
in my dreams you walk dripping from a sea-journey on the
highway across America in tears to the door of my cottage
in the Western night

A SUPERMARKET IN CALIFORNIA

What thoughts I have of you tonight, Walt Whitman, for I walked
down the sidestreets under the trees with a headache self-conscious
looking at the full moon.

In my hungry fatigue, and shopping for images, I went into the
neon fruit supermarket, dreaming of your enumerations!

What peaches and what penumbras! Whole families shopping
at night! Aisles full of husbands! Wives in the avocados, babies in
the tomatoes!—and you, Garcia Lorca, what were you doing down
by the watermelons?

I saw you, Walt Whitman, childless, lonely old grubber, poking
among the meats in the refrigerator and eyeing the grocery boys.

5 I heard you asking questions of each: Who killed the pork chops?
What price bananas? Are you my Angel?

I wandered in and out of the brilliant stacks of cans following you,
and followed in my imagination by the store detective.

We strode down the open corridors together in our solitary fancy
tasting artichokes, possessing every frozen delicacy, and never passing the cashier.

Where are we going, Walt Whitman? The doors close in an hour. Which way does your beard point tonight?

(I touch your book and dream of our odyssey in the supermarket and feel absurd.)

Will we walk all night through solitary streets? The trees add shade to shade, lights out in the houses, we'll both be lonely.

Will we stroll dreaming of the lost America of love past blue automobiles in driveways, home to our silent cottage?

Ah, dear father, graybeard, lonely old courage-teacher, what America did you have when Charon quit poling his ferry and you got out on a smoking bank and stood watching the boat disappear on the black waters of Lethe?

THE END

I am I, old Father Fisheye that begat the ocean, the worm at my
    own ear, the serpent turning around a tree,
I sit in the mind of the oak and hide in the rose, I know if any
    wake up, none but my death,
come to me bodies, come to me prophecies, come all foreboding,
    come spirits and visions,
I receive all, I'll die of cancer, I enter the coffin forever, I close
    my eye, I disappear,
I fall on myself in winter snow, I roll in a great wheel through
    rain, I watch fuckers in convulsion,
car screech, furies groaning their basso music, memory fading
    in the brain, men imitating dogs,
I delight in a woman's belly, youth stretching his breasts and
    thighs to sex, the cock sprung inward
gassing its seed on the lips of Yin, the beasts dance in Siam,
    they sing opera in Moscow,
my boys yearn at dusk on stoops, I enter New York, I play my
    jazz on a Chicago Harpsichord,
Love that bore me I bear back to my Origin with no loss, I float
    over the vomiter
thrilled with my deathlessness, thrilled with this endlessness I
    dice and bury,
come Poet shut up eat my word, and taste my mouth in your ear.

W. S. Merwin (1927-   )

W. S. Merwin was born in New York City, graduated from Princeton in 1947, and worked as a tutor in France, Portugal, and Majorca from 1949 to 1951. He is a translator—French, Spanish, Latin, and Portuguese—and lives with his British wife in the Lot area of southwest France. His first book of poems, *A Mask for Janus*, won the Yale Series of Younger Poets competition in 1952. He calls his comment on the voice of the poet "Notes for a Preface":

If he starts trying to formulate statements about the undomesti-cated phenomenon that is poetry, the man who may have been, on occasion, a poet, is likely to realize that he is virtually as thorough a layman as anyone. He can remember a few times when he wrote what he took to be poetry, but the memory is as tragically partial as that of any particular moment of sex, and doubtless he knows that the instances, as they were real, are unrepeatable. He has learned this beyond question if he has ever been tempted, by cow-ardice, to repeat them, instead of trying to call the next real crea-tures from the ark. What gifts he can muster as a summoner do not necessarily preclude him from being able to generalize about what he is doing, but it often seems so, whether he listens to other lay-men making the attempt, or makes it himself.

When statements emerge, privately he is likely to be reminded that they will help him less than his daily prayers that he may be condemned to continue. The statements usually apply to what has happened—as Aristotle would have told him—and he is concerned with something else.

Yet there is what appears to be, among all degrees of laymen, a more urgent demand for statements about poetry than for poetry itself. I am certainly no historian (though our time and its future increasingly appear to me like part of the past) and it is not a pref-erence which I share, but I have watched it as an object for a while, and imagine that I have noticed some characteristics. Those who write or hope to write poetry (and these, for other reasons, are apparently among the few who still read it) often like to formulate, attend to, collect and repeat statements about it by way of reli-quaries toward which they can direct their hopes. The devotion is understandable; the reliquaries have an interest and often a beauty of their own; sometimes the relics are genuine and even still virtuous. It is hardly necessary to remark that when the cult of relics is exalted above the vision itself it is a sign of ultimate despair.

Of those who do not look to write poems but simply to read them, evidently even among these few there are many who would rather read about them. Some reasons for this are obvious and several have been presented many times. The fact, for instance, that read-ing, of the kind that poetry assumes, is a dying activity, and the capacity for it is flattered but not fed. This, coupled as it inevitably is with the fact that contemporary poetry makes, and is chiefly famous for making, greater demands on its readers than it did in days when it was sure that they existed and could read. For those who feel that they should know about modern poetry without having to submit to it themselves, the literature about it also pro-vides the required digests for busy lives.

But these explanations are automatic and there must be others. The demand is often for a substitute, a translation, and is regularly made by those who are poorly acquainted, or uncomfortable, with the original idiom. But the original seems more and more fre-quently to be, not a particular mode of poetry, but the great language itself, the vernacular of the imagination, that at one time was common to men. It is a tongue that is loosed in the service of immediate recognitions, and that in itself would make it foreign in our period. For it conveys something of the unsoundable quality of experience and the hearing of it is a private matter, in an age in which the person and his senses are being lost in the consumer, who does not know what he sees, hears, wants, or is afraid of, until the voice of the institution has told him. Still, the voice of the institution has able apologists as well, some of whom go so far as to insist that it too is sometimes poetry.

At that point it is my turn to be glad not to understand. In any case, poetry, as I have been speaking of it, is found satisfying less and less often by those who still require any art at all. The search for substitutes in activities remarkable chiefly for their evocation of special wave-lengths that are seldom within ear-shot, or for their deliberate abandon, points to the same abdication. But there is nothing original in observing that man, if that is what he still is, has chosen to pass mutilated into the heaven of the modern world, nor in remarking that the rift between experience (which is personal, and inseparable from the whole) and activity (which may well be communal, and shared with machines) was widening, and that the species had opted for activity, activity, both as a means and, it would appear, as an end, though it meant abandoning something, and perhaps something essential, of themselves. Poetry, and the need for it, may be among what is being left behind.

Any such intimation, of course, is likely to be assailed by rotarian voices reminding in puzzlement and dudgeon that never before has the institution paid so much money toward poetry, to say nothing of attention. In our land corporations and universities give of what they have to encourage it to be itself as much as possible. And, at least partly as a result, they may truthfully claim that the production figures have never been so good. But what they are pointing to is activity, which is what the institution is capable of fostering. The encouragement of poetry itself is a labor and a privilege like that of living. It requires, I imagine, among other startlingly simple things, a love of poetry, and possibly a recurring despair of finding it again, an indelible awareness of its parentage with that Biblical waif, ill at ease in time, the spirit. No one has any claims on it, no one deserves it, no one knows where it goes. It is not pain, and it is not the subconscious, though it can hail from either as though it were at home there. On the other hand, thinking of the activists I remember the bee gorging honey (for the circumstances, as it realized, contained a menace of some kind) though its abdomen had been amputated. For some minutes it continued to devour nourishment, since its motor system was rightly informed that this was lacking. As closely as could be observed it was so far from feeling pain that it had no conception of its loss. All that it ate poured through the wound and was gone, and it died of starvation. I am haunted by its other death, before or after, in a useless gland of the lost abdomen. The fact that one is haunted by it does not mean that it stayed alive.

But then, among my peculiar failings is an inability to believe that the experience of being human, that gave rise to the arts in the first place, can continue to be nourished in a world contrived and populated by nothing but humans. No doubt such a situation is biologically impossible, but it is economically desirable, and we exist in an era dedicated to the myth that the biology of the planet, as well as anything else that may be, can be forced to adapt infinitely to the appetites of one species, organized and deified under the name of economics. It would be impossible not to be familiar with the contention that experience is merely a factor of circumstances, any circumstances, and can be equally valuable whatever they are. The argument is often presented as an excuse or consolation for activities undertaken or omitted for other reasons. The tendency of the arts, in a landscape fabricated entirely of human contraptions, to seek nourishment in accident and decay— the very places where the complex and unpredictable natural world continually re-invades the machine—may indeed be no more than an atavistic nostalgia for something no longer necessary. But it may be that the arts themselves are atavistic, or man, for that matter, as he has been defined until now, with the non-human world entering always into the definition. One of the vexed points of modern biology is precisely the definition of a species, and the point at which adaptation to changed circumstances requires a new definition for a species that has been transformed into something essentially new. I cannot escape the notion that it is because circumstances do have an effect on experience that they are not all equally valuable, and that many of the circumstances common to contemporary existence are contributing to a general destruction of what the arts until now have helped to dignify in what they called human. For one thing, the arts and their source were fed from the senses, and the circumstances that have been conceived and are being developed in the name of economics are relegating these anarchistic voices to the bee's abdomen. Indeed they must do so, for the senses, if they were not uniformed, duped, and cowed, would constitute a continuous judgement of the world they touched on, and not only of its means but of its ends. Instead of the world of the senses, which was unprovable but you never knew what it might say, the creature that is replacing the Old Adam has substituted comfort and erotic daydreams (whether or not physically enacted) and tells you that they are not only more convenient and more fun, but cleaner.

Along with the insistence that all circumstances are equally valuable, there sometimes goes an odd and guilty assertion (and all injunctions that do not proceed from the Biblical waif ventriloquize for the institution) that the artist must go along with the life of his time, as though he could do anything else. In many instances no doubt this somewhat priggish platitude bespeaks little more than a frustrated longing to escape from the salient characteristics of that life the moment occasion or courage offers. Sometimes it appears to betray, chiefly, a sense of being outside it, or just outside. But what is interesting about it is the assumption that man, the animal and artist, and the arts that have conceived him until now, are infinitely adaptable to man-made circumstances; and "adaptable," as the most unavoidable acquaintance with economics will reveal, means "simplifiable," when so used.

Going along with the life of his time in an earnest fashion may or may not benefit the attempt to give utterance to the unutterable experience of being alive, and consciously mortal, and human, in any time. It does not necessarily entail going along with all possible activities of an emergent and epidemic species which scorns all life except its own withering existence, and is busily relegating the senses its predecessors were given to apprehend their world, and the creatures with which they were privileged to share it.

Here and there a form of art has become recognizable as a feature of the era. Stemming from a more or less deliberate and exclusive immersion in the metropolitan life of our time, it resorts perforce to increasingly extreme states of consciousness as though they were the desperate retreats of truth, yet its images are frequently at a remove from any direct and integrated sensual criteria. When it provokes recognition of anything it is usually of the squalid landscapes of a world made and polluted by man alone, from which it shows that there is no escape. It is not an art which I wish to decry nor to avoid, but I would hope not to be limited by it nor identified with it, any more than I would want to do my dying in the bee's anterior part.

However that may be, absolute despair has no art, and I imagine the writing of a poem, in whatever mode, still betrays the existence of hope, which is why poetry is more and more chary of the conscious mind, in our age. And what the poem manages to find hope for may be part of what it keeps trying to say.

EAST OF THE SUN AND WEST OF THE MOON

Say the year is the year of the phoenix.
Ordinary sun and common moon,
Turn as they may, are too mysterious
Unless such as are neither sun nor moon
5   Assume their masks and orbits and evolve
Neither a solar nor a lunar story
But a tale that might be human. What is a man
That a man may recognize, unless the inhuman
Sun and moon, wearing the masks of a man,
10   Weave before him such a tale as he
—Finding his own face in the strange story—
Mistakes by metaphor and calls his own,
Smiling, as on a familiar mystery?
The moon was thin as a poor man's daughter

15 At the end of autumn. A white bear came walking
On a Thursday evening at the end of autumn,
Knocked at a poor man's door in a deep wood,
And, "Charity," when the man came he said,
"And the thin hand of a girl have brought me here.
20 Winter will come, and the vixen wind," he said,
"And what have you but too many mouths to feed,
Oh what have you but a coat like zither-strings
To ward that fury from your family?
But I though wintry shall be bountiful
25 Of furs and banquets, coins like summer days,
Grant me but the hand of your youngest daughter."

"By a swooning candle, in my porchless door,
While all I wedded or sired huddle behind me,
The night unceremonious with my hair,
30 I know I cut a poor figure," the man said;
"And I admit that your cajolery
(For opulence was once my setting-on)
Finds me not deaf; but I must ask my daughter.
And no, she says. But come again on Thursday:
35 She is more beautiful than the story goes,
And a girl who wants a week for her persuading
Merits that slow extravagance," he said.
Further in autumn by a week's persuading
The youngest girl on a white bear went riding.

40 The moon played in a painted elder tree;
He said, when they had gone a while, "We walk
In a night so white and black, how can you tell
My shoulder from a moon-struck hill, my shadow
From the towering darkness; are you not afraid?"
45 And, "You are thin and colorful who ride
Alone on a white and monstrous thing; suppose
I rose up savage in a desolate place;
Are you not afraid?" And, "What if I were to wander
Down a black ladder, in a trope of death,
50 Through seven doors all of black ice, and come
On a land of hyperbole, stiff with extremes;
Would it not make the hair rise on your head?"

The wind with moonlit teeth rippled and sulked
In the paper trees, but three times "No," she said.
55 "Oh then hold fast by the hair of my shoulders,"
He said; "hold fast my hair, my savage hair;
And let your shadow as we go hold fast
The hair of my shadow, and all will be well."
Later than owls, all night, a winter night,
60 They traveled then, until the screaming wind
Fell behind or dead, till no stars glittered

In the headlong dark; and each step dark and long
As falling in the valley of the blind;
Yet all the while she felt her yellow hair
65   Hang loose at her shoulders, as though she stood still.

They came before daylight to a stone hill
Steep as a pier glass, where no shrub grew,
Nor grass rustled, nor breeze stirred before dawn.
When the bear knocked, a door swung wide. Their eyes
70   Enormous with the dark, a hall they entered
That blazed between mirrors, between pilasters
Of yellow chrysolite; on walls of brass
Gold branches of dead genealogies
Clutched candles and wild torches whence the flames
75   Rose still as brilliants. Under a fiery
Garnet tree with leaves of glass, sunken
In a pool of sea-green beryl as in still water
A gold salmon hung. And no sound came.

The wall healed behind them. When she turned,
80   The wall steep as a pier glass, the door
Vanished like a face in ruffled water,
And they stood dumb in the echoing light
While no flame crackled, no water fell. They passed
Between the rows of burning, between the rings
85   Of extinct animals that stared from sockets
In the braziered walls; hour upon hour,
Hall upon blazing hall, and came at last
Through obsequious curtains to a closed room
Where she descended; at a beck of his head
90   A gold table leapt from the air; she dined
That night on lapwing and wine of pomegranates.

The bear had gone. She touched a silver bell.
She stood straightway in a white chamber
By a bed of lapis lazuli. Red agate
95   And yellow chrysolite the floors. A white
Carnelian window gave upon cut hills
Of amethyst and yellow serpentine
Pretending summer; when she stood naked there
Her nakedness from the lighted stones
100   Sprang a thousand times as girl or woman,
Child or staring hag. The lamps went black;
When she lay down to sleep, a young man came
Who stayed all night in the dark beside her
But was gone before dawn came to that country.

105   Nightly he came again. Once he said,
"I am the white bear, who once was a man;
In a christian body, in a green kingdom

One time I had dominion. Now I keep
Not so much as the shadow that I had,
110 And my own shape only by dark; by day
Compelled I am to that pale beast. Let it be
Ensample to your forbearance: here love
Must wander blind or with mistaken eyes,
For dissolution walks among the light
115 And vision is the sire of vanishing."
What love soever in the dark there were,
Always at daylight she wakened alone.

By day she walked in the espaliered garden
Among pheasants and clear flowers; she said,
120 "What if these pheasants amble in white glass,
Ducks strut ridiculous in stone, the streams
Slither nowhere in beryl; why should I
Complain of such inflexible content,
Presume to shudder at such serenity,
125 Who walk in some ancestral fantasy,
Lunar extravagance, or lost pagoda
That dreams of no discipline but indolence?
What shall be rigid but gems and details
While all dimensions dance in the same air?
130 And what am I if the story be not real?

But what it is," she said, "to wander in silence,
Though silence be a garden. What shall I say,
How chiseled the tongue soever, and how schooled
In sharp diphthongs and suasive rhetorics,
135 To the echoless air of this sufficiency?
Where should I find the sovereign aspirate
To rouse in this world a tinkle of syllables,
Or what shall I sing to crystal ears, and where
All songs drop in the air like stones; oh what
140 Shall I do while the white-tongued flowers shout
Impossible silence on the impossible air
But wander with my hands over my ears?
And what am I if the story be not real?

He says the place is innocent; and yet
145 I may not see his face; claims he is held
Equivocating between prince and beast
By the ministrations of an evil stepdame,
But such might be mere glittering deviltry.
Here is no nightly moon or tidal water
150 But mornings miming at mutability
Where all stands new at noon and nothing fades
Down the perfect amber of the afternoons;
All, simultaneous and unwearied, comes
Guesting again at evening. But a day

155 Must dwindle before dawn be real again;
And what am I if the story be not real?"

She said at night when he lay beside her,
"Why should I raise the singular dissent
Who delight in an undiminished country
160 Where all that was or shall be transitory
Stands whole again already? Yet I sigh
For snipes to whir and fall, for hawks to fall,
For one more mortal crimson that will fade,
For one glimpse of the twisted holly tree
165 Before my mother's door, and the short-lived
Wren by my mother's window, and the tame crane
Walking in shallow water. I would learn
Whether I dreamed then or walk now in a dream,
For what am I if the story be not real?"

170 Suddenly where no sound had been she heard
A distant lisp and crumble, like a wave,
Like the whisper of tidal water, emulous
Of its own whispers: his echoing heart. "Shall I
Pace an eternity of corridors,
175 Alone among sad topaz, the reflections
Flickering only on your emptiness,
And the soundlessness be like a sound of mourning,
That seemed a sound of joy? Nevertheless,
Go you shall if you wish; but promise,
180 Lest a malicious word undo us both,
Never to walk or talk alone," he said,
"With your mother, who is as wise as you."

It was a Sunday. Gold on the glass leaves.
She sat in the garden on the white bear's shoulders.
185 She touched a silver bell, and instantly
Saw the swaying of incorrigible meadows
Ripening, a green wind playful in barley,
The holly, contorted at her mother's door,
The fluttering wren—the brief feathers
190 Provisional about mortality—
At her mother's window, the tame crane walking
As though not real where the real shallows ran.
She had descended; the bear was gone;
She heard the whistling grass, and the holly leaves
195 Saying, "Your mother, who is wise as you."

She was greeted like a lost season.
Daylong she walked again in affluent summer,
But one day walked at last aside, and talked
Alone with her mother, who was wise as she.
200 "Equivocation between prince and beast,

The ministrations of an evil stepdame,
Might be a devilish tale; how could you tell,"
Her mother said, "should it be the devil's self
Or some marvel of ugliness you lay beside?
205 Take, better than advice, this end of candle
To light when he sleeps next you in the dark;
Only be careful that no drops fall."
The grass might whistle under the holly leaves.

On a day of no clouds he came to fetch her.
210 It was a Sunday. A soft wind stroking
The fields already white almost to harvest.
"Shall we not ride a while in the mortal air
Before we go," he asked, "for the love of fading?
But wish, when you are weary, for the sound
215 Of the silver bell, and we shall instantly
Be home again. Did all happen as I said?"
"Yes," she said, "how might it be otherwise?"
"Did you, then, walk aside with your mother?" he asked;
"Did you listen to your mother's advice?"
220 "Oh no," she said. "Then all may yet be well."
But she wished for the sound of the silver bell.

That night when she was sure he slept
She rose in the dark and struck light
To the end of candle, and held it above his face.
225 What blaze was this, what prince shaming with beauty
The sun peerless at noon? The dazzled stones
Seemed each a blond particular summer wringing
In the one thirst the lion and the nightingale.
The shadows bowed; they fell down amazed.
230 "And I with my foolish arm upraised . . .
But love so beggars me of continence,
Either I must kiss him or die," she said,
And bent, therewith, and kissed his head. Three times
The tallow folly from the candle fell.

235 "Oh why must all hope resolve to vanity?"
Waking, he cried; "Why could you not entertain
A curious patience but for one whole year,
For then had we been saved, and my spell broken.
Now this kingdom must shatter and I depart
240 For the wheeling castle of my stepmother
And marry a princess with a nose three ells long,
When I might have married you." "Oh love," she cried,
"May I not learn the way and follow you?"
"There is no way there that a body might follow:
245 Farther than dreams that palace lies,
East of the sun and west of the moon, girt
With rage of stars for sea. There no one comes."

She seemed to sleep, for she woke again
On a usual morning in a different world,
250   Bright grass blowing, birds loud in the trees;
That precious kingdom, that charmed lover
Gone. She was kneeling under a willow
In her salt tears. When she had called
And cried till she was weary she walked on
255   Slowly, walked the length of a day, and seemed
None the more weary for all her walking
But traveled, it seemed, in a landscape of exceptions
Where no evening came but a shadowy
Skeptical bird who settled in a tree
260   And sang, "All magic is but metaphor."

Under a crag, when it should have been evening,
Where there should have been shadows, by an apple tree,
She saw a hag who laughed to herself and tossed
A golden apple. "Good day, hag," she said.
265   "Can you tell me how I might find the castle
That lies east of the sun and west of the moon?"
"Whoever comes and calls me hag, haggard
May she sit also, unless it be the lady
Who should marry the prince there. Are you she?
270   Yes, she says. Yet the way I cannot tell.
Take, rather, this gold apple, mount this horse
To ride to ask my sister, and once there,
Tap him behind the left ear; he will come home."

Long she rode as the patience of stones
275   And saw again, when it should have been evening,
A hag who played with a golden carding comb.
"If withering were a signature of wisdom,
I were a miracle of sagacity,"
She said, "my brow invisible with laurel,
280   But I am bare parchment where a word might be,
And any road that might lead to that castle
Is a thing I never knew. All I can offer
By way of blessing is this gold carding comb,
But you might ask my sister; take my own horse.
285   When he has brought you where she sits, tap him
Behind the left ear; he will come home again."

The third hag said, "I have been young as you,
And shall be so again, unless the stars
Tell lies in the shifty dark, but whether
290   More pleasure is to be young and pass for fair
Or to be haggard and seem knowledgeable,
I am too wise to choose, and yet the way
That castle lies is a thing I never knew;
But there you will come, late or never. I give you,

295 Beside that wisdom, this golden spinning wheel,
And if you wish, you may ride my own horse
To ask the East Wind. When you are there,
Tap the beast once behind the left ear,
And he will be off and come to me again."

300 Oh then she rode such waste of calendars
She should have found the end of weariness
But came instead to the house of the East Wind.
"Oh Wind," she called, "which way would you blow,
Which way might I follow to come to the castle
305 That lies east of the sun and west of the moon?"
"I, bold of wing beyond the glimpse of morning,
Have found the dark where no birds sleep,
Have shivered and returned, have many times
Heard of that castle, but never blown so far
310 Nor learned the way. But I have a brother," he said,
"An infinite voyager: be pleased to sit
Between my shoulders and I shall take you there."

Though faster then than summoned ghosts they flew,
Long was that journey as the wisdom of owls
315 Before they came to the roof of the West Wind.
"For all I am prodigious of voyages,
Whistle heyday and holiday, make light
Of the poor limbs of summer and have sailed
Beyond the hueless sighing of drowned days
320 Into the dark where no shades sigh,
Have shuddered and come home a different way,
Unholy be the whisper of my name
If ever I were a wind about that tower
Or knew the way; but come with me," he said:
325 "I have a brother who has blown further than I."

"I might shriek till the world was small
As a turtle's egg; I have whipped my savagery
A pride of days beyond where the world ends
In burning, into the dark where no flames twitch,
330 Have blessed myself and hastily blown elsewhere,
But never glimpsed wrack nor wisp of that castle,
And whether there be any such place at all
I gravely doubt; but I have a brother
Wields the gale that flaps the chittering dead
335 Beyond where the world ends in ice; be sure
Unless his storm can shiver your conundrum
It is a thing unknown." The South Wind's wings
Howled, till they came to the door of the North Wind.

"Oh once," he roared, "I blew an aspen leaf
340 Beyond the glimmering world, over

The glass eaves of time, into that dark
Where no ice gleams; there, bristling, found that other
Wind of fear, but a rage stayed me until
The star-lashed sea, until I found the castle
345 That lies east of the sun and west of the moon.
But never I told a soul, for there I lay
Three weeks, frail as the aspen leaf, on the wild
Shore before I dared blow home again.
But if you be the lady that you claim,
350 Stay while I rest tonight and I shall try
Tomorrow if I can fly so far again."

Who has outflown the nightmare? Yet fast
Almost as she they flew in the morning
Beyond all boreal flickerings, headlong
355 Over the glass eaves of time and found
The breathless dark where no souls stir,
But hair in another wind; broke, almost blind,
At last over a mad famished sea;
Then long as unspoken love they whirled.
360 But he wearied. The waves snapped at his knees,
The dog-toothed waves, till he whispered, "My wings fail,"
Sinking. But she cried, "I see a white shore,
A shadowy pinnacle that may be the castle
That lies east of the sun and west of the moon."

365 What if the breakers gulped and craved his thighs?
Where he had set her on the white shore
He fell forward and slept. Already
A foot beyond the frustrate sea there drowsed,
Silence of forests, indolent, rimmed
370 With flutter of birches like birds in the tender
Sun, with thirsty osiers, pale hawthorn,
Perpetual apple trees, the capricious-limbed.
She saw in that light how the castle vanished
Above fancy among faithful clouds,
375 Saw the door, but nowhere near the door she went,
But sat under a guelder-rose and sang
"Ah, well-a-day," and played with the gold apple.

Till from an upper window of the castle
A princess with a nose three ells long
380 Called, "Who are you, singing 'well-a-day'
Under my window; and oh what will you take
And give me that golden apple?" "I am a lady
Of foreign ways singing to my own hair
A dirge for diminishing, under a pale tree,
385 Am a hazard waif blown from the scapegrace sea,
Am an aspen leaf; but nothing you own
Will I exchange for this gold apple,

Unless it should be that I might sleep tonight
Alone all night in his room with the prince
400   Who lives in this castle." And that could be arranged.

But she was returned, for earnest of gold,
Only a sleeping body and a sleep:
When she was led at evening into his room
Already he lay sleeping; for all she cried
405   His name aloud, for all she cried and kissed
His face and forehead, all night he lay sleeping.
What might she be but chorus to a dream,
But one who strokes a dream of chrysolite,
Glass pheasants, ducks ridiculous in stone,
410   A gold salmon in a beryl pool,
As reliquary, as meager communicance
Till daylight, then departs and sits again
By the tower and plays with the gold carding comb?

"Nothing whatever will I take," she said
415   When the princess called, "for my gold carding comb,
But to sleep tonight by the same prince."
But where was the unrecking fantasy,
The concord of distraught belief
She had named for love and understood by love,
420   If when she lay, and the second time, beside him
Nothing would answer to her kiss but sleep?
Must she before she wake still find a dream
Wherein she lay beside him, and he, waking,
Dreamed still of her? Although beside him, dream
425   Of yet more fortunate wakenings; till daylight;
Then sing by a gold spinning wheel, dreaming?

"I am a thirsty lady wishing I walked
Beside no water but a pool of beryl;
I sing to drown the silence of far flowers
430   And though I am deaf to all sounds other
Than a deafening heart in a distant room, I dream
I wander with my hands over my ears."
She argued with the princess as yesterday,
Parted with the gold spinning wheel. Oh must
435   Love's many mansions, the patient honeycomb
Of hope unlearn their heavens and at a sleep
Triply be consigned to cerements,
Or must salvation shrink to the unlikely
Monstrance of another's wakening?

440   Suppose the requisite vigil. Say one lay
Two nights awake beside the prince's room,
Heard crying there, as toward a vanishing spectre,
Told the prince, and he, thus wise against potions

The third night, sleepless, with wide arms received her,
445   Calling, "Oh love, is blessedness a risk
So delicate in time, that it should be
Tonight you find me? Tomorrow, always tomorrow
It is that my stepmother was to prevail,
It is that I was to marry that other princess.
450   But we are the sense of dawn beneath pretence
Of an order of darkness. Now lie in wisdom, mindful
Only of love, and leave to me tomorrow."

In the morning, to proud stepdame and coy princess,
"Call me a wry intransigent, a glass
455   Of fickle weathers, but what care I," he said,
"For decorum, though it be my wedding day?
Shall I be yoked to an unproven woman?
But who she may be can wash this shirt of mine,
Stained with three drops of tallow, white again
460   As once it was, she and no other lady
Will I marry. All wet the hands who wish;
All beat the board; all wring the linen; all wash
In the one water." Howsoever the princess
Dipped and wrung, the stains ran gray; or stepdame
465   Scrubbed, the shirt grew black as knavery.

"There is a girl outside the castle door,"
One said who loitered there and watched; "perhaps
She if she tried might wash it white again."
But vexed stepdame and angry princess
470   Raged then and screamed, "No no! Shall we have a tattered
Waif with outlandish ways for rival, and we
With our royal hands in water?" Yet the prince
Answered, "Let her come in, whoever she be."
She dipped the linen and once drew it forth
475   White as a leper; drew it forth again
White as blown snow; a third time raised it
Spotless, white as the violent moon; she said,
"How should I not, since all pallor is mine?"

The moon was musing in her high chamber
480   Among nine thousand mirrors. "Oh what am I,"
She cried, "but a trick of light, and tropically?
I walk in a wild charactry of night,
In a game of darkness figurative with tapers,
Toying with apples, and come upon myself
485   More often than is meet for sanity.
Oh, who would be shown, save in analogy,
—What for gold handsels and marvelous equerry—
As three hags sitting under an apple tree?
But I walk multifarious among
490   My baubles and horses; unless I go in a mask
How shall I know myself among my faces?"

"All metaphor," she said, "is magic. Let
Me be diverted in a turning lantern,
Let me in that variety be real.
495 But let the story be an improvisation
Continually, and through all repetition
Differ a little from itself, as though
Mistaken; and I a lady with foreign ways
To sing therein to my own hair." To the sun,
500 "You who tomorrow are my Pentecost,
Come dance with me—oh but be white, be wintry;
Oh lest I fall an utter prey to mirrors,
Be a white bear," she said "and come a-walking,
And ask my hand. I am a peasant's daughter."

505 Is it for nothing that a troupe of days
Makes repeated and perpetual rummage
In the lavish vestry; or should sun and moon,
Finding mortality too mysterious,
Naked and with no guise but its own,
510 —Unless one of immortal gesture come
And by a mask should show it probable—
Believe a man, but not believe his story?
Say the year is the year of the phoenix.
Now, even now, over the rock hill
515 The tropical, the lucid moon, turning
Her mortal guises in the eye of a man,
Creates the image in which the world is.

TO MY BROTHER HANSON
B. JAN. 28, 1926   D. JAN. 28, 1926

My elder,
Born into death like a message into a bottle,
The tide
Keeps coming in empty on the only shore.
5 Maybe it has lovers but it has few friends.
It is never still but it keeps its counsel, and

If I address you whose curious stars
Climbed to the tops of their houses and froze,
It is in hope of no
10 Answer, but as so often, merely
For want of another, for
I have seen catastrophe taking root in the mirror,
And why waste my words there?

Yes, now the roads themselves are shattered
15 As though they had fallen from a height, and the sky
Is cracked like varnish. Hard to believe,

Our family tree
Seems to be making its mark everywhere.
I carry my head high
On a pike that shall be nameless.

Even so, we had to give up honor entirely,
But I do what I can. I am patient
With the woes of the cupboards, and God knows—
I keep the good word close to hand like a ticket.
I feed the wounded lights in their cages.
I wake up at night on the penultimate stroke, and with
My eyes still shut I remember to turn the thorn
In the breast of the bird of darkness.
I listen to the painful song
Dropping away into sleep.

                    Blood
Is supposed to be thicker. You were supposed to be there
When the habits closed in pushing
Their smiles in front of them, when I was filled
With something else, like a thermometer,
When the moment of departure, standing
On one leg, like a sleeping stork, by the doorway,
Put down the other foot and opened its eye.
I
Got away this time for a while. I've come
Again to the whetted edge of myself where I
Can hear the hollow waves breaking like
Bottles in the dark. What about it? Listen, I've

Had enough of this. Is there nobody
Else in the family
To take care of the tree, to nurse the mirror,
To fix up a bite for hope when the old thing
Comes to the door,
To say to the pans of the balance
Rise up and walk?

A Scale in May

Now all my teachers are dead except silence
I am trying to read what the five poplars are writing
On the void

Of all the beasts to man alone death brings justice
But I desire
To kneel in a doorway empty except for the song

Who made time provided also its fools
Strapped in watches and with ballots for their choices
Crossing the frontiers of invisible kingdoms

10 To succeed consider what is as though it were past
    Deem yourself inevitable and take credit for it
    If you find you no longer believe enlarge the temple

    Through the day the nameless stars keep passing the door
    That have come all that way out of death
15 Without questions

    The walls of light shudder and an owl wakes in the heart
    I cannot call upon words
    The sun goes away to set elsewhere

    Before nightfall colorless petals blow under the doors
20 And the shadows
    Recall their ancestors in the house beyond death

    At the end of its procession through the stone
    Falling
    The water remembers to laugh

James Wright (1927-   )

Born in Martins Ferry, Ohio, James Wright received his B.A. from
Kenyon College in 1952, an M.A. from the University of Vienna in
1954, and a Ph.D. from the University of Washington in 1959. His
first book of poems, *The Green Wall,* won the Yale Series of Younger
Poets competition in 1956. He has taught at the University of Minnesota and was Lecturer in English at Macalaster College in 1964-1965
and a Guggenheim Fellow in 1965-1966. Married in 1952, he is the
father of two children. On the voice of the poet he writes:

> In the work of the best poets that I know, the voice of poetry is an
> articulation of true feeling and thought, at once personal and gen-
> eral, shaped in such a way as to evoke from many readers an equally
> personal response. Any poet begins with the effort to be true to
> himself. But the poets who matter most are those who discover
> and demonstrate that the effort to be true to themselves inevitably
> results in being true to others. Whatever is most truly and honestly
> personal becomes what is most widely and sympathetically humane.
> Among the innumerable privacies of our lives it would be hard
> to imagine any secret more painfully and joyfully sheltered than
> the lullabies which we sing to children; and yet many of the most
> effective of these songs were anonymously composed long before
> contemporary parents were born. I cannot think of any book of
> poetry whose voice touches and wakens me more personally than
> the *Oxford Dictionary of Nursery Rhymes* edited by Iona and Peter
> Opie; and yet the very intensity of my personal response enables
> me to enter, if only for a moment, into a community of human
> awareness—into what Dr. James Sutherland calls the invisible
> church of men everywhere.

The poetic principle which I am describing is most forcefully
articulated by Samuel Johnson in his *Preface to Shakespeare:*

Nothing can please many or please long but just representations of general nature.
Particular manners can be known to few, and few only can judge how nearly they
are copied. The irregular combinations of fanciful invention may delight awhile,
by that novelty of which the common satiety of life sends us all in quest. But the
pleasures of sudden wonder are soon exhausted, and the mind can only repose on
the stability of truth.

I admire Johnson's words for their power of integrating a guid-
ing principle of poetic craft with an affirmation of imaginative
purpose. In order to be true to himself, a poet must be true to the
truths of his time. He cannot do that without struggling to address
himself to the truths of his readers' lives.

A Song for the Middle of the Night

By way of explaining to my son the following
curse by Eustace Deschamps: "Happy is he who
has no children; for babies bring nothing but
crying and stench."

Now first of all he means the night
   You beat the crib and cried
And brought me spinning out of bed
   To powder your backside.
5 I rolled your buttocks over
   And I could not complain:
Legs up, la la, legs down, la la,
   Back to sleep again.

Now second of all he means the day
10   You dabbled out of doors
And dragged a dead cat Billy-be-damned
   Across the kitchen floors.
I rolled your buttocks over
   And made you sing for pain:
15 Legs up, la la, legs down, la la,
   Back to sleep again.

But third of all my father once
   Laid me across his knee
And solved the trouble when he beat
20   The yowling out of me.
He rocked me on his shoulder
   When razor straps were vain:
Legs up, la la, legs down, la la,
   Back to sleep again.

25 So roll upon your belly, boy,
    And bother being cursed.
You turn the household upside down,
    But you are not the first.
Deschamps the poet blubbered too,
30   For all his fool disdain:
Legs up, la la, legs down, la la,
    Back to sleep again.

To a Fugitive

The night you got away, I dreamed you rose
Out of the earth to lean on a young tree.
Then they were there, hulking the moon away,
The great dogs rooting, snuffing up the grass.
5 You raise a hand, hungry to hold your lips
Out of the wailing air; but lights begin
Spidering the ground; oh they come closing in,
The beam searches your face like fingertips.

Hurry, Maguire, hammer the body down,
10 Crouch to the wall again, shackle the cold
Machine guns and the sheriff and the cars:
Divide the bright bars of the cornered bone,
Strip, run for it, break the last law, unfold,
Dart down the alley, race between the stars.

Morning Hymn to a Dark Girl

Summoned to desolation by the dawn,
I climb the bridge over the water, see
The Negro mount the driver's cabin and wave
Goodbye to the glum cop across the canal,
5 Goodbye to the flat face and empty eyes
Made human one more time. That uniform
Shivers and dulls against the pier, is stone.

Now in the upper world, the buses drift
Over the bridge, the gulls collect and fly,
10 Blown by the rush of rose; aseptic girls
Powder their lank deliberate faces, mount
The fog under the billboards. Over the lake
The windows of the rich waken and yawn.
Light blows across the city, dune on dune.

15 Caught by the scruff of the neck, and thrown out here
To the pale town, to the stone, to burial,
I celebrate you, Betty, flank and breast
Rich to the yellow silk of bed and floors;
Now half awake, your body blossoming trees;
20 One arm beneath your neck, your legs uprisen,
You blow dark thighs back, back into the dark.

Your shivering ankles skate the scented air;
Betty, burgeoning your golden skin, you poise
Tracing gazelles and tigers on your breasts,
25 Deep in the jungle of your bed you drowse;
Fine muscles of the rippling panthers move
And snuggle at your calves; under your arms
Mangoes and melons yearn; and glittering slowly,
Quick parakeets trill in your heavy trees,
30 O everywhere, Betty, between your boughs.

Pity the rising dead who fear the dark.
Soft Betty, locked from snickers in a dark
Brothel, dream on; scatter the yellow corn
Into the wilderness, and sleep all day.
35 For the leopards leap into the open grass,
Bananas, lemons fling air, fling odor, fall.
And, gracing darkly the dark light, you flow
Out of the grove to laugh at dreamy boys,
You greet the river with a song so low
40 No lover on a boat can hear, you slide
Silkily to the water; where you rinse
Your fluted body, fearless; though alive
Orangutans sway from the leaves and gaze,
Crocodiles doze along the oozy shore.

A BREATH OF AIR

I walked, when love was gone,
Out of the human town,
For an easy breath of air.
Beyond a break in the trees,
5 Beyond the hangdog lives
Of old men, beyond girls:
The tall stars held their peace.
Looking in vain for lies
I turned, like earth, to go.
10 An owl's wings hovered, bare
On the moon's hills of snow.

And things were as they were.

In Shame and Humiliation

He will launch a curse upon the world, and as
only man can curse (it is his privilege, the primary
distinction between him and other animals),
maybe by his curse alone he will attain his object—
that is, convince himself that he is a man and not
a piano-key!

DOSTOYEVSKY, NOTES FROM UNDERGROUND

What can a man do that a beast cannot,
A bird, a reptile, any fiercer thing?
   He can amaze the ground
With anger never hissed in a snake's throat
5   Or past a bitch's fang,
Though, suffocate, he cannot make a sound.

He can out-rage the forked tongue with a word,
The iron forged of his pain, over and over,
   Till the cold blade can fall
10 And beak an enemy's heart quick as a bird,
   And then retire to cover,
To vines of hair, declivities of skull.

Outright the snake, faster than man, can kill.
A mongrel's teeth can snarl as man's cannot.
15   And a bird, unbodied soul
Soaring and dazzling, in the cloud at will
   Outbeautifies the flight
Of halt man's clavicles that flop and wheel.

Their cries last longer. Sinew of wing and coil,
20 Or sprung thighs of hounds impinge their iron
   Easy and quick, to leap
Over the brooks, the miles and days, like oil
   Flung on a surge of green.
A man limps into nothing more than sleep.

25 But under the dream he always dreams too late,
That stark abounding dream of wretchedness
   Where stones and very trees
Ignore his name, and crows humiliate,
   And fiends below the face,
30 Serpents, women, and dogs dance to deny his face—

He will not deny, he will not deny his own.
Thrashing in lakes or pools of broken glass,
   He hunches over to look
And feel his mouth, his nostrils, feel of the bone,
35   A man's ultimate face:
The individual bone, that burns like ice.

That fire, that searing cold is what I claim:
What makes me man, that dogs can never share,
   Woman or brilliant bird,
40   The beaks that mock but cannot speak the names
   Of the blind rocks, of the stars.
Sprawling in dark, I burn my sudden pride.

Let my veins wither now, my words revolt
Serpent or bird or pure untroubled mind.
45   I will avow my face
Unto my face and, through the spirit's vault,
   Deliberate underground,
Devour the locusts of my bitterness.

That angel, wheeled upon my heart, survives,
50   Nourished by food the righteous cannot eat
   And loathe to move among.
They die, fastidious, while the spirit thrives
   Out of its own defeat.
The pure, the pure! will never live so long.

AT THE EXECUTED MURDERER'S GRAVE
FOR J. L. D.

Why should we do this? What good is it to us?
Above all, how can we do such a thing? How can
it possibly be done?

                    FREUD

1
My name is James A. Wright, and I was born
Twenty-five miles from this infected grave,
In Martins Ferry, Ohio, where one slave
To Hazel-Atlas Glass became my father.
5   He tried to teach me kindness. I return
Only in memory now, aloof, unhurried,
To dead Ohio, where I might lie buried,
Had I not run away before my time.
Ohio caught George Doty. Clean as lime,
10   His skull rots empty here. Dying's the best
Of all the arts men learn in a dead place.
I walked here once. I made my loud display,
Leaning for language on a dead man's voice.
Now sick of lies, I turn to face the past.
15   I add my easy grievance to the rest:

2
Doty, if I confess I do not love you,
Will you let me alone? I burn for my own lies.
The nights electrocute my fugitive,

My mind. I run like the bewildered mad
20 At St. Clair Sanitarium, who lurk,
Arch and cunning, under the maple trees,
Pleased to be playing guilty after dark.
Staring to bed, they croon self-lullabies.
Doty, you make me sick. I am not dead.
25 I croon my tears at fifty cents per line.

3

Idiot, he demanded love from girls,
And murdered one. Also, he was a thief.
He left two women, and a ghost with child.
The hair, foul as a dog's upon his head,
30 Made such revolting Ohio animals
Fitter for vomit than a kind man's grief.
I waste no pity on the dead that stink,
And no love's lost between me and the crying
Drunks of Belaire, Ohio, where police
35 Kick at their kidneys till they die of drink.
Christ may restore them whole, for all of me.
Alive and dead, those giggling muckers who
Saddled my nightmares thirty years ago
Can do without my widely printed sighing
40 Over their pains with paid sincerity.
I do not pity the dead, I pity the dying.

4

I pity myself, because a man is dead.
If Belmont County killed him, what of me?
His victims never loved him. Why should we?
45 And yet, nobody had to kill him either.
It does no good to woo the grass, to veil
The quicklime hole of a man's defeat and shame.
Nature-lovers are gone. To hell with them.
I kick the clods away, and speak my name.

5

50 This grave's gash festers. Maybe it will heal,
When all are caught with what they had to do
In fear of love, when every man stands still
By the last sea,
And the princes of the sea come down
55 To lay away their robes, to judge the earth
And its dead, and we dead stand undefended everywhere,
And my bodies—father and child and unskilled criminal—
Ridiculously kneel to bare my scars,
My sneaking crimes, to God's unpitying stars.

6

60 Staring politely, they will not mark my face
From any murderer's, buried in this place.
Why should they? We are nothing but a man.

7

Doty, the rapist and the murderer,
Sleeps in a ditch of fire, and cannot hear;
65   And where, in earth or hell's unholy peace,
Men's suicides will stop, God knows, not I.
Angels and pebbles mock me under trees.
Earth is a door I cannot even face.
Order be damned, I do not want to die,
70   Even to keep Belaire, Ohio, safe.
The hackles on my neck are fear, not grief.
(Open, dungeon! Open, roof of the ground!)
I hear the last sea in the Ohio grass,
Heaving a tide of gray disastrousness.
75   Wrinkles of winter ditch the rotted face
Of Doty, killer, imbecile, and thief:
Dirt of my flesh, defeated, underground.

EISENHOWER'S VISIT TO FRANCO, 1959

". . . we die of cold, and not of darkness."
UNAMUNO

The American hero must triumph over
The forces of darkness.
He has flown through the very light of heaven
And come down in the slow dusk
5   Of Spain.

Franco stands in a shining circle of police.
His arms open in welcome.
He promises all dark things
Will be hunted down.

10   State police yawn in the prisons.
Antonio Machado follows the moon
Down a road of white dust,
To a cave of silent children
Under the Pyrenees.
15   Wine darkens in stone jars in villages.
Wine sleeps in the mouths of old men, it is a dark red color.

Smiles glitter in Madrid.
Eisenhower has touched hands with Franco, embracing
In a glare of photographers.
20   Clean new bombers from America muffle their engines
And glide down now.
Their wings shine in the searchlights
Of bare fields,
In Spain.

A Prayer to Escape from the Market Place

I renounce the blindness of the magazines.
I want to lie down under a tree.
This is the only duty that is not death.
This is the everlasting happiness
Of small winds.
Suddenly,
A pheasant flutters, and I turn
Only to see him vanishing at the damp edge
Of the road.

The Minneapolis Poem
to john logan

1

I wonder how many old men last winter
Hungry and frightened by namelessness prowled
The Mississippi shore
Lashed blind by the wind, dreaming
Of suicide in the river.
The police remove their cadavers by daybreak
And turn them in somewhere.
Where?
How does the city keep lists of its fathers
Who have no names?
By Nicollet Island I gaze down at the dark water
So beautifully slow.
I wish my brothers good luck
And a warm grave.

2

The Chippewa young men
Stab one another shrieking
Jesus Christ.
Split lipped homosexuals limp in terror of assault.
High school backfields search under benches
Near the Post Office. Their faces are the rich
Raw bacon without eyes.
The Walker Art Center crowd stare
At one another,
And the Guthrie Theater crowd stare
At the Guthrie Theater.

3

Tall Negro girls from Chicago
Listen to light songs.
They know when the supposed patron
Is a plainclothesman.

30 A cop's palm
Is a roach dangling down the scorched fangs
Of a light bulb.
The soul of a cop's eyes
Is an eternity of Sunday daybreak in the suburbs
35 Of Juarez, Mexico.

4

The legless beggars are gone, carried away
By white birds.
The Artificial Limbs Exchange is gutted
And sown with lime.
40 The whalebone crutches and hand-me-down trusses
Huddle together dreaming in a desolation
Of dry groins.
I think of poor men astonished to waken
Exposed in broad daylight by the blade
45 Of a strange plough.

5

All over the walls of comb cells
Automobiles perfumed and blindered
Consent with a mutter of high good humor
To take their two naps a day.
50 Without sound windows glide back
Into dusk.
The sockets of a thousand blind bee graves tier upon tier
Tower not quite toppling.
There are men in this city who labor dawn after dawn
55 To sell me my death.

6

But I could not bear
To allow my poor brother my body to die
In Minneapolis.
The old man Walt Whitman our countryman
60 Is now in America our country
Dead.
But he was not buried in Minneapolis
At least.
And no more may I be
65 Please God.

7

I want to be lifted up
By some great white bird unknown to the police,
And soar for a thousand miles and be carefully hidden
Modest and golden as one last corn grain,
70 Stored with the secrets of the wheat and the mysterious lives
Of the unnamed poor.

In Response to a Rumor That the Oldest Whorehouse in Wheeling, W. Va., Has Been Condemned

I will grieve alone,
As I strolled alone, years ago, down along
The Ohio shore.
I hid in the hobo jungle weeds
Up stream from the sewer main,
Pondering, gazing.

I saw, down river,
At Twenty-third and Water Streets
By the vinegar works,
The doors open in early evening.
Swinging their purses, the women
Poured down the long street to the river
And into the river.

I do not know how it was
They could drown every evening.
What time near dawn did they climb up the other shore,
Drying their wings?

For the river at Wheeling, W. Va.,
Has only two shores:
The one in hell, the other
In Bridgeport, Ohio.

And nobody would commit suicide, only
To find beyond death
Bridgeport, Ohio.

The Queen from the Cold Haunch of the Moon

I breathe bouquet of onions from
A pensioner's cell beyond my walls.
Between the dark and the day light
She wakes, my earnest of old night,
My landlady, and prowls the halls,
Sniffing. Deliberate queen, she flares
Supremely thin fastidious
Nostrils, I swear to God she does.
I see her, though my door's well shut,
Chained within, bolted without.
She smiles the evening to me.
My elbows ache, I curse the rain,
She flicks her tongue, she smiles again,
I brace my midriff, undreamed of shears
Haggle and saw my knees, my spine

Clenches, I damn her gods, she mine,
I dribble a bright gold spittle, I
Beg her pity my few gray hairs,
I sprawl wheezing, I shrill, I die,
20   I pay the rent. She goes downstairs.

RIP

It can't be the passing of time that casts
That white shadow across the waters
Just offshore.
I shiver a little, with the evening.
5   I turn down the steep path to find
What's left of the river gold.
I whistle a dog lazily, and lazily
A bird whistles me.
Close by a big river, I am alive in my own country,
10   I am home again.
Yes: I lived here, and here, and my name,
That I carved young, with a girl's, is healed over, now,
And lies sleeping beneath the inward sky
Of a tree's skin, close to the quick.
15   It's best to keep still.
But:
There goes that bird that whistled me down here
To the river a moment ago.
Who is he? A little white barn owl from Hudson's Bay,
20   Flown out of his range here, and lost?
Oh, let him be home here, and, if he wants to,
He can be the body that casts
That white shadow across the waters
Just offshore.

Anne Sexton (1928-   )

Anne Sexton was born in Newton, Massachusetts, grew up in
Wellesley, and was a student of Robert Lowell at Boston University.
She has had a mental breakdown, and recovered. With her husband
and two daughters, she lives in Weston, Massachusetts. She has been a
Robert Frost Fellow at The Bread Loaf Writers Conference and a
recipient of a traveling fellowship from the American Academy of
Arts and Letters. Here is her comment on the voice of the poet:

> To begin with, I think it is a kind of prostitution (or perhaps might
> I do better to call it a small advertisement?) for the poet to try to
> tell how or why he might be distinctive. For me to talk about "my

voice" is an afterthought. I never meant it to happen. Both my face and my voice belong to me and although I certainly admire others I seem to be stuck with my own. Life gets mapped onto your face as you grow, as you age. My poems, despite a highly motivated wish to take on other styles and "voices" keep right on singing the same old song. The influences, such as they are, seem to be invisible to all critics for I have not heard them mentioned in connection with my work.

Many of my poems are written in the first person, or close to it, and yet they are not always my story. I try to assume, for a moment, someone else's life. But no matter how much I try to get inside their mouth, the poem itself ends up sounding like mine. As in this collection surely I have not been *The Farmer's Wife* and in *The Truth the Dead Know* perhaps it did not happen quite that way. Thus I would prefer not to be praised or blamed for some brutally frank documentary of my life. Truth is not always factual or logical. I think, in my case, it is associative.

MUSIC SWIMS BACK TO ME

Wait Mister. Which way is home?
They turned the light out
and the dark is moving in the corner.
There are no sign posts in this room,
5   four ladies, over eighty,
in diapers every one of them.
La la la, Oh music swims back to me
and I can feel the tune they played
the night they left me
10   in this private institution on a hill.

Imagine it. A radio playing
and everyone here was crazy.
I liked it and danced in a circle.
Music pours over the sense
15   and in a funny way
music sees more than I.
I mean it remembers better;

remembers the first night here.
It was the strangled cold of November;
20   even the stars were strapped in the sky
and that moon too bright
forking through the bars to stick me
with a singing in the head.
I have forgotten all the rest.

25   They lock me in this chair at eight a.m.
and there are no signs to tell the way,

just the radio beating to itself
and the song that remembers
more than I. Oh, la la la,
30   this music swims back to me.
The night I came I danced a circle
and was not afraid.
Mister?

ELIZABETH GONE

1

You lay in the nest of your real death,
Beyond the print of my nervous fingers
Where they touched your moving head;
Your old skin puckering, your lungs' breath
5   Grown baby short as you looked up last
At my face swinging over the human bed,
And somewhere you cried, *let me go let me go.*

You lay in the crate of your last death,
But were not you, not finally you.
10   They have stuffed her cheeks, I said;
This clay hand, this mask of Elizabeth
Are not true. From within the satin
And the suede of this inhuman bed,
Something cried, *let me go let me go.*

2

15   They gave me your ash and bony shells,
Rattling like gourds in the cardboard urn,
Rattling like stones that their oven had blest.
I waited you in the cathedral of spells
And I waited you in the country of the living,
20   Still with the urn crooned to my breast,
When something cried, *let me go let me go.*

So I threw out your last bony shells
And heard me scream for the look of you,
Your apple face, the simple crèche
25   Of your arms, the August smells
Of your skin. Then I sorted your clothes
And the loves you had left, Elizabeth,
Elizabeth, until you were gone.

THE FARMER'S WIFE

From the hodge porridge
of their country lust,

their local life in Illinois,
where all their acres look
5   like a sprouting broom factory,
they name just ten years now
that she has been his habit;
as again tonight he'll say
honey bunch let's go
10   and she will not say how there
must be more to living
than this brief bright bridge
of the raucous bed or even
the slow braille touch of him
15   like a heavy god grown light,
that old pantomime of love
that she wants although
it leaves her still alone,
built back again at last,
20   mind's apart from him, living
her own self in her own words
and hating the sweat of the house
they keep when they finally lie
each in separate dreams
25   and then how she watches him,
still strong in the blowzy bag
of his usual sleep while
her young years bungle past
their same marriage bed
30   and she wishes him cripple, or poet,
or even lonely, or sometimes,
better, my lover, dead.

RINGING THE BELLS

And this is the way they ring
the bells in Bedlam
and this is the bell-lady
who comes each Tuesday morning
5   to give us a music lesson
and because the attendants make you go
and because we mind by instinct,
like bees caught in the wrong hive,
we are the circle of the crazy ladies
10   who sit in the lounge of the mental house
and smile at the smiling woman
who passes us each a bell,
who points at my hand
that holds my bell, E flat,
15   and this is the gray dress next to me
who grumbles as if it were special

to be old, to be old,
and this is the small hunched squirrel girl
on the other side of me
20 who picks at the hairs over her lip,
who picks at the hairs over her lip all day,
and this is how the bells really sound,
as untroubled and clean
as a workable kitchen,
25 and this is always my bell responding
to my hand that responds to the lady
who points at me, E flat;
and although we are no better for it,
they tell you to go. And you do.

THE TRUTH THE DEAD KNOW
FOR MY MOTHER, BORN MARCH 1902, DIED MARCH 1959
AND MY FATHER, BORN FEBRUARY 1900, DIED JUNE 1959

Gone, I say and walk from church,
refusing the stiff procession to the grave,
letting the dead ride alone in the hearse.
It is June. I am tired of being brave.

5 We drive to the Cape. I cultivate
myself where the sun gutters from the sky,
where the sea swings in like an iron gate
and we touch. In another country people die.

My darling, the wind falls in like stones
10 from the whitehearted water and when we touch
we enter touch entirely. No one's alone.
Men kill for this, or for as much.

And what of the dead? They lie without shoes
in their stone boats. They are more like stone
15 than the sea would be if it stopped. They refuse
to be blessed, throat, eye and knucklebone.

THE STARRY NIGHT

That does not keep me from having a terrible
need of—shall I say the word—religion. Then
I go out at night to paint the stars.
  VINCENT VAN GOGH IN A LETTER TO HIS BROTHER

The town does not exist
except where one black-haired tree slips
up like a drowned woman into the hot sky.
The town is silent. The night boils with eleven stars.

APPENDIX A

A NOTE ON THE HISTORY OF AMERICAN POETRY SINCE WHITMAN

When we think of history we usually think of a span of time characterized by certain events of importance. Frequently the events are wars, which tend in the nature of things to be vivid measuring sticks of political and social change. Thus to think of American history of the last hundred years or so is to think of or to measure by the cataclysm we call the Civil War (1861-1865), followed by the relatively minor Spanish-American War (1898), followed in the twentieth century by two more cataclysms, World War I (1914-1918) and World War II (1939-1945), and then by the Cold War with its two hot wars, Korea (1950-1953) and Vietnam, U.S. military involvement in the latter dating from about 1963. For the United States the period is also poignantly measured by the assassination of two popular presidents, Abraham Lincoln in 1865 and John F. Kennedy in 1963.

It would hardly make sense to consider the history of American poetry apart from such events, and yet poetry proves peculiarly uncooperative in fitting itself to what we think of as political, social, and economic history, or just plainly as history. The problem arises from the implication that when we say the word *poetry* what we really mean is poetry of the highest quality, which, to be sure, is a matter of continuous debate as well as a certain consensus. The death of Lincoln was followed by Whitman's great elegy *When Lilacs Last in the Dooryard Bloom'd*. The death of Kennedy was followed by a memorial volume of poems by various poets called *Of Poetry and Power*—but this volume does not contain a single great poem. The fact that it does not is not something for which the poets, men of excellent talent, should be censured. It is just one of those things, the great problem of matching the power of language to the potential of a subject.

Poetry, then, may or may not relate to the events vivid in our minds as history. But there is a sense in which poetry, that is, the best poetry, cannot help but relate in its history to history viewed as major events. Poetry must in some way reflect the temper of the age in which it is written, irrespective of the manner in which it alludes to events, although exceptions are as possible as individuality or eccentricity are possible in any given age, and in some cases the temper of the poet in one age may be more like the temper of the next age—thus Emily Dickinson is properly thought of as modern rather than as a nineteenth-century poet though she died in 1886. Perhaps the best example in the twentieth century of poetry reflecting the temper, or an aspect of the temper, of an age is that of T. S. Eliot in the Twenties. World War I produced little war poetry of consequence, but it was followed in 1922 by *The Waste Land*, which caught a postwar mood of disillusion and a sense of a fragmentation of values. Similarly, Robert Frost had no direct connection with the First World War, yet he too was reflecting the temper of his age in the sense that he persistently sought to find order and value in a world that seemed to be characterized by fragmentation. Like World War I, World War II did not produce a great war poetry, a kind of across the board extension of Randall Jarrell's classic *The Death of the Ball Turret Gunner*. The novel, rather, seemed to emerge as the vehicle for the war experience, as it had after World War I with, most notably, *A Farewell to Arms* (1929). With the explosion of the atomic bomb in 1945 the temper of the modern age was confirmed. It would not be an age of serenity, since nuclear power precludes the possibility of a firm personal security for any individual. Yet there is not a great poetry of the bomb, though psychologically speaking the bomb is everywhere. The postwar period in America is, moreover, characterized by great material prosperity, which has inevitably tended to suggest to the poet the need to go beyond things to values. In an extreme form this need manifests itself as the strident voice of the Beatnik, but this movement of the Fifties seems ready for oblivion in the Sixties, except of course for what *might be* a small permanent achievement, particularly in the work of Allen Ginsberg, who does not, however, seem at present to be a *developing* talent. But an historical evaluation of the achievement of American poetry following World War II will clearly have to wait for the perspective of time.

I have in effect suggested two obvious orientations in the viewing of the history of American poetry since Whitman. The first is that of major events, which begins as mere chronology but moves to the intensity of emotion realized in such poems as *When Lilacs Last in the Dooryard Bloom'd*. The second is the temper of the age as the poet reflects that temper whether or not he is writing on the subject that, say, would occupy the daily newspapers. A third orientation, equally obvious, is that of form. Is the poet writing in a manner that has clear antecedents in poetic traditions? Does he, for example, write in rhymed quatrains, a form which has a long and honorable history in poetry written in English? Does he write in the traditional iambic meter? Or is he an innovator, struggling with new rhythms, seeking a new form? Here a distinction must be made. A poet may be very modern and very much himself but write in an old way. Robert Frost, with his avowed love of iambic meter, is a good example. Conversely, a poet may prefer new forms but otherwise be quite traditional—E. E. Cummings and Dylan Thomas immediately come to mind. T. S. Eliot would perhaps be somewhere between, with a strong lean to innovation. But whether a poet in terms of his form is traditional or an innovator should not be allowed to obscure what he is in other respects. Put another way, we always have to guard against taking novelty for achievement.

With these three orientations in mind we may consider the main outlines of the history of American poetry since Whitman. The first edition of *Leaves of Grass*, which Whitman published himself, appeared in 1855, the ninth and final edition in 1892. Although Whitman developed as a poet significantly over the thirty-seven-year period between, his goal was clear from the start. He himself expressed it explicitly in the characteristic *Song of Myself*, which opens:

> I celebrate myself, and sing myself,
> And what I assume you shall assume,
> For every atom belonging to me as good belongs to you.

He is elsewhere in the poem equally explicit. Life for him is a mystery. "I am the poet of the Body and I am the poet of the Soul." "Your facts are useful, and yet they are not my dwelling." "I believe a leaf of grass is no less than the journey-work of the stars." Add to his romantic assertion of the unity of man and nature his desire to be the voice of democracy, to celebrate the common man, and one has the essential Whitman. He was a strong man, physically robust, a man who took complete delight in the pleasures of the senses in his search for unity in human life and for human brotherhood. He was also sensual, an erotic poet who offended the fastidious of his own time. One catches his expansive and democratic spirit in such lines as the opening of *To a Common Prostitute:* "Be composed— be at ease with me—I am Walt Whitman, liberal and lusty as Nature,/ Not till the sun excludes you do I exclude you." Or, his feeling for another as summed up in this quiet statement from *When Lilacs Last in the Dooryard Bloom'd:* "Here, coffin that slowly passes,/I give you my sprig of lilac." But it should be stressed that when Whitman speaks, perhaps identifying himself particularly as Walt Whitman, he is simultaneously creating a person, a mythic Walt Whitman, complete lover of the known universe for whom, as he says in the Preface to the 1855 edition of *Leaves of Grass,* "Past and present and future are not disjoined but joined."

When Whitman died on March 26, 1892, Robert Frost, born March 26, 1874, was celebrating his eighteenth birthday. Like Whitman, who published *Leaves of Grass* when he was thirty-six, Frost would be a late comer, publishing his first volume of poems, *A Boy's Will,* in 1913 when he was thirty-nine. Although Frost did not labor to identify the speaker in his poems as Robert Frost, he had something very much in common with Whitman, namely, that he was creating a mythic character, a mythic Robert Frost, the New England Yankee. There is a continuity, then, in what must be regarded in the history of American poetry as the incredibly difficult achievement of both Whitman and Frost in creating mythic characters, or complex imaginative realizations of their individual experiences of self and country. The difference between them is inevitably that Whitman is romantic and Frost is modern, that is, Frost, rather than asserting, explicitly and implicitly, the unity of man and nature, tends to assert the fact of man's separation from nature. One need only recall, for example, two poems placed in nearly every beginner's poetry anthology, *Stopping by Woods on a Snowy Evening* and *Desert Places.* Or consider the concluding stanza of the less known but provocative *The Strong Are Saying Nothing:*

> Wind goes from farm to farm in wave on wave,
> But carries no cry of what is hoped to be.
> There may be little or much beyond the grave,
> But the strong are saying nothing until they see.

The relationship between Whitman and Frost suggests, then, a fourth orientation to the history of American poetry—that history as it is written in terms of mythic characterization. Which immediately raises the question, After Frost, who? At the moment it looks as if critics, editors, and literary historians are saying nothing until they see.

Given the "mythic" orientation to the history of American poetry over the last hundred years with Whitman and Frost as two key figures, Frost dominating the contemporary scene until his death in 1963, we may glance at the history of American poetry since World War I. The period immediately following the war is perhaps dominated by T. S. Eliot's *The Waste Land*, a poem which has already been taken as at least an expression of the temper of the times and at most as a mythic embodiment of twentieth-century disillusion, or the experience of a world without belief. But the premise of the myth is surely too simple, as Eliot must have known since he is preeminently faithful to dramatizing the quality of the experience of a loss of faith as opposed to arguing the thesis that faith has been lost or cannot be experienced. Or to put the matter another way, *The Waste Land* is a fine poem and will remain a fine poem, but there is a sense in which it may become less and less believable as time goes on and historical perspective sees it as an exaggeration of the condition of life following World War I. Was the "lost generation" that lost? Was the disintegration in the life of Hart Crane, for example, representative of an age or more like an individual instance of something that can happen in any age but which modern industrial society, admittedly depersonalized, encourages? Or is the social decay observed by Robinson Jeffers really at the center of life in the first half of the twentieth century? Frost, it would seem, ought to remain more steadily believable than the early Eliot because he does not relate so tightly to the events of history, nor does he put too much of a burden of truth on a simple static character like Prufrock. The same might be said of Wallace Stevens, William Carlos Williams, or of Eliot himself in *Ash Wednesday* and the *Four Quartets*. In sum, I would suggest that the early Eliot as a myth-maker is more subject to challenge than Frost, Stevens, or Williams, though his resources as a poet are of course formidable.

We may conclude in a manner appropriate to the twentieth century, namely, by raising questions rather than by offering answers. I am of course suggesting that the history of American poetry may next be written in terms of a complex achievement involving the poet's relation (direct and indirect) to the events of history, to the temper of the time in which he lives, to his decisions, needs, or discoveries of the form proper to what he has to say, and finally, perhaps, to his power to create myth or mythic character, that is, to continue the work that Whitman started, which might be a better way to say it since *myth* is now a term in vogue and may go out of vogue. Who, then, are the American poets writing now, particularly those in mid-career, who might be placed in the second half of the twentieth century as poets with the stature of Frost are placed in the first half? I hope I have offered some candidates in this anthology, but I would not be surprised if I have rudely overlooked a flowering genius, nor would I be surprised if Frost's successor, as it were, were now attending, just beginning, or leaving college, or deciding, perhaps, that to succeed Frost he (or she) had better not bother with college at all.

APPENDIX B

BIBLIOGRAPHY

The following selected bibliography is divided into three parts. The first is a list of useful biographical reference works. The second is a list of general works, mainly of criticism, which the student will find valuable in the study of modern poetry. The general works of criticism contain, of course, specific discussion of individual poets and individual poems, and thus invite use of table of contents and index. The third is an alphabetical list of authors with a full but not exhaustive list of their writings followed by works of biography, bibliography, and criticism. In the case of a number of the contemporaries there is naturally little criticism of importance; no attempt is made to list each book review or relatively casual mention of a contemporary or his work.

1. Biographical Reference Works:

CURRENT BIOGRAPHY YEARBOOK. New York, H. W. Wilson Company.

Kunitz, Stanley J., and Howard Haycraft, eds. TWENTIETH CENTURY AUTHORS. A Biographical Dictionary of Modern Literature. New York, H. W. Wilson Company, 1942. First Supplement, ed. Stanley J. Kunitz. New York, H. W. Wilson Company, 1955.

Millet, Fred, ed. CONTEMPORARY AMERICAN AUTHORS. New York, Harcourt, Brace and World, Inc., 1944.

2. General Works:

Beach, Joseph Warren. OBSESSIVE IMAGES: SYMBOLISM IN THE POETRY OF THE 1930's AND 1940's. Minneapolis, University of Minnesota Press, 1960.

Blackmur, R. P. FORM AND VALUE IN MODERN POETRY. New York, Anchor Books, 1957.

Bogan, Louise. ACHIEVEMENT IN AMERICAN POETRY, 1900-1950. Chicago, Henry Regnery Company, 1951.

Bowra, C. M. THE BACKGROUND OF MODERN POETRY. London, Oxford University Press, 1946.

Bradbury, John M. RENAISSANCE IN THE SOUTH: A CRITICAL HISTORY OF THE LITERATURE. Chapel Hill, University of North Carolina Press, 1963.

Brooks, Cleanth. MODERN POETRY AND THE TRADITION. Chapel Hill, University of North Carolina Press, 1939.

Cambon, Glauco. RECENT AMERICAN POETRY. Minneapolis, University of Minnesota Press, 1962.

————. THE INCLUSIVE FLAME: STUDIES IN MODERN AMERICAN POETRY. Bloomington, Indiana, Indiana University Press, 1965.

Commager, Henry S. THE AMERICAN MIND: AN INTERPRETATION OF AMERI-
CAN THOUGHT AND CHARACTER SINCE THE 1880's. New Haven, Yale
University Press, 1950, 1959.

Cowley, Malcolm, ed. WRITERS AT WORK, THE PARIS REVIEW INTERVIEWS, Second Series. New York, Viking Press, Inc., 1963.

Daiches, David. POETRY AND THE MODERN WORLD. Chicago, University of
Chicago Press, 1940.

Deutsch, Babette. POETRY IN OUR TIME. New York, Holt, Rinehart and Winston, Inc., 1952.

Fiedler, Leslie. WAITING FOR THE END. New York, Dell Publishing Company,
Inc., 1965.

Frohock, Wilbur, STRANGERS TO THIS GROUND; CULTURAL DIVERSITY IN CON-
TEMPORARY AMERICAN WRITING. Dallas, Southern Methodist University
Press, 1961.

Gregory, Horace, and Marya Zaturenska. A HISTORY OF AMERICAN POETRY,
1900-1940. New York, Harcourt, Brace and World, Inc., 1946.

Gross, Harvey. SOUND AND FORM IN MODERN POETRY; A STUDY OF PROSODY
FROM THOMAS HARDY TO ROBERT LOWELL. Ann Arbor, University of
Michigan Press, 1964.

Hungerford, Edward B., ed. POETS IN PROGRESS: CRITICAL PREFACES TO TEN
CONTEMPORARY AMERICANS. Evanston, Illinois, Northwestern University
Press, 1962.

Jarrell, Randall. POETRY AND THE AGE. New York, Alfred A. Knopf, Inc.,
1953.

Miller, J. Hillis. POETS OF REALITY: SIX TWENTIETH-CENTURY WRITERS. Cambridge, Massachusetts, Harvard University Press, 1965.

Mills, Ralph J., Jr. CONTEMPORARY AMERICAN POETRY. New York, Random
House, Inc., 1965.

O'Conner, William Van. SENSE AND SENSIBILITY IN MODERN POETRY. Chicago, University of Chicago Press, 1948.

Pearce, Roy Harvey. THE CONTINUITY OF AMERICAN POETRY. Princeton,
Princeton University Press, 1961.

Quinn, Sister M. B. THE METAMORPHIC TRADITION IN MODERN POETRY;
ESSAYS ON THE WORK OF EZRA POUND, WALLACE STEVENS, WILLIAM CARLOS
WILLIAMS, T. S. ELIOT, HART CRANE, RANDALL JARRELL, AND WILLIAM BUT-
LER YEATS. New Brunswick, New Jersey, Rutgers University Press, 1955.

Rosenthal, M. L. THE MODERN POETS, A CRITICAL INTRODUCTION. New York,
Oxford University Press, 1960; Galaxy Books, 1965.

Spender, Stephen, and Donald Hall, eds. THE CONCISE ENCYCLOPEDIA OF
ENGLISH AND AMERICAN POETS AND POETRY. New York, Hawthorn Books,
Inc., 1963.

Spiller, Robert, and others, eds. LITERARY HISTORY OF THE UNITED STATES,
3 vols. New York, The Macmillan Company, 1948. Bibliography Supplement, 1959.

Tate, Allen. ON THE LIMITS OF POETRY, SELECTED ESSAYS: 1928-1948. New
York, Swallow Press, 1948.

———. SIXTY AMERICAN POETS, 1896-1944, rev. ed. New York, Washington Square Press, Inc., 1954.

Thorp, Willard. AMERICAN WRITING IN THE TWENTIETH CENTURY. Cambridge, Massachusetts, Harvard University Press, 1960.

Waggoner, H. H. THE HELL OF ELOHIM: SCIENCE AND VALUES IN MODERN AMERICAN POETRY. Norman, University of Oklahoma Press, 1950.
Winters, Ivor. IN DEFENSE OF REASON. Denver, University of Denver Press, 1937.

3. List of Authors:

CONRAD AIKEN

COLLECTED POEMS. New York, Oxford University Press, 1953.

EARTH TRIUMPHANT AND OTHER TALES IN VERSE (1914)
A JIG OF FORSLIN (1916)
TURNS AND MOVIES, AND OTHER TALES IN VERSE (1916)
THE CHARNEL ROSE, SENLIN: A BIOGRAPHY, AND OTHER POEMS (1918)
PRIAPUS AND THE POOL (1922)
THE PILGRIMAGE OF FESTUS (1923)
PRIAPUS AND THE POOL AND OTHER POEMS (1925)
SENLIN: A BIOGRAPHY (1925)
BRING! BRING! AND OTHER STORIES (1925)
PRELUDE (1929)
JOHN DETH: A METAPHYSICAL LEGEND AND OTHER POEMS (1930)
PRELUDES FOR MEMNON (1931)
THE COMING FORTH BY DAY OF OSIRIS JONES (1931)
LANDSCAPE WEST OF EDEN (1934)
TIME IN THE ROCK: PRELUDES TO DEFINITION (1936)
AND IN THE HUMAN HEART (1940)
BROWNSTONE ECLOGUES AND OTHER POEMS (1942)
THE SOLDIER: A POEM (1944)
THE KID (1947)
SKYLIGHT ONE: FIFTEEN POEMS (1949)
USHANT; AN ESSAY (1952)
A LETTER FROM LI PO AND OTHER POEMS (1955)
SHEEPFOLD HILL: FIFTEEN POEMS (1958)
COLLECTED SHORT STORIES (1960)
SELECTED POEMS (1961)
THE MORNING SONG OF LORD ZERO, POEMS OLD AND NEW (1963)
COLLECTED NOVELS (1964)
A SEIZURE OF LIMERICKS (1964)

Brown, Ashley. "An Interview with Conrad Aiken," *Shenandoah,* XV, 1 (1963), 18-40.
Denney, Reuel. CONRAD AIKEN. Minneapolis, University of Minnesota Press, 1964.
Hoffman, Frederick J. CONRAD AIKEN. New York, Twayne Publishers, Inc., 1962.
Martin, Jay. CONRAD AIKEN, A LIFE OF HIS ART. Princeton, Princeton University Press, 1962.

ELIZABETH BISHOP

NORTH AND SOUTH   (1946)
POEMS: NORTH AND SOUTH, A COLD SPRING   (1955)
QUESTIONS OF TRAVEL: POEMS AND A STORY   (1965)
THE DIARY OF HELENA MORLEY   (1966)   A translation.

PHILIP BOOTH

LETTER FROM A DISTANT LAND   (1957)
THE ISLANDERS   (1961)

JOHN CIARDI

HOMEWARD TO AMERICA   (1940)
OTHER SKIES   (1947)
LIVE ANOTHER DAY   (1949)
MID-CENTURY AMERICAN POETS   (1950)
FROM TIME TO TIME   (1951)
THE INFERNO; A VERSE RENDERING FOR THE MODERN READER   (1954)
AS IF: POEMS NEW AND SELECTED   (1955)
I MARRY YOU: A SHEAF OF LOVE POEMS   (1958)
THIRTY-NINE POEMS   (1959)
THE REASON FOR THE PELICAN   (1959)
SCRAPPY THE PUP   (1960)
I MET A MAN   (1961)
IN THE STONEWORKS   (1961)
THE MAN WHO SANG THE SILLIES   (1961)
THE PURGATORIO; A VERSE TRANSLATION FOR THE MODERN READER   (1961)
IN FACT   (1962)
THE WISH-TREE   (1962)
YOU READ TO ME, I'LL READ TO YOU   (1962)
DIALOGUE WITH AN AUDIENCE   (1963)
JOHN J. PLENTY AND FIDDLER DAN; A NEW FABLE OF THE GRASSHOPPER AND
   THE ANT   (1963)
YOU KNOW WHO   (1964)
PERSON TO PERSON   (1964)
THE KING WHO SAVED HIMSELF FROM BEING SAVED   (1965)

White, William. JOHN CIARDI, A BIBLIOGRAPHY. Detroit, Wayne State University Press, 1959.

HART CRANE

THE COLLECTED POEMS OF HART CRANE, ed. Waldo Frank. New York, Liveright Publishing Corp., 1933.

WHITE BUILDINGS: POEMS   (1926)
THE BRIDGE: A POEM   (1930)
THE LETTERS OF HART CRANE, ed. Brom Weber   (1952, 1965)

Andreach, Robert J. STUDIES IN STRUCTURE: THE STAGES OF THE SPIRITUAL LIFE IN FOUR MODERN AUTHORS. New York, Fordham University Press, 1965.

Dembo, L. S. HART CRANE'S SANSKRIT CHARGE; A STUDY OF THE BRIDGE. Ithaca, New York, Cornell University Press, 1960.

Hazo, Samuel. HART CRANE: AN INTRODUCTION AND INTERPRETATION. New York, Barnes and Noble, Inc., 1963.

Horton, Philip. HART CRANE: THE LIFE OF AN AMERICAN POET. New York, W. W. Norton and Company, Inc., 1937; Compass Books, 1957.

Quinn, Vincent. HART CRANE. New York, Twayne Publishers, Inc. 1963.

Rowe, H. D. HART CRANE: A BIBLIOGRAPHY. Denver, Alan Swallow, Publisher, 1955.

Spears, Monroe K. HART CRANE. Minneapolis, University of Minnesota Press, 1965.

Weber, Brom. HART CRANE: A BIBLIOGRAPHICAL AND CRITICAL STUDY. New York, Bodley Press, 1948.

E. E. CUMMINGS

POEMS, 1923-1954. New York, Harcourt, Brace and World, Inc., 1954.

TULIPS AND CHIMNEYS   (1923)
XLI POEMS   (1925)
&   (1925)
IS 5   (1926)
HIM   (1927)
W (VIVA)   (1931)
EIMI   (1933)
NO THANKS   (1935)
TOM   (1935)
ONE OVER TWENTY   (1936)
COLLECTED POEMS   (1938)
50 POEMS   (1940)
1 X 1   (1944)
SANTA CLAUS: A MORALITY   (1946)
XAIPE: 71 POEMS   (1950)
95 POEMS   (1958)
100 SELECTED POEMS   (1959)
73 POEMS   (1963)

Firmage, George. E. E. CUMMINGS, A BIBLIOGRAPHY. Middletown, Connecticut, Wesleyan University Press, 1960.

Friedman, Norman. E. E. CUMMINGS; THE GROWTH OF A WRITER. Carbondale, Southern Illinois University Press, 1964.

Lauter, Paul. E. E. CUMMINGS: INDEX TO FIRST LINES AND BIBLIOGRAPHY OF WORKS BY AND ABOUT THE POET. Denver, Alan Swallow, Publisher, 1955.

Marks, Barry Alan. E. E. CUMMINGS. New York, Twayne Publishers, Inc., 1964.

Norman, Charles. E. E. CUMMINGS, THE MAGIC-MAKER, rev. ed. New York, Duell, Sloan and Pearce, 1964.

Von Abele, Rudolph. "'Only to Grow'; Change in the Poetry of E. E. Cummings," *PMLA*, LXX (1955), 913-933.

Watson, Barbara. "The Dangers of Security: E. E. Cummings' Revolt Against the Future," *Kenyon Review*, XVIII (1956), 519-537.

JAMES DICKEY

DROWNING WITH OTHERS   (1962)
THE SUSPECT IN POETRY   (1963)
HELMETS   (1964)
BUCKDANCER'S CHOICE   (1965)

ALAN DUGAN

POEMS   (1961)
POEMS 2   (1963)

RICHARD EBERHART

COLLECTED POEMS 1930-1960. New York, Oxford University Press, 1960.
COLLECTED VERSE PLAYS. Chapel Hill, University of North Carolina Press, 1962.

A BRAVERY OF EARTH   (1930)
READING THE SPIRIT   (1936)
SONG AND IDEA   (1940)
POEMS: NEW AND SELECTED   (1944)
BURR OAKS   (1947)
RUMINATION   (1947)
BROTHERHOOD OF MEN   (1949)
AN HERB BASKET   (1950)
SELECTED POEMS   (1951)
UNDERCLIFF: POEMS, 1946-1953   (1953)
THE OAK   (1957)
GREAT PRAISES   (1957)
THE QUARRY   (1964)

Hoffman, Daniel. "Hunting a Master Image: the Poetry of Richard Eberhart," *The Hollins Critic*, I, 4 (1964), 1-12.

Mills, Ralph J., Jr. "Reflections on Richard Eberhart," *Chicago Review*, XV, 4 (1962), 81-99.

T. S. ELIOT

THE COMPLETE POEMS AND PLAYS, 1909-1950. New York, Harcourt, Brace and World, Inc., 1962.
COLLECTED POEMS, 1909-1962. New York, Harcourt, Brace and World, Inc., 1963.

PRUFROCK AND OTHER OBSERVATIONS (1917)
POEMS (1919)
THE SACRED WOOD, ESSAYS ON POETRY AND CRITICISM (1920)
THE WASTE LAND (1922)
HOMAGE TO JOHN DRYDEN (1924)
POEMS, 1909-25 (1925)
DANTE (1929)
ASH-WEDNESDAY (1930)
SWEENEY AGONISTES (1932)
THE USE OF POETRY AND THE USE OF CRITICISM (1933)
AFTER STRANGE GODS (1933)
ELIZABETHAN ESSAYS (1934)
THE ROCK: A PAGEANT PLAY (1934)
MURDER IN THE CATHEDRAL (1935)
ESSAYS ANCIENT AND MODERN (1936)
OLD POSSUM'S BOOK OF PRACTICAL CATS (1939)
THE FAMILY REUNION: A PLAY (1939)
THE IDEA OF A CHRISTIAN SOCIETY (1939)
FOUR QUARTETS (1943)
NOTES TOWARD THE DEFINITION OF CULTURE (1949)
THE COCKTAIL PARTY: A COMEDY (1950)
THE CONFIDENTIAL CLERK: A PLAY (1954)
ON POETRY AND POETS (1957)
THE ELDER STATESMAN (1959)

Drew, Elizabeth. T. S. ELIOT: THE DESIGN OF HIS POETRY. New York, Charles Scribner's Sons, 1949.
Gallup, D. C. T. S. ELIOT: A BIBLIOGRAPHY INCLUDING CONTRIBUTIONS TO PERIODICALS AND FOREIGN TRANSLATIONS. New York, Harcourt, Brace and World, Inc., 1953.
Gardner, Helen. THE ART OF T. S. ELIOT. New York, E. P. Dutton and Co., Inc., 1950.
Headings, Philip R. T. S. ELIOT. New York, Twayne Publishers, Inc., 1964.
Howarth, Herbert. NOTES ON SOME FIGURES BEHIND T. S. ELIOT. Boston, Houghton, Mifflin Company, 1964.
Kenner, Hugh, ed. T. S. ELIOT, A COLLECTION OF CRITICAL ESSAYS. Englewood Cliffs, New Jersey, Spectrum Books, 1962.
Knoll, Robert E. STORM OVER THE WASTE LAND. Chicago, Scott, Foresman and Company, 1964.
Martin, Philip M. MASTERY AND MERCY, A STUDY OF TWO RELIGIOUS POEMS: THE WRECK OF THE DEUTSCHLAND BY G. M. HOPKINS AND ASH-WEDNESDAY BY T. S. ELIOT. London, Oxford University Press, 1957.

Matthiessen, F. O. THE ACHIEVEMENT OF T. S. ELIOT: AN ESSAY ON THE NATURE OF POETRY. New York, Oxford University Press, Inc. 1959.

Smith, Grover. T. S. ELIOT'S POETRY AND PLAYS: A STUDY IN SOURCES AND MEANING. Chicago, University of Chicago Press, 1956.

Thompson, Eric. T. S. ELIOT, THE METAPHYSICAL PERSPECTIVE. Carbondale, Southern Illinois University Press, 1963.

Unger, Leonard. T. S. ELIOT. Minneapolis, University of Minnesota Press, 1961.

————. "A Tribute, T. S. Eliot: The Intimate Voice." *Southern Review*, I, 3, New Series (July 1965), 731-734.

Williamson, George. A READER'S GUIDE TO T. S. ELIOT: A POEM-BY-POEM ANALYSIS. New York, The Noonday Press, 1953.

Wright, George T. THE POET IN THE POEM: THE PERSONAE OF ELIOT, YEATS, AND POUND. Berkeley, University of California Press, 1960.

ROBERT FROST

COMPLETE POEMS OF ROBERT FROST, 1949. New York, Holt, Rinehart and Winston, Inc., 1949.

A BOY'S WILL   (1913)
NORTH OF BOSTON   (1914)
MOUNTAIN INTERVAL   (1916)
NEW HAMPSHIRE: A POEM   (1923)
WEST-RUNNING BROOK   (1928)
A FURTHER RANGE   (1936)
A WITNESS TREE   (1942)
COME IN AND OTHER POEMS   (1943)
A MASQUE OF REASON   (1945)
POEMS   (1946)
STEEPLE BUSH   (1947)
A MASQUE OF MERCY   (1947)
YOU COME TOO   (1959)
IN THE CLEARING   (1962)
THE LETTERS OF ROBERT FROST TO LOUIS UNTERMEYER   (1963)

Brower, Reuben A. THE POETRY OF ROBERT FROST; CONSTELLATIONS OF INTENTION. New York, Oxford University Press, 1963.

Cook, Reginald. THE DIMENSIONS OF ROBERT FROST. New York, Holt, Rinehart and Winston, Inc., 1958.

Cox, James M., ed. ROBERT FROST: A COLLECTION OF CRITICAL ESSAYS. Englewood Cliffs, N.J., Spectrum Books, 1962.

Cox, Sidney. A SWINGER OF BIRCHES: A PORTRAIT OF ROBERT FROST. New York, New York University Press, 1957.

Gould, Jean. THE AIM WAS SONG. New York, Dodd, Mead and Company, 1964. (biography)

Lynen, John. THE PASTORAL ART OF ROBERT FROST. New Haven, Yale University Press, 1960.

Mertins, Louis, and Mertins, Esther. THE INTERVALS OF ROBERT FROST: A CRITICAL BIBLIOGRAPHY. Berkeley, University of California Press, 1947.

Reeve, Franklin D. ROBERT FROST IN RUSSIA. Boston, Little, Brown and Company, 1964.

Sergeant, Elizabeth Shepley. ROBERT FROST; THE TRIAL BY EXISTENCE. New York, Holt, Rinehart and Winston, Inc., 1960.

Smythe, Daniel. ROBERT FROST SPEAKS. New York, Twayne Publishers, Inc., 1964.

Thompson, Lawrence. FIRE AND ICE; THE ART AND THOUGHT OF ROBERT FROST. New York, Holt, Rinehart and Winston, Inc., 1942.

————. ROBERT FROST. Minneapolis, University of Minnesota Press, 1959.

ALLEN GINSBERG

HOWL AND OTHER POEMS   (1956)
EMPTY MIRROR; EARLY POEMS   (1961)
KADDISH AND OTHER POEMS   (1961)
REALITY SANDWICHES, 1953-60   (1963)
THE YAGE LETTERS   (with William Burroughs, 1963)

Kostelanetz, Richard. "Ginsberg Makes the World Scene," *New York Times Magazine,* 6 (July 11, 1965), 22ff.

RANDALL JARRELL

BLOOD FOR A STRANGER   (1942)
LITTLE FRIEND, LITTLE FRIEND   (1945)
LOSSES   (1948)
THE SEVEN LEAGUE CRUTCHES   (1951)
POETRY AND THE AGE   (1953)
PICTURES FROM AN INSTITUTION: A COMEDY   (1954)
SELECTED POEMS   (1955)
THE WOMAN AT THE WASHINGTON ZOO: POEMS AND TRANSLATIONS   (1960)
A SAD HEART AT THE SUPERMARKET: ESSAYS AND FABLES   (1961)
GINGERBREAD RABBIT   (1963)
THE BAT-POET   (1964)
THE LOST WORLD   (1965)
THE ANIMAL FAMILY   (1965)

Adams, Charles Marshall. RANDALL JARRELL, A BIBLIOGRAPHY. Chapel Hill, University of North Carolina Press, 1958.

ROBINSON JEFFERS

TAMAR AND OTHER POEMS   (1924)
ROAN STALLION, TAMAR, AND OTHER POEMS   (1925)
THE WOMEN AT POINT SUR   (1927)
CAWDOR AND OTHER POEMS   (1928)

THURSO'S LANDING AND OTHER POEMS (1932)
GIVE YOUR HEART TO THE HAWKS AND OTHER POEMS (1933)
SOLSTICE AND OTHER POEMS (1935)
SUCH COUNSELS YOU GAVE TO ME AND OTHER POEMS (1937)
THE SELECTED POETRY OF ROBINSON JEFFERS (1938)
BE ANGRY AT THE SUN AND OTHER POEMS (1941)
MEDEA: FREELY ADAPTED FROM THE MEDEA OF EURIPIDES (1946)
THE DOUBLE AXE AND OTHER POEMS (1954)
THE SELECTED POEMS OF ROBINSON JEFFERS (1959)
THE BEGINNING AND THE END AND OTHER POEMS (1963)

Carpenter, Frederic I. ROBINSON JEFFERS. New York, Twayne Publishers, Inc., 1962.
Monjian, Mercedes C. ROBINSON JEFFERS, A STUDY IN INHUMANISM. Pittsburgh, University of Pittsburgh Press, 1958.
Squires, Radcliffe. THE LOYALTIES OF ROBINSON JEFFERS. Ann Arbor, University of Michigan Press, 1956.

STANLEY KUNITZ

SELECTED POEMS 1928-1958. Boston, Little, Brown and Company, 1958.

INTELLECTUAL THINGS (1930)
PASSPORT TO THE WAR: A SELECTION OF POEMS (1944)

ROBERT LOWELL

LAND OF UNLIKENESS (1944)
LORD WEARY'S CASTLE (1946; with changes, 1947)
POEMS, 1938-1949 (1950)
THE MILLS OF THE KAVANAUGHS (1951)
LIFE STUDIES (1959)
PHAEDRA (1961)
IMITATIONS (1961)
FOR THE UNION DEAD (1964)

Mazzaro, Jerome. THE ACHIEVEMENT OF ROBERT LOWELL, 1939-1959. A bibliography. Detroit, University of Detroit Press, 1960.
————. THE POETIC THEMES OF ROBERT LOWELL. Ann Arbor, University of Michigan Press, 1965.
Staples, Hugh B. ROBERT LOWELL, THE FIRST TWENTY YEARS. New York, Farrar, Straus & Giroux, Inc., 1962.

W. S. MERWIN

A MASK FOR JANUS (1952)
THE DANCING BEARS (1954)

GREEN WITH BEASTS   (1956)
THE POEM OF THE CID   (1959)
THE DRUNK IN THE FURNACE   (1960)
PERSIUS, SATIRES   (1961)
SOME SPANISH BALLADS   (1961)
THE MOVING TARGET   (1963)

MARIANNE MOORE

COLLECTED POEMS. New York, The Macmillan Company, 1951.
A MARIANNE MOORE READER. New York, The Viking Press, Inc., 1961.

POEMS   (1921)
OBSERVATIONS   (1924)
SELECTED POEMS   (1935)
THE PANGOLIN AND OTHER VERSE   (1936)
WHAT ARE YEARS   (1941)
NEVERTHELESS   (1944)
ROCK CRYSTAL   (1945)
THE FABLES OF LA FONTAINE   (1954)
PREDILECTIONS   (1955)
LIKE A BULWARK   (1956)
O TO BE A DRAGON   (1959)
THE ABSENTEE; A COMEDY IN FOUR ACTS   (1962)

Engel, Bernard F. MARIANNE MOORE. New York, Twayne Publishers, Inc., 1964.
Fowlie, Wallace. "Marianne Moore," *Sewanee Review*, LX (1952), 537-547.
Garrigue, Jean. MARIANNE MOORE. Minneapolis, University of Minnesota Press, 1965.
Quarterly Review of Literature, IV (1948). Marianne Moore issue.

EZRA POUND

PERSONAE: COLLECTED POEMS. New York, New Directions Publishing Corp., 1956.

A LUME SPENTO   (1908)
PERSONAE   (1909)
EXULTATIONS   (1909)
CANZONI   (1911)
RIPOSTES   (1912)
CANZONI AND RIPOSTES   (1913)
PERSONAE AND EXULTATIONS   (1913)
CATHAY: TRANSLATIONS BY EZRA POUND   (1915)
LUSTRA   (1916)
PAVANNES AND DIVIGATIONS   (1918)
THE FOURTH CANTO   (1919)

QUIA PAUPER AMAVI   (1919)
HUGH SELWYN MAUBERLEY   (1920)
UMBRA: THE EARLY POEMS   (1920)
POEMS 1918-1921   (1921)
A DRAFT OF XVI CANTOS   (1925)
PERSONAE: THE COLLECTED POEMS OF EZRA POUND   (1926)
A DRAFT OF THE CANTOS 17-27 OF EZRA POUND   (1928)
HOMAGE TO SEXTUS PROPERTIUS   (1934)
ELEVEN NEW CANTOS: XXXI-XLI   (1934)
THE FIFTH DECAD OF CANTOS   (1937)
CULTURE   (1938)
CANTOS LII-LXXI   (1940)
THE PISAN CANTOS   (1948)
THE CANTOS OF EZRA POUND   (1948)
SEVENTY CANTOS   (1950)
PERSONAE: COLLECTED SHORTER POEMS   (1950)
THE LETTERS OF EZRA POUND, 1907-1941   (1950, ed. D. D. Paige)
CANTOS 1-84   (1954)
THE LITERARY ESSAYS OF EZRA POUND   (1954)
THE TRANSLATIONS OF EZRA POUND   (1954; enlarged ed., 1963)
DIPTYCH: ROME-LONDON   (1958)
THRONES 96-109 DE LOS CANTARES   (1959)
LOVE POEMS OF ANCIENT EGYPT   (1962)
EP TO LU: NINE LETTERS WRITTEN TO LOUIS UNTERMEYER BY EZRA POUND
   (1963)

Davie, Donald. EZRA POUND: POET AS SCULPTOR. New York, Oxford University Press, 1964.

Dekker, George. THE CANTOS OF EZRA POUND. New York, Barnes and Noble, Inc., 1963.

Dembo, L. THE CONFUCIAN ODES OF EZRA POUND: A CRITICAL APPRAISAL. Berkeley, University of California Press, 1963.

Edwards, John, and William W. Vasse. ANNOTATED INDEX TO THE CANTOS OF EZRA POUND, CANTOS I-LXXXIV. Berkeley, University of California Press, 1957.

Eliot, T. S. EZRA POUND: HIS METRIC AND POETRY. New York, Alfred A. Knopf, Inc., 1917.

Espey, J. J. EZRA POUND'S MAUBERLEY: A STUDY IN COMPOSITION. Berkeley, University of California Press, 1955.

———. A PRELIMINARY CHECKLIST OF THE WRITINGS OF EZRA POUND, ESPECIALLY HIS CONTRIBUTIONS TO PERIODICALS. New Haven, Connecticut, Kirgo-Books, 1953.

Gallup, Donald. A BIBLIOGRAPHY OF EZRA POUND. London, Hart-Davis, 1963.

Leary, Lewis, ed. MOTIVE AND METHOD IN THE CANTOS OF EZRA POUND. New York, Columbia University Press, 1954.

MacLeish, Archibald. POETRY AND OPINION: THE PISAN CANTOS OF EZRA POUND, A DIALOGUE ON THE ROLE OF POETRY. Urbana, University of Illinois Press, 1950.

Norman, Charles. EZRA POUND. New York, The Macmillan Company, 1960.

O'Conner, William Van. EZRA POUND. Minneapolis, University of Minnesota Press, 1963.

Rosenthal, M. L. A PRIMER OF EZRA POUND. New York, The Macmillan Company, 1960.

Russell, Peter, ed. AN EXAMINATION OF EZRA POUND: A COLLECTION OF ESSAYS. Norfolk, Connecticut, New Directions Publishing Corp., 1950.

Sullivan, John P. EZRA POUND AND SEXTUS PROPERTIUS; A STUDY IN CREATIVE TRANSLATION. Austin, University of Texas Press, 1964.

Sutton, Walter, ed. EZRA POUND: A COLLECTION OF CRITICAL ESSAYS. Englewood Cliffs, New Jersey, Spectrum Books, 1963.

JOHN CROWE RANSOM

POEMS ABOUT GOD   (1919)
ARMAGEDDON   (1923)
CHILLS AND FEVER: POEMS   (1924)
GRACE AFTER MEAT   (1924)
TWO GENTLEMEN IN BONDS   (1927)
GOD WITHOUT THUNDER; AN UNORTHODOX DEFENSE OF ORTHODOXY   (1931)
THE WORLD'S BODY   (1938)
THE NEW CRITICISM   (1941)
SELECTED POEMS   (1945)
SELECTED POEMS   (1952)
POEMS AND ESSAYS   (1955)
SELECTED POEMS   (1963)

Koch, Vivienne. "The Achievement of John Crowe Ransom," *Sewanee Review*, LVIII (1950), 227-261.

Ransom, John Crowe. "'Prelude to an Evening'; A Poem Revised and Explicated," *Kenyon Review*, XXV (1963), 70-80.

Stallmann, R. W. "John Crowe Ransom: A Checklist," *Sewanee Review*, LVI (1948), 442-476.

Stewart, John Lincoln. THE BURDEN OF TIME: THE FUGITIVES AND AGRARIANS; THE NASHVILLE GROUPS OF THE 1920'S AND 1930'S, AND THE WRITING OF JOHN CROWE RANSOM, ALLEN TATE, AND ROBERT PENN WARREN. Princeton, Princeton University Press, 1965.

————. JOHN CROWE RANSOM. Minneapolis, University of Minnesota Press, 1962.

Warren, Robert Penn. "John Crowe Ransom: A Study in Irony," *Virginia Quarterly Review*, XI (1935), 93-112.

THEODORE ROETHKE

THE COLLECTED VERSE OF THEODORE ROETHKE: WORDS FOR THE WIND. New York, Doubleday, 1958; Indiana University Press, 1961.

OPEN HOUSE   (1941)

THE LOST SON AND OTHER POEMS   (1948)
PRAISE TO THE END!   (1951)
THE WAKING: POEMS 1933-1953   (1953)
I AM! SAYS THE LAMB   (1961)
SEQUENCE, SOMETIMES METAPHYSICAL, POEMS   (1963)
THE FAR FIELD   (1964)
ON THE POET AND HIS CRAFT: SELECTED PROSE OF THEODORE ROETHKE. Ralph
   J. Mills, Jr., ed. (1965)

Burke, Kenneth. "The Vegetal Radicalism of Theodore Roethke," *Sewanee
   Review*, LVIII (1950), 68-108.
Martz, William J., ed. THE ACHIEVEMENT OF THEODORE ROETHKE. Chicago,
   Scott, Foresman and Company, 1966.
Matheson, John W. THEODORE ROETHKE; A BIBLIOGRAPHY. Seattle, Wash-
   ington, M.A. Thesis, 1958.
Mills, Ralph J., Jr. THEODORE ROETHKE. Minneapolis, University of Min-
   nesota Press, 1963.
Staples, Hugh B. "The Rose in the Sea-Wind: A Reading of Theodore
   Roethke's 'North American Sequence'," *American Literature*, XXXVI
   (1964), 189-203.
Stein, Arnold, ed. THEODORE ROETHKE: ESSAYS ON THE POETRY. Seattle,
   University of Washington Press, 1965.

ANNE SEXTON

TO BEDLAM AND PART WAY BACK   (1960)
ALL MY PRETTY ONES   (1962)

KARL SHAPIRO

POEMS   (1935)
PERSON PLACE AND THING   (1942)
V-LETTER AND OTHER POEMS   (1944)
ESSAY ON RIME   (1945)
TRIAL OF A POET AND OTHER POEMS   (1947)
A BIBLIOGRAPHY OF MODERN PROSODY   (1948)
POEMS, 1940-1953   (1953)
BEYOND CRITICISM   (1953; reissue, A PRIMER FOR POETS, 1965)
POEMS OF A JEW   (1958)
IN DEFENSE OF IGNORANCE   (1960)
THE BOURGEOIS POET   (1964)
THE WRITER'S EXPERIENCE   (1964)
A PROSODY HANDBOOK   (1965)

Bradley, Sam. "Shapiro Strikes at the Establishment," *University of Kansas
   City Review*, XXIX (1963), 275-279.
Rubin, Louis D., Jr. "The Search for Lost Innocence: Karl Shapiro's *The
   Bourgeois Poet*," *The Hollins Critic*, I, 5 (1964), 1-16.
White, William. KARL SHAPIRO: A BIBLIOGRAPHY. Detroit, Wayne State
   University Press, 1960.

LOUIS SIMPSON

THE ARRIVESTES, POEMS 1940-49   (1949)
GOOD NEWS OF DEATH AND OTHER POEMS   (1955)
A DREAM OF GOVERNORS   (1959)
JAMES HOGG: A CRITICAL STUDY   (1962)
RIVERSIDE DRIVE   (1962)
AT THE END OF THE OPEN ROAD   (1963)
SELECTED POEMS   (1965)

W. D. SNODGRASS

HEART'S NEEDLE   (1959)
"Finding a Poem," *Partisan Review*, XXVI, 2 (1959), 276-284.

WILLIAM STAFFORD

DOWN IN MY HEART   (1947)
WEST OF YOUR CITY   (1960)
TRAVELING THROUGH THE DARK   (1962)
THE RESCUED YEAR   (1966)

WALLACE STEVENS

THE COLLECTED POEMS OF WALLACE STEVENS. New York, Alfred A. Knopf, Inc., 1954.

HARMONIUM   (1923; enlarged ed., 1931)
IDEAS OF ORDER   (1935)
OWL'S CLOVER   (1936)
THE MAN WITH THE BLUE GUITAR AND OTHER POEMS   (1937)
PARTS OF A WORLD   (1942)
NOTES TOWARD A SUPREME FICTION   (1942)
ESTHÉTIQUE DU MAL   (1945)
THREE ACADEMIC PIECES   (1947)
TRANSPORT TO SUMMER   (1947)
THE AURORAS OF AUTUMN   (1950)
THE NECESSARY ANGEL; ESSAYS ON REALITY AND THE IMAGINATION   (1951)
OPUS POSTHUMOUS   (1957)

Benamou, Michel. "Wallace Stevens and the Symbolist Imagination," *ELH*, XXXI (1964), 35-63.
Borroff, Marie, ed. WALLACE STEVENS, A COLLECTION OF CRITICAL ESSAYS. Englewood Cliffs, New Jersey, Spectrum Books, 1963.
Bowra, C. M. THE CREATIVE EXPERIMENT. London, The Macmillan Company, 1949.

Brown, Ashley, and Robert S. Haller. THE ACHIEVEMENT OF WALLACE STEVENS. Philadelphia, J. B. Lippincott Company, 1962.

Enck, John J. WALLACE STEVENS: IMAGES AND JUDGMENTS. Carbondale, Southern Illinois University Press, 1964.

Frye, Northrop. "The Realistic Oriole; a Study of Wallace Stevens," *Hudson Review*, X (1957), 353-370.

Fuchs, Daniel. THE COMIC SPIRIT OF WALLACE STEVENS. Durham, North Carolina, Duke University Press, 1963.

Kermode, Frank. WALLACE STEVENS. New York, Grove Press, Inc., 1961.

Morse, Samuel French. "Wallace Stevens, Bergson, Pater," *ELH*, XXI (1964), 1-34.

Morse, Samuel French, Jackson R. Bryer, and Joseph N. Riddel. WALLACE STEVENS CHECKLIST AND BIBLIOGRAPHY OF STEVENS CRITICISM. Denver, Colorado, Alan Swallow, Publisher, 1963.

Nemerov, Howard. "The Poetry of Wallace Stevens," *Sewanee Review* LXV (1957), 1-14.

O'Conner, William Van. THE SHAPING SPIRIT: A STUDY OF WALLACE STEVENS, Chicago, Henry Regnery Company, 1950.

Pack, Robert. WALLACE STEVENS, AN APPROACH TO HIS POETRY AND THOUGHT. New Brunswick, New Jersey, Rutgers University Press, 1958.

Pearce, Roy Harvey, and J. Hillis Miller, eds. THE ACT OF THE MIND; ESSAYS ON THE POETRY OF WALLACE STEVENS. Baltimore, The Johns Hopkins Press, 1965.

Ransom, John Crowe. "The Planetary Poet," *Kenyon Review*, XXVI (1964), 233-264.

Riddel, Joseph N. THE CLAIRVOYANT EYE: THE POETRY AND POETICS OF WALLACE STEVENS. Baton Rouge, Louisiana State University Press, 1965.

Tindall, William York. WALLACE STEVENS. Minneapolis, University of Minnesota Press, 1961.

Walsh, Thomas F. CONCORDANCE TO THE POETRY OF WALLACE STEVENS. University Park, Pennsylvania State University Press, 1963.

Wells, Henry W. INTRODUCTION TO WALLACE STEVENS. Bloomington, Indiana University Press, 1964.

RICHARD WILBUR

THE POEMS OF RICHARD WILBUR. New York, Harcourt, Brace and World, Inc., 1963.

THE BEAUTIFUL CHANGES AND OTHER POEMS   (1947)
CEREMONY AND OTHER POEMS   (1950)
MOLIERE'S THE MISANTHROPE   (1955)
THINGS OF THIS WORLD   (1956)
CANDIDE: A COMIC OPERA   (with Lillian Hellman and others, 1957)
POEMS, 1943-1956   (1957)
ADVICE TO A PROPHET   (1961)
LOUDMOUSE   (1963)

WILLIAM CARLOS WILLIAMS

THE COLLECTED EARLIER POEMS OF WILLIAM CARLOS WILLIAMS. New York, New Directions Publishing Corp., 1951.

THE COLLECTED LATER POEMS OF WILLIAM CARLOS WILLIAMS. New York, New Directions Publishing Corp., 1950.

POEMS (1909)
THE TEMPERS (1913)
A BOOK OF POEMS: AL QUE QUIERE! (1917)
KORA IN HELL: IMPROVISATIONS (1920)
SOUR GRAPES: A BOOK OF POEMS (1921)
SPRING AND ALL (1923)
IN THE AMERICAN GRAIN (1925)
COLLECTED POEMS, 1921-31 (1934)
AN EARLY MARTYR AND OTHER POEMS (1935)
ADAM AND EVE AND THE CITY (1936)
THE BROKEN SPAN (1941)
THE WEDGE (1944)
PATERSON (Book One, 1946; Book Two, 1948; Book Three, 1949; Book Four, 1951; Book Five, 1958)
THE PINK CHURCH (1948)
MAKE LIGHT OF IT; COLLECTED STORIES (1950)
THE AUTOBIOGRAPHY OF WILLIAM CARLOS WILLIAMS (1951)
THE BUILD-UP, A NOVEL (1952)
THE DESERT MUSIC AND OTHER POEMS (1954)
SELECTED ESSAYS (1954)
JOURNEY TO LOVE (1955)
THE SELECTED LETTERS OF WILLIAM CARLOS WILLIAMS (1957, ed. J. C. Thirlwall)
I WANTED TO WRITE A POEM: THE AUTOBIOGRAPHY OF THE WORKS OF A POET (1958, ed. Edith Heal)
PATERSON (1958)
THE FARMER'S DAUGHTERS; COLLECTED STORIES (1961)
MANY LOVES, AND OTHER PLAYS; THE COLLECTED PLAYS OF WILLIAM CARLOS WILLIAMS (1961)
PICTURES FROM BRUEGHEL, AND OTHER POEMS (1962)

Brinnin, John M. WILLIAM CARLOS WILLIAMS. Minneapolis, University of Minnesota Press, 1963.

Koch, Vivienne. WILLIAM CARLOS WILLIAMS. Norfolk, Connecticut, New Directions Publishing Corp., 1950.

Wagner, Linda Welshimer. THE POEMS OF WILLIAM CARLOS WILLIAMS: A CRITICAL STUDY. Middletown, Connecticut, Wesleyan University Press, 1964.

JAMES WRIGHT

THE GREEN WALL (1957)
SAINT JUDAS (1959)
THE BRANCH WILL NOT BREAK (1963)

APPENDIX C

POETS READING THEIR OWN POEMS: A LIST OF RECORDINGS

Listening to a poet read his own poems adds a marvelous dimension to the whole experience of modern poetry. The clear place to begin is with a poet you like. Following this choice of taste, the listening experience adds at least two others, the quality of the poet's voice and the manner in which he reads his poems. If possible listen first to records in the usual English department and library collections; this will, of course, act as a spur to the acquisition of a small personal library of poets reading their own poems, and perhaps, though not included on the following list, of others reading the works of various poets. Such a library will prove to be a long-term pleasure.

Other than the fact that nearly all records of poets reading their own poems are 12″ monaural LPs there are no uniform standards. Some albums—among the following, Ciardi, Kunitz, Roethke, "San Francisco Poets," and the Library of Congress Recording Laboratory—include the text of the poems, a real asset. Most of the poets give the title of each poem before they read it, which is helpful. On the whole the records are technically of good quality, but they should be inspected immediately upon receipt. Delivery time may vary from one week to several months.

The following list is alphabetical by poet and includes records in which the poet is one of several on a single record; these albums are listed first and are thereafter abbreviated under author. If two or more records of a single poet reading his own work are available, the table of contents for each is included. Library of Congress tapes, done by most poets but not commercially available, are not included.

Caedmon Treasury of Modern Poets, TC 2006. Abbreviated CTMP
Library of Congress Recording Library, PL5, PL7, PL9, PL10, PL11, PL 20, PL21, PL22, PL27, PL29. Abbreviated LC-PL with number.
Pleasure Dome. An Audible Anthology of Modern Poetry Read by Its Creators, ed. Lloyd Frankenberg. Columbia ML 4259. Abbreviated PD.
San Francisco Poets, Evergreen Records EVR-1. Abbreviated SFP.

Aiken, Conrad

> Caedmon TC 1039. A Letter from Li Po, The Blues of Ruby Matrix, Time in the Rock—Selections.
> Carillon 307. The Things, The Poet in Granada, The Fluteplayers, The Cicada, Landscape West of Eden; Proem to the Kid, 1, 11, 19; Mayflower, The Orchard.
> CTMP
> LC-PL 11
> LC-PL 20

Bishop, Elizabeth

CTMP
LC-PL 9
PD

Ciardi, John

"As If," Folkways FP 97/8
LC-PL 27 (one side; W. D. Snodgrass on other side)
"The Inferno," Cantos 1-8, Folkways FP 97
Children's records:
    "I Met a Man," Pathways of Sound POS 1031
    "You Read to Me, I'll Read to You," Spoken Arts SP 835
    "You Know Who," Spoken Arts SP 914

Cummings, E. E.

Caedmon TC 1017
CTMP
LC-PL 5
LC-PL 22
PD

Dugan, Alan

LC-PL 29

Eberhart, Richard

Carillon 314
CTMP
LC-PL 21

Eliot, T. S.

"T. S. Eliot Reads His *Four Quartets*," Angel 45012
"T. S. Eliot Reading Poems and Choruses," Caedmon TC 1045. The Love Song of J. Alfred Prufrock, Portrait of a Lady, Preludes, Mr. Eliot's Sunday Morning Service, Ash-Wednesday, A Song for Simeon, Marina, Triumphal March, O Light Invisible, Murder in the Cathedral, II, Opening Chorus, Family Reunion, II, A Chorus.
"Twentieth Century Poetry in English—T. S. Eliot," Library of Congress Recording Laboratory, PL 3. The Waste Land, Ash Wednesday, Landscapes, Sweeney Among the Nightingales.
"Old Possum's Book of Practical Cats," Spoken Arts 758
LC-PL 20
PD

Frost, Robert

Caedmon TC 1060. The Road Not Taken, The Pasture, Mowing, Birches, After Apple-Picking, The Tuft of Flowers, My November Guest, Acquainted with the Night, Tree at My Window, West-Running Brook, Death of the Hired Man, Witch of Coös, Mending Wall, One More Brevity, Departmental, A Considerable Speck, Why Wait for Science, Etherealizing; Provide, Provide; One Step Backward Taken, Choose Something Like a Star, Happiness Makes up in Height, Reluctance.

Carillon 320. Spring Pools, A Young Birch, The Sound of Trees, The Oven Bird, The Onset, Stopping by Woods on a Snowy Evening, An Old Man's Winter Night, Desert Places, The Need of Being Versed in Country Things, The Line-Gang, A Roadside Stand, The Silken Tent, Never Again Would Bird's Song Be the Same, Design, The Wood Pile, The Star-Splitter, Neither Out Far Nor in Deep, The Most of It, Triple Bronze, The Courage to Be New, No Holy Wars for Them, The Gift Outright, Couplets, My Objection to Being Stepped On, Away!

Decca DL 9033. Mending Wall, The Runaway, The Woodchuck, Stopping by Woods on a Snowy Evening; Provide, Provide; Birches, The Death of the Hired Man, Choose Something Like a Star, Once by the Pacific, The Gift Outright, One Step Backward Taken, Departmental, Two Tramps in Mud Time, A Lone Striker, A Considerable Speck, Come In, Spring Pools, Closed for Good, A Soldier, Happiness Makes Up in Height, It Is Almost the Year 2000, Fire and Ice, Why Wait for Science.

"Twentieth Century Poetry in English—Robert Frost," Library of Congress Recording Laboratory, PL 6. The Witch of Coös, The Mountain, Come In, Mowing, The Pasture, Reluctance, Stopping by Woods on a Snowy Evening, The Most of It, An Old Man's Winter Night; Provide, Provide; The Runaway, Acquainted with the Night, Choose Something Like a Star, A Drumlin Woodchuck, Why Wait for Science, Departmental, A Considerable Speck, One Step Backward Taken, On Looking Up by Chance at the Constellation, A Soldier, The Gift Outright, Directive.

CTMP

LC-PL 20

Ginsberg, Allen

"*Howl* and Others," Fantasy 7006
SFP

Jarrell, Randall

LC-PL 7

Jeffers, Robinson

LC-PL 5
LC-PL 20

Kunitz, Stanley

Carillon 302
LC-PL 22
LC-PL 29

Lowell, Robert

Carillon 301
LC-PL 11
LC-PL 22

Merwin, W. S.

"A Mask for Janus and Other Poetry," Spoken Word 122
LC-PL 22

Moore, Marianne

Caedmon TC 1025. The Fish, The Steam Roller, Spenser's Ireland, Nevertheless, The Wood-Weasel, A Carriage from Sweden, The Mind Is an Enchanting Thing, Nine Nectarines, Armour's Undermining, Modesty, Rigorists, A Face, Propriety, What Are Years, Translations from the Fables of La Fontaine.
Carrillon 312. The Plumet Basilisk, O to Be a Dragon, The Arctic Ox or Goat, The Frigate Pelican, Melchior Vulpius, To a Chameleon, Leonardo da Vinci's, Saint Nicholas, A Jellyfish, Bird-Witted, In This Age of Hard Trying, Efforts of Affection, The Pangolin, Voracities and Verities.
LC-PL 20
PD

Pound, Ezra

Caedmon TC 1122. Hugh Selwyn Mauberly, Cantico del Sole, Moeurs Contemporaines, Cantos 1, 4, 36, 84.
Caedmon TC 1155. Cantos 45, 51, 76, 99; The Gypsy, The Exile's Letter.

Ransom, John Crowe

Carillon 306
LC-PL 20

Roethke, Theodore

"Words for the Wind," Folkways FL 9736
LC-PL 10

LC-PL 22
LC-PL 29

Shapiro, Karl

LC-PL 7

Simpson, Louis

Carillon 305

Snodgrass, W. D.

LC-PL 27 (one side; John Ciardi on other side)
LC-PL 29

Stevens, Wallace

Caedmon TC 1068
CTMP
LC-PL 20

Wilbur, Richard

Spoken Arts 747
CTMP
LC-PL 22
LC-PL 29

Williams, William Carlos

Caedmon TC 1047
CTMP
LC-PL 20
PD

INDEX OF TITLES AND FIRST LINES

Poem titles are in roman type and first lines of poems are in *italics*. Page numbers in *italics* indicate a reference to the Introduction.